Go the Distance

The Complete Resource for Endurance Horses

by Nancy S. Loving, DVM

Foreword by Kerry J. Ridgway, DVM

Trafalgar Square Publishing
North Pomfret, Vermont

First published in 1997 by
Trafalgar Square Publishing
North Pomfret, Vermont 05053

Library of Congress Cataloging-in-Publication Data
    Loving, Nancy S.
    Go the distance : the complete resource for endurance horses /
    Nancy S. Loving ; foreword by Kerry J. Ridgway.
    p.   cm.
    Includes index.
    ISBN: 1-57076-044-6 (hc)
    1. Endurance horses. 2. Endurance riding (Horsemanship)
    I. Title.
    SF296.E5L68 1997
    636.1'0888—dc21   97-17545
                                                    CIP

Illustrations:
All the photographs in the book were taken by the author with the exception of photograph 29 on page 44, which appears courtesy of Dr. Jeannie Waldron. The line drawings through-out are by Patty Naegeli with the exception of the drawings on pages 21,51,52, which are by Laurie Prindle. The competition judging forms appear compliments of the following associations: American Endurance Ride Conference (AERC), North American Trail Ride Conference (NATRC), Eastern Competitive Trail Riders Association (ECTRA), and British Endurance Riding Association (BERA).

Cover and Book Design by Edith Crocker
Typeface: Caslon 10.5/14

Printed in Canada
10 9 8 7 5 6 4 3

Acknowledgments

This book is dedicated to our gallant horses and to all the riders, veterinarians, ride managers, and volunteer staff that make the sport possible. I especially want to acknowledge the following for lending their inspiration through the years:

My unwavering and most ardent supporter, and best friend, Roger

The "love affairs" I share with my horses Wichi and Jeep

My veterinary buddies of the Race of Champions – Jeannie, Don, Ray, Tony, and Liz, who keep me laughing

My riding buddy, Cheryl, with whom I share so many miles of Rocky Mountain wilderness

To Susan, my creative inspiration

And, to my family, for always being there

Table of Contents

Foreword

IN MY LONG YEARS OF DISTANCE RIDING INVOLVEMENT, the operative words that I most believed in — that I fought long and hard to see the sport adopt as a worthy standard — was the concept "fit to continue." This term, this concept, should have meaning for the true distance riding competitor and aficionado that goes far beyond just the sense of the "race" itself. It should be the operative concept to every aspect of selecting, training, conditioning, shoeing, feeding, trailering, as well as in competing and meeting veterinary criteria. It is my strong belief that it even applies when it is appropriate to retire your old campaigner; he should, barring the unforeseeable, still be "fit to continue!"

Dr. Nancy S. Loving's book, "Go the Distance," gives every distance riding competitor the knowledge and the tools to accomplish this definitive goal. I have long championed endurance riders as being generally more knowledgeable about their horses with respect to care and physiology than nearly any other group of horse people. Distance riders have always had a voracious and insatiable appetite for knowledge and improvement. However, at the time that I came into endurance and competitive riding most of that knowledge came from the seat of our pants, from tradition and a little from science. Through the deep and special interest of key veterinarians in this sport, among whom Dr. Loving stands credentialed and tall, science has come to distance riding. Science has also come to distance riding because of the wonderful cooperation of the distance riding competitors themselves. "Go The Distance" puts these gains in our scientific knowledge into words and concepts that are easy to understand, and even more importantly, to apply.

It is most appropriate that such a book as this comes from a veterinarian, but even more so that such a book be authored by a veterinarian who knows the sport from the top side of the horse as well. Every section of this book achieves high marks because it reflects what riding and competing veterinarians know from the veterinary side, tempered by what we have learned from being competitors.

This is not just a book for people new to the sport nor is it just a book for the elite competitor. It is a book that belongs in the library of every person who aspires to compete in long distance riding, and especially the sport of endurance riding. It should not be left on a shelf — it should become dog-eared from easy accessibility and from frequent reading.

Through thirty years of lecturing and writing about distance riding I always have cautioned my audiences that "today's truths, are tomorrow's lies." That is to say, that which we so firmly think we know today may not stand the scrutiny of time and new knowledge. However, though the axiom still holds, the material contained in Dr. Loving's book has been developed and proven through the last 30 plus years. It is timely, and I feel confident in predicting that its content will continue to provide a standard for the good of the horses for many years to come.

Kerry M. Ridgway, DVM

A rider with 8,000 competitive miles, FEI, AHSA & AERC judge,
and Endurance Hall of Fame member since 1991

Introduction

VERY FEW EQUINE SPORTS create as intense an interaction between a horse and his rider as do long distance and cross country equine events. Like the mythical centaur, you will feel joined with your horse in such a way that your thoughts are reflected in your horse's responses. Developing a horse to perform in endurance, competitive trail, ride-and-tie competitions, or cross country riding and jumping becomes more than just part of your day; it becomes a lifestyle.

Distance riders wax poetic when describing the joy felt in sharing the miles with their equine "friends"; in the inspiration derived from traveling miles of beautiful trails; the friendships forged with other participants in the sport; and the thrill of the challenge.

There may be no greater demand on the whole horse than when this remarkable animal gives of his full athletic potential over many miles. Every organ system in the horse's body must adapt to the effort. The integrated process of conditioning becomes its own adventure, taking time as well as strategy. The horse learns to love his work, his enthusiasm apparent even after 50 or 100 miles of open trail.

I have written this book because endurance riding is my passion. Years in the saddle on top of my horses, years spent as part of the veterinary staff at competitions that attract the finest endurance talent, years managing the health and veterinary care of many wonderful horses on a daily basis: these facets of my life all inspired this book.

In the process of watching, listening, and experiencing long distance riding, I have learned that success is in the details. I want to share these observations and principles with you so that you can maximize your horse's natural talent while you and your horse stay safe and sound.

Good luck, and Happy Trails...
Nancy S. Loving, DVM
1997

A Note to the Reader

The author has provided a glossary for her readers. The words defined in the glossary appear throughout the book in *italicized type* as an indication to readers that they may refer to page 239 at the rear of the book for term definitions.

1 Selection of an Endurance Prospect

Setting the Standard

It would seem on the surface that a long-distance horse should be a fairly straightforward investment. You have only to decide gender, age, breed, and how much money you are willing to pay. But there is far more to it than that. You should consider the horse from every angle, not limiting your evaluation to physical characteristics and soundness.

Probably the first thing everyone looks at upon approaching a horse is appearance. But **pretty** does not get you very far down the endurance trail. Sweet disposition counts for an awful lot, but must be supported by athletic ability and structural soundness. On the other hand, a great body will not always compensate for a bad attitude or a lazy disposition.

The perfect horse is a fabulous mover and a great looker; is ambitious, has four correct legs, and has no metabolic or structural abnormalities. Horses like this do exist, but more often than not, we are faced with accepting some imperfections.

What is acceptable and what is not? There are no exact formulas for this, since it boils down to your individual needs and tastes. There is no question that any potential distance horse should undergo a thorough veterinary exam **prior** to purchase. Once you've bought that horse, your emotions often make it hard to walk away from a poor choice. It is hard enough to do that when you have not actually bought the horse; imagine having to find a new home for an unsuitable buy, especially one that could have been prevented. A discussion with your veterinarian is money well spent to help you sort through potential problems.

Before you even get to the point of including the veterinarian in your decision-making process, you can ferret out quite a bit of information about your potential equine partner. Some guidelines will help you set a standard against which to measure the potential purchase. These same principles can also help you decide if you are able to convert a horse that is currently part of your family to a new sport of distance riding.

The Growing Years

As you start the search for the perfect horse, look into how the horse has been raised. If you are contemplating buying a young horse, consider his current living environment. You should also realize that a horse should be at least four years old before starting an intense conditioning program.

The development of your endurance prospect starts long before the horse is old enough to be ridden. Ideally, a young growing horse should be raised in an environment that allows healthy stress on the *musculoskeletal* system. (Musculoskeletal refers to the muscles and the skeleton, and the interaction of these structures to create locomotion.) A young horse should live outside, pastured with other horses, or have regular turn-out for play. Then he will receive sufficient stimulus to form solid, dense bone, tough feet, and sound joints. Ligaments and tendons slowly strengthen while a young, active horse develops the *neuromuscular* coordination important to rigorous athletics. (Neuromuscular relates to the nerves and the muscles, and their interaction to provide agility, coordination, and strength of movement and locomotion.)

Stall or paddock confinement does not allow development of an athlete's potential. A horse that is kept in a confined space must be given adequate exercise throughout its growing years. Part of its training should include long-lining, driving, or being ponied off another horse at least several days a week. A young horse that has had restricted exercise may require two to three years for its bones to condition to the level an active horse may reach within a year. This is partly because the tissues and bone of a stall-raised horse are less responsive to the stress of exercise.

While assessing the environment in which your potential distance horse has been raised, also check that sound health management practices have been followed. The horse should have been dewormed regularly (every 2 months) starting at the age of six weeks, vaccinated for appropriate infectious diseases, and should have received regular foot care. Balanced nutritional management also is critical in building strong, healthy bones and joints.

Breed Type

In selecting a specific breed for endurance work, consider that Arabians or Arabian crosses excel at endurance sports. Both respond rapidly to cardiovascular conditioning, as compared to warmblood or heavily muscled breeds.

Ancestry is important but not essential to developing a premier athlete.

The musculature of an endurance athlete should be long, sloping, and flat. This type of muscle structure is typically associated with a preponderance of muscle fibers called *slow twitch* and *fast twitch high oxidative* that work efficiently during *aerobic* work of endurance sports (Photos 1 & 2). Bulky, short muscles (typical of warmbloods, Quarter Horses, and Appaloosa breeds as examples) contain more *fast twitch low oxidative* muscle fibers that are better adapted for *anaerobic* work, like sprinting or fast acceleration for short intense efforts (Photo 3). This is significant in selecting a horse, since bulky muscles tend to rely more on *anaerobic* energy *metabolism* that generates toxic by-products, like *lactic acid* (or lactate). A heavy-muscled horse also has more trouble dissipating internal body heat. (For more detail on muscle fiber types, refer to Chapter 5.)

Thin skin, which is inherent to many Arabians and Thoroughbreds, facilitates heat transfer that dissipates internal body heat generated by working muscles. A horse with an abundance of blood vessels visible near the surface of the skin probably has good skin circulation that is essential for cooling (Photo 4).

Color

Horses with white leg markings may be a liability. Irritation of pink skin under the white hair on the lower limbs can cause a horse to be lame (Photo 5). These "scratches," often caused by sensitivity to alkaline or abrasive soils, could put a horse out of competition for several weeks to allow healing. The easiest way to tell if a horse has pink skin is by wetting the legs: pink skin is most apparent when wet.

Lighter colored horses seem to have an easier time cooling in hot weather. Darker colored coats tend to absorb solar radiation.

Body Shape and Size

Body shape is important, not only because a narrow body works as a better heat radiator, but it is easier on the rider who must sit astride for 50-100 miles of competition. (Note: see page 244 for a mile to kilometer conversion chart.) A barrel-shaped body is uncomfortable to straddle over the long term, and it tends to retain more of a horse's body heat. The bulkier the torso of the horse, the more depth blood vessels must travel to bring heat from the core to the skin (Figure 1).

In much the same way, size has some effect on a horse's ability to cool. Reports show that most elite equine endurance competitors range from 14.0

Photo 1 An ideal endurance prospect in a balanced, free moving trot.

Photo 2 A fit horse with the desired long, sloping muscle structure.

Photo 3 A horse with bulky, short musculature, usually not considered suitable for distance sports.

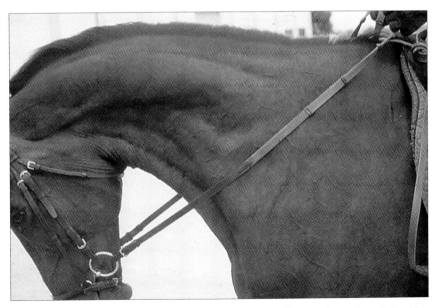

Photo 4 A horse with an abundance of blood vessels visible near the surface of the skin. This promotes good blood circulation that is essential for cooling.

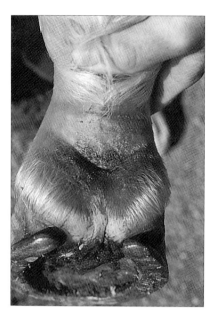

Photo 5 A pink-skinned horse that has developed pastern scratches. Horses with this lack of pigment are more likely to develop scratches.

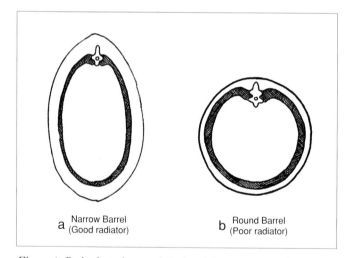

Figure 1 Body shape has much to do with success over a long distance. A narrow-barreled horse (a) radiates heat more efficiently than one with a bulky torso (b).

to 15.1 hands. A big horse requires more work to move its body; more work means more heat buildup in the tissues. A smaller horse has an increased body surface relative to its mass; this allows better heat dispersal and cooling. Despite these rules of thumb, you must match the horse and rider in size; a heavyweight rider needs a larger horse.

Movement Quality

The quality of a horse's movement is critical to its success. A distance horse must have an efficient gait with a ground-covering stride. You don't want a horse with high knee action that wastes energy and increases the number of steps the horse must travel over the miles. More steps taken means more wear and tear on joints, tendons, ligaments, and feet. A horse that lands with a hard impact increases concussion on its limbs and creates a jarring ride. On the other hand, if the foot flight is too low, a horse may tend to stumble. Ultimately, smooth gaits decrease both a rider's and a horse's fatigue.

Mental Attitude

A long-distance horse must be a durable athlete and must be of a mind and temperament that invites you to spend time with him. Years are devoted to the making of an accomplished endurance horse. Hours and hours are spent not only in training and conditioning, but in attending to many other aspects of daily management such as feeding, grooming, massaging, trailering, to name just a few time-consuming tasks. Your horse and you will come to know each other on the most basic level. To create a successful partnership, you both must respect each other and delight in each other's company. Trust is the operative word.

An endurance horse should have a bold, confident, and ambitious attitude. He should be eager to move down the trail, but not be uncontrollable. The horse should be responsive to the rider's commands.

It's also of great importance that the horse be a good eater and drinker. A horse that eats and drinks well is able to refuel at vet checks to safely sustain him through a ride. Maintaining adequate body condition enables the horse to have plenty of energy reserves throughout a ride.

Traveling is an important part of the life of a competitive horse. A nervous or finicky horse often will not take good care of himself while being hauled long distances to events. A confident horse that continues to eat and drink while traveling and while working maintains both body weight and hydration. This is a critical aspect to successful completion of an arduous competition.

Physical Attributes

The *cardiovascular* system is the limiting factor in performance of an equine athlete. Muscles require ample energy, oxygen, and removal of waste products by the circulatory system in order to perform to maximum potential. A big strong heart (a genetic contribution) and a well-developed blood circulation (a training contribution) determine if a horse will be a superior athlete.

Any horse exercising for more than one or two minutes is limited by the ability of its heart to continue to pump blood throughout the body. An accomplished endurance competitor has a large-sized heart, although the only way to evaluate its dimensions is by an ultrasound exam of the heart (echocardiography).

A low resting heart rate (24-36 beats per minute) is preferred. Heart sounds should be audible over a large area of the chest when listening with a stethoscope. The span of the area across which you can hear heart sounds also gives an impression of the size of the heart.

The depth of the heart girth (the depth of the chest measured from the withers around under the barrel to the withers on the other side of the horse) is more important than its width. A deep heart girth may be an indication of a large heart. The increased rib spring created by a deep chest also provides ample room for lung expansion that is critical to acquiring oxygen during exercise. Do not confuse a deep chest with a wide chest, because width limits the rearward front leg swing. If the elbows are restricted and can't clear the barrel, the stride is subsequently shortened. Also, if the elbows don't clear a wide chest, a horse is more likely to develop girth galls and rubs.

Wide nostrils allow a horse to bring in more air, and with it the oxygen needed for his muscles. Many Arabians that have been bred for horse shows have faces with pinched-in nostrils that may limit air intake. This is obviously not a positive attribute for an endurance prospect.

Conformation

There is, of course, no perfect horse, but we can construct some ideals against which we might measure the prospective endurance athlete. The first thing you should do is stand the horse squarely on a level surface, and stand back. Do you like the overall picture you see? Look at the horse from the front, side, and back.

Try to identify areas of asymmetry that might hint at chronic muscle disuse due to an injury. Look at the muscles for signs of atrophy, or areas of over-development. Stand on a fence with the horse positioned in front of you and peer down his back looking for asymmetry in the spine or in muscles

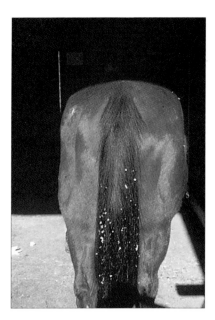

Photo 6 A horse with hip atrophy, which resulted in muscle asymmetry. Notice that the muscles of the left haunch appear rather sunken-looking compared to the well-rounded muscling of the right haunch.

around the spine. Stand behind the horse and examine the muscling from the rear, noting any asymmetry resulting in hip atrophy. (Photo 6).

BACK

A horse's back must be strong and able to accommodate the saddle plus the rider's weight. A horse with a sore back may relieve irritating pressure by changing the way he moves. This leads to fatigue and ultimately to lameness problems, particularly in the hind end.

The withers of an endurance horse should be prominent enough to prevent a saddle from sliding forward, but not so high that the saddle pinches or rubs them. Withers that are low with heavily-muscled shoulders are undesirable, since the saddle and rider can slide forward towards the neck. This creates muscle soreness and moves the rider's center of gravity over the front limbs. The horse then carries more weight on the front legs, its shoulders are restricted in their movement, and it moves less efficiently. A tail crupper may be necessary to hold the saddle back on a horse where this occurs.

NECK LENGTH

A horse's length of stride is correlated with the length of its neck. The legs can only reach to the point of the nose when the neck is fully extended. A short

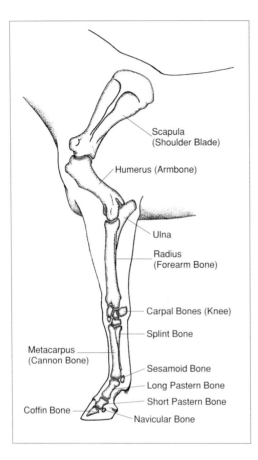

Scapula
(Shoulder Blade)

Humerus (Armbone)

Ulna

Radius
(Forearm Bone)

Carpal Bones (Knee)

Splint Bone

Metacarpus
(Cannon Bone)

Sesamoid Bone

Long Pastern Bone

Short Pastern Bone

Coffin Bone

Navicular Bone

Figure 2 A gently sloping shoulder with a long, vertical arm bone enables a horse to move smoothly. A horse with a more vertical shoulder is limited in his motion.

neck decreases a horse's scope and flexibility, but too long a neck increases the weight over the front limbs and hastens fatigue. Look for a horse that falls between the two extremes.

SHOULDER

The relationship of the scapula (shoulder blade) to the humerus (arm bone) is critical to a horse's scope and reach. Ideally, you would like to see an angle created by the joining of the shoulder blade and arm bone that is greater than ninety degrees, preferably 105 degrees. This "sloping" shoulder, with a long, vertical arm bone enables a horse to move with a fluid freedom of movement (Figure 2). Conversely, a short, more horizontal arm bone limits a horse's stretch and creates a jarring ride with increased impact on the horse's legs and on the rider.

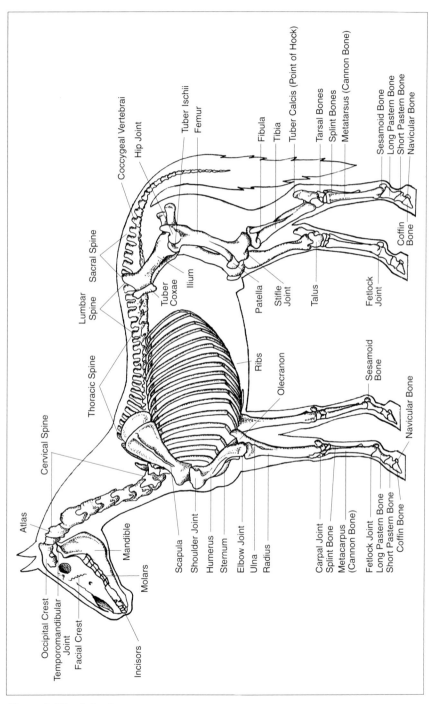

Figure 3 The skeletal system.

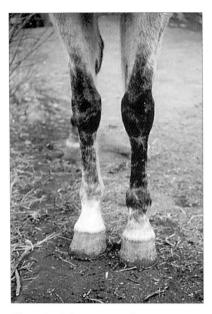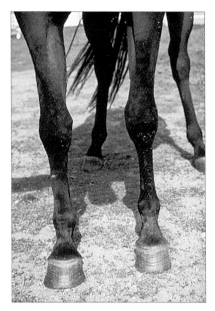

Photo 7 A short cannon bone.   *Photo 8 A long cannon bone.*

CANNON LENGTH

Think of the skeleton of the horse as being the scaffold to which the muscles and tendons attach (Figure 3). The muscles work like levers and pulleys, with the greatest mechanical efficiency gained by a long forearm and a relatively short cannon bone (Photo 7). This combination allows a horse to have a longer stride reach. Too long a cannon increases the stretch and strain on the superficial flexor tendons and on the suspensory ligaments (Photo 8).

BONE SUBSTANCE

Strong, dense bones are essential to the performance horse. Horses inherit bone size from the sire and dam, whereas bone density is dependent on training. As the horse grows exercise encourages the deposit of minerals in bone and adds to its density. Ideally, the cannon bone should have a circumference of at least eight inches for a one thousand pound horse. (The measurement is taken just below the carpal joints at the top of the cannon bone (Photo 9). The average nine hundred pound Arabian would then need a minimum of 7 1/4 inches of bone to safely assume the load associated with long distance work. Bone that is too slender is at risk for fractures and failure.

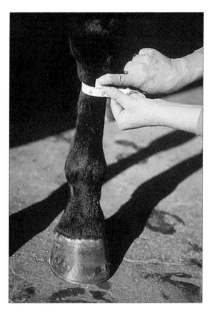

Photo 9 *Measuring the circumference of the cannon bone just below the carpal joints (the knee).*

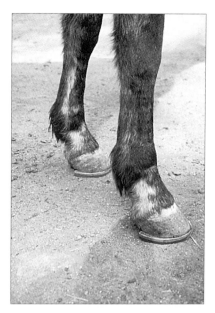

Photo 10 *A medium pastern.*

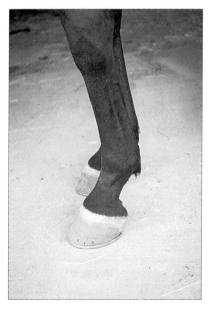

Photo 11 *A long pastern.*

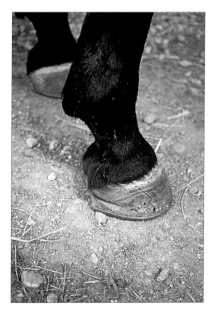

Photo 12 *A short pastern.*

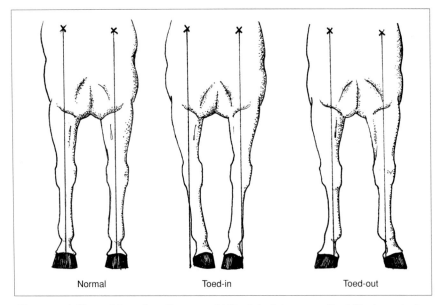

| Normal | Toed-in | Toed-out |

Figure 4 a) Normal front leg alignment b) Toed-in (pigeon-toed) c) Toed-out (splay-footed)

PASTERN

A medium length pastern is preferred (Photo 10). Too long a pastern length (Photo 11) adds strain on the fetlock joints and on the superficial flexor tendons that are commonly involved in a bowed tendon injury.

Too short a pastern creates a jarring ride, adding concussion to the limbs as well as to the rider (Photo 12). A short pastern also is associated with the development of navicular disease, due to increased impact on the heels from a choppy stride, and to strain of the deep digital flexor tendon as it runs across the bottom of the navicular bone.

LEG FAULTS

If you could create the perfect horse, it would have a perfectly straight set of legs, with no crookedness in sight. However, most horses have some slight aberration from normal. (On occasion, deviations from normal may be created by imbalanced trimming or growth of the feet and thus are correctable.) Some conformational faults are more tolerable than others; the following list includes some that are less desirable:

- Toed-in: Toed-in conformation implies that the toes point slightly towards each other rather than straight ahead (Figure 4). This conforma-

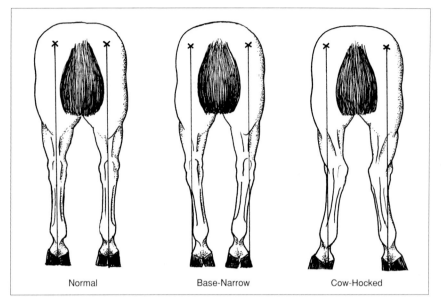

| Normal | Base-Narrow | Cow-Hocked |

Figure 5 a) Normal hind leg alignment b) Base-narrow c) Cow-hocked

tion often leads to development of ringbone (degenerative joint disease of the pastern or coffin joints).

• Toed-out, especially if base-narrow: The base-narrow horse stands with its elbows and forearms wider apart than its lower legs. Toed-out means just that, the toes aim out in a duck-footed position (Figure 4). This increases the likelihood of interference injury and places great stress on the inside aspect of the joints and feet.

• Long cannon bones: This increases the risk of developing a bowed tendon or inflammation of the suspensory ligaments.

• Long pasterns: This increases the possibility of developing a bowed tendon, suspensory injury, or fetlock joint disease.

• Bench knee: This means the cannon bone is offset so it is not set directly in the middle of the knee joint. This places more stress on the inside of the leg and can lead to development of a splint.

• Splint: A bony enlargement that develops around part of the pencil-thin splint bone located alongside the cannon bone. Irritation to a splint bone results from conformational problems, excess concussion, or from trauma related to an interference injury by the opposite leg. Splints rarely create a permanent lameness problem, but when they do form,

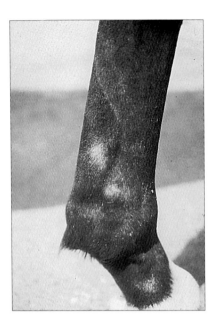

Photo 13 A horse with windpuffs of both the flexor tendon sheath and the fetlock joint.

sufficient healing time (2-4 months) must be allowed before returning a horse to work. Usually splints are nothing more than a cosmetic issue unless they are related to an interference injury due to serious conformation flaws (toed-out or bench-kneed), or if they impinge on the suspensory ligament.

- Windpuffs: A windpuff refers to any distention of a joint or tendon sheath (Photo 13) due to increased synovial fluid within a joint or tendon sheath. This indicates inflammation due to stress from abnormal conformation or concussion; an older endurance athlete often develops windpuffs due to inevitable wear and tear on the joints and tendons, but a young horse should have clean, tight joints and tendons with no swelling.
- Cow-hocked: Fetlock joints that reach further to the side than do the hocks, causing extreme stress to be placed on the hock joints (Figure 5). Most Arabians toe out behind but are not technically cow-hocked. This is commonly seen in draft breeds.
- Sickle-hocked: The hock joints must swing and extend, push and support with each stride. In a sickle-hocked horse, the lower limbs of the hind legs angle beneath the horse rather than dropping straight down in line with the point of the buttocks (Figure 6). More stress is placed

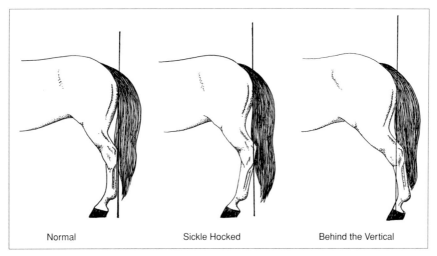

| Normal | Sickle Hocked | Behind the Vertical |

Figure 6 a) Normal hind leg alignment (side view) b) Sickle hocked c) Behind the vertical

on a horse with this conformation fault, which can lead to degenerative joint disease.

- Post-legged: This type of conformation describes a lack of angulation between the stifles and hock joints (Photo 14). The joints experience excessive compression forces with each step, ultimately leading to degenerative joint disease of the hocks or stifles.

As you examine the horse's legs, look for indications of interference wounds. Fresh scabs or thickened scars on the insides of the cannon bones or fetlocks hint that a horse may hit himself with one of his other legs. Often these concerns are related to some degree of toeing in or toeing out of the limbs. Keep in mind that as a distance horse tires over long mileage, he will have a greater tendency to hit himself. Chronic interference injuries may necessitate that the horse wear splint or ankle boots when ridden. (In competitive trail riding where leg boots are disallowed, use them for protection during training and conditioning.)

The Foot as the Foundation for Athletic Performance

There is no question that strong feet are one of the most important features of longevity in an endurance athlete. A horse's feet must be able to withstand the continual concussion and pounding sustained during years of conditioning and competition (Photo 15).

A long-distance horse works consistently on broken terrain that is often

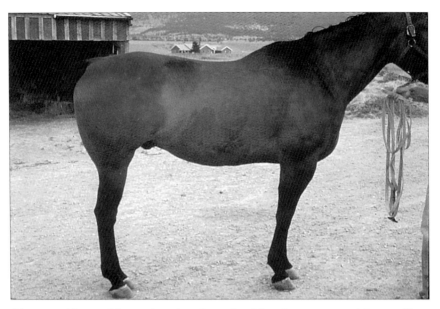

Photo 14 A horse with post-legged conformation. Note the extreme straightness of its hind legs from hip through stifle and hock to pastern.

Photo 15 A good-sized foot that is broad in width with strong bars and frog.

hard and rocky. Common career-threatening problems include bruising of superficial and deep foot structures. Some of these injuries have as much to do with incorrect shoeing practices as with unsound structural stability, but the better the conformation and inherent strength of the hoof structures, the fewer management tricks will be required to keep your horse sound over the long term.

A horse's feet will remodel in response to uneven stresses placed upon them, so they are useful visual reflectors of other problems. Foot size and shape, and configurations in the hoof wall give clues about less-than-perfect alignment in the body. Imbalances may result from pain or because of conformational imperfections. (For detail, please refer to Chapter 3.)

CHARACTERISTICS OF GAIT

What kinds of characteristics do you look for in the gait of your prospective distance horse? With some practice, you will begin to recognize when a horse moves energetically and with lightness. As you watch the horse's gait, you will come to appreciate how efficiently he moves. Each gait should appear effortless, with no wasted motion. This makes a lot of difference in how well the horse will hold up structurally after thousands of miles.

The durability of the feet has a lot to do with how much impact the hoof assumes with each step. You don't want to see a horse landing really hard on the front end; hard impact means increased wear and tear. You also don't want a short, choppy-strided horse that requires many extra steps to move down the trail compared to a big mover. Besides being related to conformational structure, short strides may also result from foot discomfort. Similarly, a horse that seems to protect himself as he negotiates a downhill slope may be doing so because of painful foot problems. A horse that shortens up his stride or looks "ouchy" on gravel or a rocky surface is also communicating to you that his feet are sore and tender.

CUPPED SOLES AND FOOT SIZE

An endurance athlete should have a good size foot relative to its body. Ideally, you'd like to see a deep cup to the sole so every rock and pebble won't lame your horse. Flat feet can pose problems for a distance horse since they are prone to bruising. You must discern if the flatness of the foot is a result of overzealous trimming, or because that is the genetic makeup of that horse. Consider that if you do purchase a flat-footed horse, or one with inherently thin soles, you will need to pay particular attention to shoeing concerns. You may need to maintain the horse in special shoes and/or pads. There is certainly nothing wrong with this, but it will cost you added expense and care over the long term. Such a horse does not tolerate trimming or shoeing mistakes very easily so you need to be especially selective in choosing your farrier.

A contracted, narrow foot ("mule-shaped") may not absorb concussion as well as a wide foot, and may not be able to hold on to Easy Boots®. (An Easy

Boot® is a polyurethane boot that is used over horseshoes in rocky terrain or as a shoe replacement if your horse loses a shoe out on the trail.)

In defense of many strong-footed horses that do eventually suffer bruising or heel soreness, I might point out that miles and miles of concussion takes its toll. This is especially so in the highly competitive individuals who consistently finish in the "top ten" or who push themselves hard time after time in competition and training. In some cases, the hoof wall cannot sustain that degree of loading over a competitive season; the hoof tubules weaken and start to collapse. Deep bruising develops, and short of growing out a new, tough hoof, the rider bumps up against continual frustration as a horse goes lame during or after competition. There is nothing inherently wrong with feet like these; it is just that our sport does exact a price. So, with that in mind, why start with a liability?

THE SIGNIFICANCE OF PADS OR SPECIAL SHOES

As you review the horse's athletic history, look to see if the horse is shod with pads or special shoes, or if he ever has been in the past? If so, find out the reason for this from the seller. Egg bar shoes have great merit, but they are also used as therapy for a number of serious foot problems, such as laminitis or navicular disease. The horse may be shod in pads due to owner preference or for practical purposes because of local terrain, but it may also be that the horse has tender feet or thin soles that require pads in order to stay functionally sound. You need to know which situation you are dealing with. (See Chapter 3 for more detail on special shoeing.)

Horses that have been kept in a stall, as opposed to being mostly turned out, or those shod with pads for a long time, experience a drop of their soles. The soles soften and lose their natural cupped configuration — even if there had been a cup in the first place. It is possible to toughen feet on many horses by removing the pads, slowly introducing firmer ground surfaces, turning the horse out in rocky pastures, and routinely applying tincture of iodine to the soles. But, this is not always the case. Ask a million questions, and talk to the seller's veterinarian about the reasons behind special shoeing methods.

HEALTH OF THE HOOF HORN

The superficial portion of a horse's hoof wall consists of a material referred to as hoof horn. Comparable to your fingernail, hoof horn is comprised of layers of insensitive tissue. In the deeper portions of a horse's hoof, sensitive tissue is arranged in layers in a tubular configuration to provide a concussion absorbing

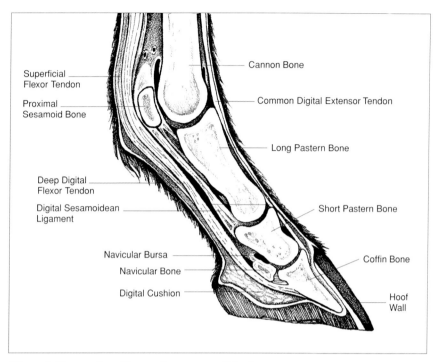

Figure 7 External and internal structures of the foot.

function (Figure 7). Hoof horn forms between the tubular sensitive tissue to build a tough, durable hoof capsule that remains flexible enough to temporarily deform and expand as the horse loads and unloads the foot with each step.

Let's look at the quality of the hoof horn itself. It cannot be overstated that tough, durable feet make for happier horses and much happier owners. If you see feet with fissure cracks on the hoof face or a thin or separating white line, beware. Sometimes weakness of the hoof wall results from improper shoeing over the long term. If the feet have been fitted with too small shoes or have been allowed to grow with underrun heels where the angle of the heel is greater than that of the toe, they lose a lot of their inherent strength. The walls will become thin over time, making the hooves more prone to chipping and cracking. Horseshoe nails tend to wiggle in a weakened hoof wall. The shoe loosens as the nails shift, and it is more easily thrown. Also, shoes that vibrate or flex because the nails are not secured tightly will create lameness problems. This shoe shift may not be apparent to you. You don't always hear a shoe clicking when it moves very slightly. Corns easily develop at the heels where a loose shoe repeatedly moves up and down.

Poor quality hoof horn may be due to shoeing problems or to genetic tendencies. If the dam, sire, or brothers and sisters of the horse are nearby, inspect their hooves as comparisons to the horse you are considering. This might give you an indication of the heritability of foot strength.

EXAMINING THE BAREFOOT HORSE

A barefoot horse provides an excellent opportunity to examine how a horse tends to wear the ground surface of his foot. The wear point on the bottom of the toe indicates where the *breakover point* occurs. As the horse's hoof lifts off the ground, he will roll off a point on the end of the toe. Ideally, this point is in the center of the hoof wall of the toe, but if the hoof twists slightly or does not land quite square, the breakover point may be to either side of center. This is visible as a point of greater wear on a bare foot. Without shoes on his feet, you can also estimate the thickness of the white line on the bottom of the hoof. A thick white line is usually a plus and indicates ample hoof density and strength. A white line that has points of separation, tends to flake apart, and is very thin, may indicate some underlying structural weakness in the laminae.

FOOT SYMMETRY

Look at the length of the toes, then compare the front feet to each other, and the back feet to each other. Are the feet similar in size? You can measure the length of the toes from the middle of the coronary band down the center of the hoof to the tip of each toe. How about the width of each foot? Measure across the widest part of the hoof as you look at the bottom surface of the foot. Is one foot more contracted or narrower than another? If so, this may be a hint that the horse doesn't bear as much weight on the limb with the smaller foot. This could be due to persistent discomfort or chronic lameness. In many cases, horses do not have exactly the same size feet on each side. Slight deviations are expected, but large differences should be addressed by veterinary evaluation.

To gain a baseline of information, measure all the way around each hoof from the coronary band to the ground surface. Or, make paper tracings of each hoof to facilitate measurement of each portion of the foot (Photos 16 & 17). Compare the inside of one foot to its outside measurements. Compare each foot to the other. These measurements give you an idea of foot balance and levelness. They tell you if the hoof horn is longer on one side than another, or if the coronary bands are pushed up from impact stress.

Photo 16 A paper tracing shown on a hoof model to compare hoof uniformity.

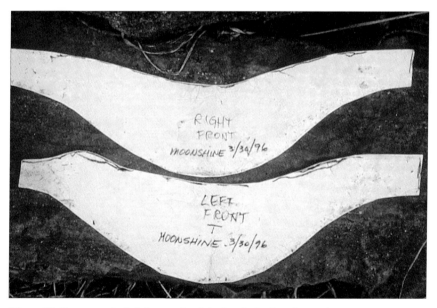

Photo 17 Compare the left foot to the right foot by laying the tracings out next to one another. Note the difference between the two tracings shown here.

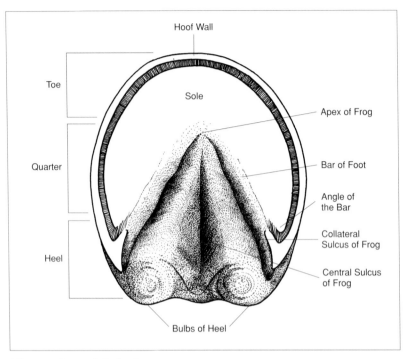

Figure 8 Parts of the hoof.

SYMMETRY OF CORONARY BANDS AND HEEL BULBS

Study the coronary bands and heel bulbs for symmetry. The slope of the coronary bands tips you off to long-occurring stresses in the feet. Ideally, the coronary bands should be parallel to the ground surface. The coronary band should also be perpendicular to the vertical axis of the leg, only slightly dropping away towards the quarters of the heels. More impact on one side of the foot than the other causes the coronary band or the heel bulbs, or both to be "driven" upwards. This kind of impact and similar asymmetric loading forces experienced by the foot are felt throughout the limb.

FROG ALIGNMENT

Pick up each foot and peer at the underside (Figure 8). Study the alignment of the frog. You'd like to see it nicely centered in the foot. If it sits off to one side more than another, you will also probably see flares in the hoof face (Figure 9). These asymmetrical features tell you that one side of the hoof repeatedly receives more impact than another. The steeper side of the hoof is assuming

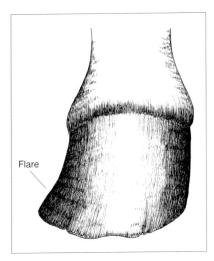

Figure 9 A hoof showing a noticeable flare.

Photo 18 A hoof with ridges, which indicate any number of possible causes including dietary or weather changes, a bout with fever, shearing forces from concussion or chronic laminitis.

the greater load. Circulation is increased on that side of the foot so the hoof wall grows faster in response. The side with the flare receives less impact, and subsequently relatively less circulation. What this boils down to is a lack of balance, either due to trimming or to conformation. Shoeing imbalances can be rectified in time, but conformation is there to stay. Be sure to know which applies to the animal you are considering.

The horse should have a large frog with good bars. The bars add structural stability and strength to the foot. An unshod foot that appears balanced and level indicates that the horse lands squarely on the foot as it moves.

RIDGES, GROOVES, AND DISHING IN THE HOOF WALL

Any dishing — a concave appearance — in the face of the hoof wall is an excellent reason to pursue *radiographs* (x-ray films) if the horse is very suitable in other respects. The radiographs will diagnose the significance of the abnormality. In the best case, growth rings develop due to dietary changes, seasonal and weather changes, or as a result of a past bout of fever (Photo 18). Sometimes the dishing occurs because of *shearing forces* in the hooves from being shod with too long a toe. Long toes increase the leverage in the foot, and cause tearing of the laminae. Sometimes a dished appearance results from low-grade or chronic laminitis. Any alteration in the mechanical integrity of the sensitive laminae of the foot is a good reason to turn down a horse as an endurance prospect. Although the horse may appear sound at the time and may not have had any recent laminitis crisis, this individual would be at greater risk for recurrence of the inflammatory problem. The punishment assumed by strong feet is profound; a foot that has suffered a serious laminitis event in the past cannot withstand what it takes to get a horse fit and into competition. This is not to say the horse is not fit for pleasure riding; it just makes for a bad gamble as a distance competitor.

You might also see horizontal hoof cracks that indicate an inflammatory event from too much concussion during training or competition. Again, these changes warrant radiographic examination to determine if there are underlying problems in the coffin bone.

Before Involving the Veterinarian

Some simple efforts on your part will help in your information-gathering process. Here are some helpful guidelines:

- Ride the horse on several occasions. This gives you an opportunity to see if his gaits are comfortable and if you get along with the horse and he is responsive to you.
- Ride the horse under variable circumstances, such as in crowded areas, on the trail, and on different terrains. A horse that moves nicely on flat ground may be a disaster on hilly or rocky terrain. Is the horse ambitious? Does he like to work? Does he have brakes? Can you control his speed? Does he move with rhythm?
- Ride the horse off its accustomed property or trails. Then you can see how the horse reacts to "lions and tigers and bears," and how much he places trust in you to get him through scary situations.
- Ride the horse with other horses and off by itself. Is the horse herd bound, or insecure when in the lead or by itself? Does the horse fuss at other horses, try to kick, or crowd the trail? Many bad habits are able to be trained away, but you should know in advance what you are in for.
- Watch the horse free in the paddock or pasture. This enables you to see how the horse socializes in a herd, whether he has any vices (like wood chewing, cribbing, or fence pacing) or other unusual habits. You can also discern how he moves and conducts himself during free play.
- Study the horse's interaction with other horses while being ridden or in

a herd. From a competitive standpoint, this is important to the future performance of an endurance prospect. Is he timid? Too bold? Aggressive? Easy going? Lazy? A leader? A follower?

By now, you have an idea if the horse should be pursued to the next level in the selection process.

- Have a knowledgeable friend or trainer accompany you on one of your visits. This individual often offers a more objective viewpoint.
- Research the medical and surgical history of the horse. The seller should be willing to disclose medical records from the horse's veterinarian or veterinarians.
- Discuss deworming and vaccination history, and feeding practices. This gives you an idea about the seller's attention to routine care and the management of special dietary needs.

If the horse is broke to ride, watch him being ridden by someone else.

- Does the horse object to the girth or seem "cold backed" when saddled? These reactions could be related to back pain, or may be behavioral problems that necessitate a future investment in training.
- Does he resent bridling? Sometimes this is a behavioral issue, sometimes it can be caused by teeth or ear problems.
- Does he seem stiffer to one side than the other? This issue may be based on lack of proper training, lack of muscle strength, physical discomfort from musculoskeletal problems, or saddle fit.
- Does he refuse to pick up one lead? Or to hold the canter once started?
- Does he wring his tail, or throw his head when asked to work?
- Does he move in a nice, round frame or does he carry his head high with a hollowed back? A well-developed muscling on the underside of the neck blatantly tells you the horse moves in an inverted, hollow frame, with head in the air, and has done so for a long time (Photo 19). This will tip you off to how much training time you will need to put into this horse to maximize his gait efficiency on the trail.
- Ride him out on the trail, incorporating hills so you can see if he is sure-footed with good neuromuscular control.

If this is a mature horse that has campaigned in the past, get details:

- Discuss his training schedule, and the foundation that was laid before he was ever put into a competition.
- Also look at the interval between competitive events. A horse that has

Photo 19   A well-developed muscling on the underside of the neck is a clear indication that this horse has been worked in an inverted, hollow frame with its head in the air.

competed on an every two to three week basis during a season has been subjected to considerable and unnecessary stress on the musculoskeletal system. A month interval between 50 mile rides, and six to eight weeks between 100 mile rides is a better recipe for longevity.

- Research the horse's competitive record if one exists. Discuss with the seller the possible reasons for failure to complete an event. By asking astute questions, you will gather clues about the person's horsemanship abilities. The seller's remarks will give you an indication of general concern for the horse's welfare. You may note a pattern of complacency that might have precipitated problems that had more to do with rider error than actual structural or *metabolic problems* of the horse. Ask about the record of other horses this seller may also have trained and competed to see if there is a pattern of mishaps. If a horse had inherent problems, what was done on follow-up care, and what happened during future events?

It is often helpful to take home a videotape of your potential dream horse while you are at the crossroads of "to buy" or "not to buy." With electronic gadgetry, we now have the luxury of bringing a horse into our homes and "living" with him for many days before coming to a decision.

- Videotape the horse standing still from front, back, and sides. Video him moving directly away from you, and directly towards you, at both a walk and a trot. Video him on the longe line or free in a round pen, and then again under saddle. Take the tape home and watch it over and over. You can scrutinize many elements of a horse without needing a veterinarian's expertise during the initial screening process. Think about all the aforementioned characteristics both with the horse in front of you, and again on the videotape. It's amazing how much more objective you can be when the horse is not snuffling in your pockets for treats and worming his way into your heart. If you don't feel fully qualified, then ask a friend or trainer to offer opinions. Remember though, that often all that you get is **opinion** and not necessarily fact. But sometimes other people bring up issues that you might have overlooked.

- Once you think you have narrowed your search down to a particular horse, offer your veterinarian a consulting fee to review the video so glaring problems will be recognized before you go through an entire prepurchase exam process. Many veterinarians own sophisticated VCR equipment that facilitates a gait analysis. The videotape can be played on single frame rate and in slow motion to enable detection of subtle gait inconsistencies that are not visible to the naked eye.

The Veterinary Exam

Now that you have picked this horse apart, and considered how well you get along with his personality, you can move forward to the next step: the prepurchase exam. A complete prepurchase exam does cost money, but it is a valuable investment. Don't shortcut the process by asking a veterinarian to do a partial exam. Have your veterinarian perform a thorough soundness evaluation with flexion tests and careful palpation and manipulation of all limbs and back. The physical exam also consists of examination of heart, lungs, eyes, teeth, skin, neurological function, and everything else that is physically available to hands-on assessment.

If we put our potential spouses through such a diligent exam process, none of us would be married! Fortunately, in regards to our spouses, love conquers all. But we can and should be ever so picky about buying a distance horse; rarely is the match a matter of love at first sight. You should try to be objective and clinical in your initial evaluation, knowing that you will spend a huge amount of time with your horse. Make sure you like the horse and the horse likes you because you are to be a hard-working team. A strong human-horse bond brings out the best performance potential in both of you.

2 Wise Investments in Tack and Equipment

Outfitting for Long-distance Riding

On the surface it would seem that the main ingredients needed to become involved in riding sports are a good horse, a saddle, and a bridle. But in reality, long-distance riding sports have stimulated development of better equipment suited for spending many hours in the saddle. A small industry has arisen out of this need for both horse and rider to be as comfortable as possible. We'll explore some essential pieces of equipment, and also take a look at the not-so-essential but fun tools of the trail.

For the Horse

Bridle and Headstall

The variety of materials you can use in bridles includes leather, nylon webbing, biothane (a vinyl material), or even braided horse hair. You want the bridle to fit comfortably and not cause any rub spots on the poll or cheeks. Find the width that your horse is happiest with. Remember that your horse will sweat a lot, and you repeatedly will be soaking his head and neck with water for cooling. The material you choose should withstand this kind of environmental abuse.

The style of headstall is probably of most significance for this discussion. Throughout a ride, there will be times when you'll want to tie your horse. This can be accomplished by leaving a rope halter on underneath the bridle and attaching a lead rope to the halter for tying. Or, many headstalls come equipped with a nose band and halter ring as an integral part of the bridle. The bit can easily be detached from the headstall so your horse can eat and drink without having to change head gear. This makes it faster for you to bridle up and go.

Importance of Proper Saddle Fit

Without a proper saddle fit, it is possible that no amount of correct equitation or training will permit a horse to reach its potential. Just as a poorly fitting shoe affects a person's athletic performance, a poorly fitting saddle will dampen your horse's abilities to move comfortably and to concentrate on the task at hand.

Let's consider how a bad fit impedes your horse's locomotion. In order to optimally support a rider's weight, a horse must move in some degree of self-carriage. This means the poll and croup should be carried in a level or slightly rounded attitude, rather than the head and neck raised upwards with the hind legs trailing behind and failing to aid the back in supporting the rider's weight. A horse that moves with a low, hollow back takes twice as many strides to cover a similar distance as a horse that moves in self-carriage. This causes more wear and tear on the limbs, as well as being extremely uncomfortable for both horse and rider.

Some of the longest muscles in the horse, the **longissimus dorsi** muscles sit to either side of the spine. These muscles run all the way from the sacrum, along the length of the back, on under the shoulder blades where they then fan out to attach to the base of the neck and withers. Your saddle sits directly over these muscles. Not only are these muscles important for stabilizing the lateral movement of your horse, but they also lift the back to assist self-carriage and engagement of the hindquarters. When the back is well-rounded in extension, spaces are opened between the joint surfaces of each vertebrae, allowing the spine a full range of motion.

A horse that is uncomfortable under saddle moves with its back hollowed. This causes the spinous processes (the long fins that extend upward off each vertebrae) to overlap. Over time, calcification or degenerative arthritis may develop. The result is chronic pain for your horse.

A horse experiencing pain from muscular bruising or bone irritation often guards against it by "splinting" its back muscles, in effect creating a rigid, un-bending structure. With this body posture, a horse loses its freedom of move-ment and muscular strength. Ultimately, rear end muscles and joints become sore due to the tension felt throughout the back and hindquarters.

Any aspect of a poor saddle fit that stimulates a horse to hollow its back will detract from natural extension (rounding) of the back. A saddle that pinches at the withers causes a horse to hollow its back. The saddle then loses complete contact with the back, thereby decreasing the surface area for dispersal of a rider's weight, and abnormal pressure points develop under areas of excessive load.

Correct Saddle Positioning

Comfort is the key to performance. You should position a saddle behind the scapula (shoulder blade), not over it, or it will interfere with movement of your horse's front end.   This is particularly true for a horse with a great amount of shoulder rotation that contributes to a big, flowing stride. The scapula is extremely mobile in the horse. Unlike a human, horses have no collar bone, so the shoulder blade attaches to the horse's trunk by muscles, ligaments, and soft tissue. With each stride, these muscular attachments contract to move the scapula, pivoting it at a point located about two-thirds of its length up from the body. At its top, the shoulder blade may rotate three to four inches with each stride.

Commonly, people make the mistake of placing a saddle too far forward on the horse's back. If you haven't allowed enough room for the shoulder blade to rotate, then the saddle jabs the shoulder muscles with each step. This creates discomfort, and ultimately causes tissue to thicken and develop lumps at the areas of impingement. By restricting movement, a saddle causes a horse's gait to shorten and become choppy. To eliminate pressure on the shoulder blades, such a horse may throw his and the rider's weight onto the forehand, subsequently the horse appears to be moving "downhill."

A horse that shortens its gait to compensate for an ill-fitting saddle often develops soreness in the triceps muscles of the shoulder. Muscles below the shoulder tighten in response to the soreness, resulting in a limitation to elasticity and suspension in the stride (See Figure 14, page 93 for the muscular system). Tension in these muscles also diminishes stretch of the complementary tendons in the lower limb. This creates conditions for increased concussion impact on tendons, the navicular structures, and the feet. Similarly in the rear end, soreness in the back and loin muscles stimulates compensation in muscles of locomotion in the hindquarters. *Tying-up* syndrome, or *myositis*, a serious condition, may result. (See Chapter 9.)

How to Check for Saddle Fit

To check for appropriate saddle fit, start by placing the saddle on your horse's back and loosely tightening the girth. Hold your horse's front leg out in front and measure to see if there is three to four inches of freedom between the top of the shoulder blade and the saddle tree. Now turn your horse's head and neck sideways to see what happens when the muscles bulge with bending. If the tree is too narrow, the saddle will dig into the back. This often occurs on a wide horse. Any restriction to bending mobility will hamper a horse's performance in any kind of athletic effort.

Next, snugly girth up the saddle and stand in the stirrups. Put your hand under the saddle to see if there is adequate room for your horse's movement. Do the same thing while someone pulls your horse's leg forward. The panels of an English saddle should mold well to fit the shoulders and withers, with no excessive gaps. The skirts of a Western saddle should not smash into the shoulders; if they do, then the tree is too narrow.

While a friend sits in the saddle, check clearance under the pommel. You should be able to vertically stack two to three fingers between the withers and the gullet of the saddle. If there is too much room in the gullet allowing more than two to three fingers to fit, then the saddle tree is too narrow. A saddle that is perched too high on the withers painfully pinches the withers. If fewer than two fingers fit between the withers and gullet, then the tree is too wide; the saddle will then rest on the withers and the spine. As you stand behind your horse, you should be able to peer all the way along the gullet of the saddle, with no point coming into contact with the spine. If you cannot see light under the entire length of the saddle, then the tree is too wide. Persistent contact on the spinous processes will create irreparable damage to your horse's back.

The panels of the saddle should distribute a rider's weight over the greatest amount of contact area possible. To check for correct fit, oil the bottom of your saddle, powder your horse's back, and set the saddle directly on its back. You'd like to see the powder dust the largest possible surface area on the bottom of the saddle. If the powder only adheres in a thin line on the bottom of the panels or if the panels only pick up a small area of powder off the back, then the panels are too narrow. Narrow panels cause a saddle to pinch and apply excessive pressure on specific spots along the back.

Panels can also be too wide, sitting off to the sides of the supporting muscles along the back. When panels are too wide, the gullet sits too low and presses on the withers with each step. Panels that are too straight do not contact the entire back, so that the powder doesn't evenly coat the bottom of the panels. What you will see is that instead of the powder fully dusting the panel leather, spots will be skipped where the panels don't contact your horse's back at all. Less weight is then distributed along their full length. Remember, an uncomfortable horse will hollow its back, further decreasing the degree of surface area contact. Panels that do not make full contact cause the front and back of the saddle tree to dig in with painful pressure points. The horse becomes sore at the depression behind the shoulder blade where the forks of the saddle rest, and at the rear of the panels as they curve upward to form the cantle.

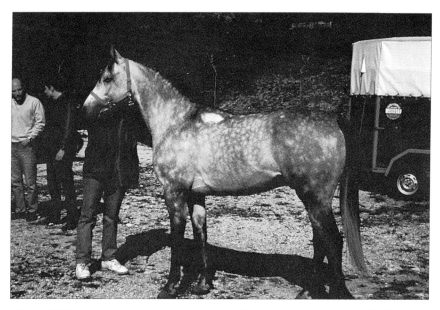

Photo 20 This horse has an obvious patch of white hair on the withers, an indication of poor saddle fit.

Currently, there are computerized programs available to evaluate where pressure points may be occurring on your horse's back from a particular saddle. These computer assessments are helpful in identifying problems, but keep in mind that nothing simulates what happens when a horse works on hilly terrain. Muscular movement is quite different as a horse goes up and down hills as compared to working in a flat, level arena. A saddle will shift and twist with the change in muscle length and contraction in rough terrain.

It is best to try a saddle for a month or so to get an idea if it will work on your horse. Check the underside of the saddle pad for abnormal dry spots, and look at your horse's back after a good, sweaty workout. Dry spots indicate that there is either excessive pressure on that area that limits function of the sweat glands, or the saddle is not contacting that area at all. Ruffled and wavy hairs suggest that the saddle is sliding and rotating around that point, potentially creating muscle and skin pain from friction (Photo 20). Worn hairs on the back under the rearmost part of the saddle indicate that the saddle is shifting too much, independent of your horse's movement. The saddle is probably too rigid and won't accommodate movement of each side of your horse's back as he travels over unlevel terrain.

Saddle Balance

As you sit in a saddle, check its balance by feeling where it tends to place you. You shouldn't have to push on the stirrups or stand in them to feel comfortable. If the saddle sits too far forward, you will be thrown back against the cantle. If it is too low in front, you will be thrown forward with impingement on your horse's shoulder rotation. You should feel like you are sitting in the deepest portion of the saddle, and not on your crotch. The seat should feel level. If the deepest part of the saddle is at the rear, your horse will develop sore loins; if the deepest point is over the pommel, the saddle sits too low and impinges on the withers because of too wide a tree. In an English saddle, the cantle should be about one to two inches higher than the pommel. If the cantle is even with or sits lower than the pommel, then the tree is too narrow, causing the saddle to sit too high in front.

As for your actual fit in the seat of an English saddle, a rule of thumb is that you should be able to fit one hand's width behind you before you run out of cantle. In a Western saddle, you should be able to fit two to three fingers between your thigh and the swell.

Padding can only correct problems to a minor degree. You should not have to add more than one inch of padding to modify saddle fit. Too much padding causes a saddle to shift, which can intensify bruising under pressure points, or can create friction sores. In many cases, a thin pad protects the spine and compensates for reduced fat "padding" along the side of the spine that results from increasing fitness. Your horse's back muscles will become lean with conditioning, causing a saddle that once fit quite well to no longer fit at all. You need to continually check your saddle fit as your horse ages and develops fit musculature.

The only way in which you will be able to achieve a balanced seat is if your saddle is balanced for your horse's physique. Your horse will transmit its delight in its comfort by performing to potential, with ears forward, eagerly responding to your demands.

Saddle Types

This is an individual decision according to the way you prefer to ride. The variety of saddles are many, anything from a hunt seat close-contact saddle, to a western saddle, to an Australian outback saddle, to a saddle specifically built for endurance riding.

The most important element of what type of saddle to buy is how well it fits both you and your horse. You both must be comfortable because long-

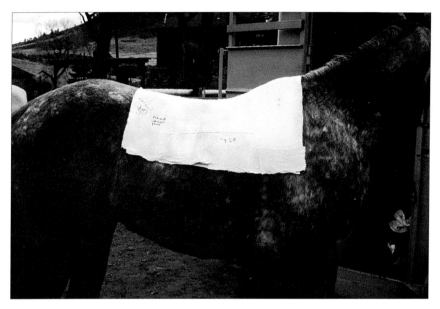

Photo 21 A plaster cast is used by a saddle maker to build a custom saddle that fits an individual horse's back exactly.

distance riding causes the slightest discomfort to escalate to nerve-wracking pain. If your horse is uncomfortable, his performance will suffer. If you are uncomfortable, you will suffer and want to quit.

One of the advantages to buying a saddle designed for endurance is that many of these factors have been considered. The seat of an endurance saddle is comfortable and supportive, making it easier for you to ride in a balanced position. The panels are wide enough to distribute even weight along your horse's back, minimizing the chance of developing soreness. These saddles are lightweight so your horse doesn't have to carry unnecessary pounds. And, endurance saddles have built-in "D" rings to which you can attach all the many accessories you might want to bring along.

In the long-distance sport horse industry today, we have excellent craftsmen who will build a custom saddle to your horse's specifications. You can make a plaster casting of your horse's back and have the saddle built exactly to the molded cast (Photo 21). This saves a lot of frustration, and ultimately saves time and money if you have a horse with a difficult-to-fit back.

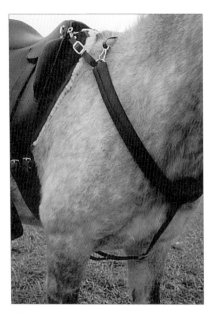

Photo 22 Neoprene breast plate fitted correctly to accommodate ample shoulder movement.

Photo 23 A breast plate properly placed on the chest so it does not interfere with breathing.

Saddle Pads

Saddle pads and blankets should not be used as a substitute for a poor fitting saddle. However, saddle blankets do provide a layer of cushion to soften the pressure of the saddle on the back. And, while these pads absorb sweat and dirt from your horse's skin, they are easily washable so the bottom of the saddle doesn't become caked with dried sweat and grime.

Wool has been a favored saddle blanket material for its great absorbent properties. Natural or synthetic fleece wool also serve as excellent materials. Cotton and polar fleece are other nonabrasive padding materials for your horse's back.

Frequent washing of your saddle blankets prevents friction areas on your horse's back and promotes good hygiene for the skin. Be sure all soap and detergents are rinsed thoroughly from the pads.

Girths, Breast Collars, and Cruppers

Whenever you use any of these items, find the material that least chafes your horse. Neoprene has proven to be an excellent material for this purpose. If you

Photo 24 A rump rug keeps the large hindquarter muscles warm during work on a cold, windy or rainy day.

do use a breast collar to help hold the saddle from sliding backwards, make sure it doesn't restrict shoulder movement. The shoulder straps should run well in front of the shoulder blades, and not across the shoulders. Also, make sure the breast collar doesn't sit so high on the chest that it restricts your horse's breathing (Photos 22 & 23).

A crupper should not rub the tender underside of the tail. It should be fastened such that it develops tension only when your horse is going downhill when it is needed to keep the saddle from sliding forward.

Rump Rugs

In wet and windy weather, one piece of equipment you should have tied onto your saddle is a rump rug (Photo 24). Fondly referred to by some as "haunch heaters," they do just that. They keep the hindquarter muscles warm while your horse's muscles are working hard. Cold rain or winds tend to chill down the rump muscles too quickly and contribute to muscle cramping. Most rump rugs are made of water repellent material; Gore-Tex® or Ultrex® are excellent materials for this purpose.

As an example of the usefulness of a rump rug to your horse's performance, we can review the situation at the 1993 Race of Champions in South Dakota. Despite being July, the weather turned nasty, quickly dropping to 38 degrees with 25 mph winds. To top that off, it poured for most of the day and night; not exactly summertime conditions. Those horses wearing rump rugs came through the ride looking very well. Those whose rumps were exposed to the elements for many hours suffered metabolic problems, or entered vet checks looking muscle weary and exhausted due to hours spent bracing their bodies against the chill. An inexpensive investment, a rump rug can truly make the difference in your horse's performance.

Blankets

At veterinary check points along a ride, your horse may stand for as long as an hour during a rest period. When you suddenly pull working muscles to a stop, they are prone to rapid chilling if there is wind or rain. It is a good idea to have a blanket or "cooler" on hand to keep hindquarter muscles from chilling down too rapidly.

In rainy weather, many blanket materials tend to become waterlogged. Instead of keeping your horse warm, a wet blanket works like a refrigerator and speeds up the evaporative cooling process, causing a horse to chill quickly. This can be prevented by using a Gore-Tex® or Ultrex® sheet over a thin blanket. Then if your horse was wet before you blanketed him, he will continue to evaporate away the moisture from his hair, and it will be wicked out through the breathable Gore-Tex® material.

Nylon is not a good material because it tends to keep moisture and heat against a horse's skin in hot, humid weather, and to cause a horse to become chilled in cool weather. Wool, polypropylene, or Hollofil® liners are best for covering up the rump muscles at stopping points.

Leg Boots

There are two schools of thought on the use of leg boots for your distance horse. If your horse is not entirely correct in its conformation or tends to hit itself when shod, then you may need to use splint boots to prevent interference injuries. If your horse tends to interfere (strike one leg with the opposite leg) when he gets muscle weary, you might want to put on boots. If you ride in terrain that is littered with sharp rocks, cactus, brush, or a lot of downed timber, you may want to use leg boots to protect your horse from "attack" by ground obstacles.

If your horse is careful in negotiating prickly terrain and his limbs do not contact each other, then it is best not to use leg boots since they can cause irritation. Riding in sandy soil or for more than 50 miles are situations where leg boots are not advisable. Sand seeps in around the edges and abrades the skin. The legs stay quite warm over the course of a 100 mile competition, and sweaty leg boots could create abrasions in a thin-skinned horse.

Should you decide to use splint boots, the best material to select is neoprene. It rubs minimally on thin skin and is easily and quickly cleaned at vet checks. Velcro® closures allow you to quickly put them on and take them off at checks, and enable you to adjust the tension to a safe comfort level for your horse.

For the Rider

The Helmet

An essential piece of equipment that every rider should own and wear is a helmet. With the advancement in plastic technology, we now have safe helmets that weigh nearly nothing and are comfortable to wear. Just like wearing a seat belt when driving in your car, think of wearing your helmet as an insurance policy. You just never know when you might fall off and crack your head on a rock or hard ground. Most people these days have very expensive brains that they have spent a lifetime filling with information, not to speak of decades of developing a personality loved by friends and family. Protect this investment!

Shoes for You

You will find your feet living in a pair of shoes for a **long** time over an endurance course. Most critically, shoes should be both supportive and comfortable. Your shoes should breathe to dissipate sweat. You shouldn't feel any rubbing or restriction from your shoes. In other words, your feet should feel not at all. Make sure there is ample room for your feet so circulation doesn't get restricted over the course of the miles.

It is best to ride in shoes with a riding heel so your foot won't slip through the stirrup and become dangerously trapped. If you prefer to ride in running shoes, then use a stirrup with a basket on the front.

If you like to get off and run with your horse, plan on using foot gear that gives you ankle support and provides cushioning. Regular running shoes are designed for flat, even ground. Remember that rocks and gullies tend to jump out of nowhere in terrain where many competitions are held. A twisted ankle or bruised foot will really ruin your riding adventure.

Photo 25 A wide, shock-absorbing
stirrup that provides the rider with
comfort and support over many miles.

Photo 26 A saddle fitted with a
shearling cover over the stirrup leathers
that prevents rubbing of the rider's legs.

Stirrups

Endurance technology has provided us with a plethora of stirrup styles, each designed with ample width to provide maximum support for your feet (Photo 25). This feature keeps your feet from going numb by providing a substantial platform to rest your foot on. Some companies claim their stirrups have shock-absorbing capabilities.

Riding Pants

Lycra tights make for an extremely comfortable ride in hot weather. They don't chafe your legs, yet they breathe in the heat and dry quickly when drenched with sweat or rain. If you prefer denim material, many brands of riding jeans are available. Just make sure that whatever pants you buy, there is no seam running across your knees or crotch. Preferably buy something with a knee patch to maximize longevity of the riding pants.

For winter wear, synchilla tights are comfortable and warm.

Half chaps

Suede or leather half chaps provide additional protection from leg chafing as you trot the miles. These leggings keep your horse's sweat from soaking through the calves of your riding pants. It is best to buy half chaps that have an adjustable buckle at the top so they don't slide down your calves as the leather wears and stretches.

Seat Savers

Another way of making yourself more comfortable in the saddle for long hours at a stretch is to cover your saddle seat with a sheepskin or synthetic wool "seat saver." These provide some cushioning for your behind and crotch while keeping you from sliding around in the saddle.

If you like to ride in shorts, or are an avid ride-and-tie person, you might consider a full shearling saddle cover that covers the saddle flaps and stirrup leathers (Photo 26). Or, you can purchase sheepskin covers solely for your stirrup leathers. The only down-side to using more padding is the increased bulk between your legs, and if you get caught in the rain, these covers get wet and stay wet; when waterlogged they are heavy.

Rain Gear

There is nothing as fine as a good Gore-Tex® or Ultrex® rain suit or coat to fend off the elements. This material, or something comparable, breathes so you don't bake inside, yet it keeps you dry. It also serves as an excellent windbreaker. You can find this material in a "duster" style raincoat that rolls into a small, lightweight tube that can be tied to your saddle.

Sun Protection

Nothing wears on a person so much as sunburn. Don't leave home without your sun block and lip protection. You can also use a wet bandanna around your neck as well to prevent sunburn.

Miscellaneous Equipment

Stethoscope

A stethoscope is a handy piece of equipment to carry with you at all times to monitor your horse's heart rate and its rhythm, and to assess the activity of the intestines by listening to intestinal noises. You don't need a particularly expensive stethoscope to accomplish these tasks; one can be had for a very modest amount of money that will adequately do the job.

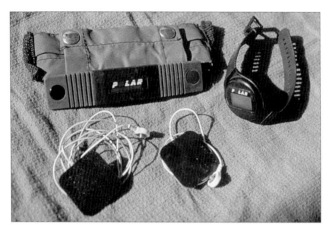

Photo 27 A heart rate monitor. The components are (clockwise from the top left) the transmitter and carrying case, the watch receiver, and two electrodes.

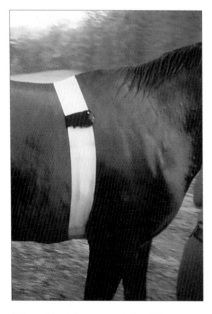

Photo 29 A thermistor reads the skin temperature while the horse is working.

Photo 28 A heart rate belt will continue to track the horse's heart rate after the saddle and heart rate monitor are removed.

To monitor your horse's heart rate, the bell or diaphragm end of the stetho-scope is placed on the horse's body wall just behind the horse's left elbow close to the armpit, and on a level with the elbow.

Heart Rate Monitors

This piece of equipment should be part of every serious long-distance rider's essential equipment (Photo 27). A heart rate monitor measures your horse's heart rate while he is exercising, something you are unable to accomplish with a stethoscope. Small electrodes are placed under the saddle and girth in con-tact with the skin. The electrodes pick up electrical signals from the heart, and the heart beats are continually averaged over a 6-10 second time span. These signals are then transmitted to a digital receiver watch to continually update changes in the heart rate with changes in work intensity. (For a detailed discus-sion, please refer to Chapter 6.)

Heart Rate Belt

Once you have pulled off your saddle at the vet checks, a handy piece of equip-ment to have is a heart rate belt so you can continue to track your horse's heart rate (Photo 28). This is a stretchable belt with electrodes that cinches around your horse's girth and maintains contact with a heart rate monitor. This frees up your hands to take care of your horse while your heart rate wristwatch continues to keep tabs on your horse's recovery. This can help you get through the pulse and respiration (P&R) checks as quickly as possible by knowing immediately when your horse has reached heart rate recovery criteria.

Thermistors

One of the more recent technological advances has been the development of a temperature gauge that reads your horse's skin temperature while working (Photo 29). The thermistor is attached to the front of the saddle near the pommel and the heat sensor pad is usually placed along the withers. When used in conjunction with a heart rate monitor, you can ride your horse more accurately within the safety zone. Usually, a horse's skin temperature will stay below 100°F (38°C) while exercising within the safe margin. If the thermistor gives a higher reading, the horse's internal temperature is heating up too much and too quickly for him to eliminate the heat load. One word of caution: when using neoprene saddle inserts or foam gel saddle pads, check that the heat sensor pad has not slipped further back beneath the saddle as this gives a falsely high reading. Greater skin heat builds beneath these synthetic materials even

Photo 30 A sponge secured to a saddle ready for immediate use at a stream along the trail.

though the horse's body is cooling adequately. If the thermistor reads less than 94°F (36°C), this may indicate that circulation to the skin is not enough to maintain adequate cooling and the horse may also be overheating internally. In both cases, exhaustion will likely set in. The thermistor is a handy device that should prove to be invaluable to a horse's safety, especially when exercising in hot and humid climates.

Sponges

Part of your technique for cooling your horse along the trail and in vet checks includes the use of a sponge. However, all sponges are not created equal. Buy the sponge that was once a live animal in the sea as it will save you a lot of frustration. When you dip the organic sponge into water, it soaks up water immediately and in quantity. This enables you to dip the sponge in a stream or creek while "on the fly." A synthetic sponge, on the other hand, forces you to stop and wait while it absorbs enough water to sink and finally fill with water. Attach a grommet into the sponge so you can tie a string onto it to hang off your saddle and to allow you to dunk it in water while you stay on top of your horse (Photo 30).

Water Holders, Fanny Packs, and Saddle Packs

Your horse must drink a lot and often while exercising, and so must you. You can buy any of a number of different holders in which to put your water bottles. Some people prefer a fanny pack made specifically for the purpose of holding two water containers. These are commonly found in bicycle shops and sporting goods stores.

Other people put the water bottles into specific compartments within a pommel or cantle pack designed for that purpose. This really is a matter of individual preference. The downside of having the water bottles affixed to your saddle is that if you get separated from your horse, there goes your water. However, if you think you might fall off, you might not want to land on a fanny pack full of bottles and trail supplies.

Collapsible Water Bucket

Once again the wonder materials, Gore-Tex® and Ultrex®, can be made into a handy collapsible water pail for you to dip into a creek or tank and then carry to your horse for drinking or sponging. These buckets can be purchased from endurance equipment suppliers. You can also carry a gallon plastic "pail" on your saddle that might have once been a large liquid bleach container but now has been cleaned and had the bottom cut off. This is a light weight "scoop" that is handy for dousing your horse's neck and chest with water when you reach water or the vet check.

Rider Card Pouch

At long-distance competitions, you will be asked for your rider card at each vet check. Everybody is happiest when the card is neat, dry, and readable. The best way to ensure this is to carefully fold the rider card and place it in a Ziploc® bag. To make your job of finding it much easier, purchase a pouch specifically designed for holding your rider card. Then it'll be hard to misplace, and will stay in good condition. At times when you are doing training rides or venturing into new territory, a rider card pouch makes a good map holder.

Equipment for Riding in the Dark

If you plan to get involved in 100 mile competitions, you will inevitably find yourself riding in the dark, whether it be at the start of the ride, the finish, or both. You can buy head lamps that attach around your helmet and brow bands and stirrup guards that light up like a beacon so pedestrians and cars can more readily see you at night.

If you use any kind of battery-driven equipment, check that the batteries are working just before each ride. Carry a good flashlight on your person, just in case. Glow sticks can be found at scuba diving shops. These can be hung from a horse's breast collar to somewhat light the trail so you can see rocks and holes as you move along in the dark.

Ice Boots

After you finish an arduous training ride or a competition, it is a good idea to cool down your horse's legs to minimize the inflammatory process that results from miles of pounding concussion. Commercially available ice boots make this process really easy. You can freeze the boots or methylcellulose inserts and store them in a cooler until you are ready to use them. Then, dampen your horse's legs and apply the boots for 20-30 minutes. If there is a chance your horse will chill from leaving the boots on this long, then apply them at 5-10 minute intervals, or massage the legs with ice cubes.

3 Athletic Foot Care

Without strong, healthy feet, an equine athlete works at a serious disadvantage. If a horse doesn't receive appropriate trimming and balancing of its feet, and without properly fitted shoes, even the most talented can go lame. At the very least, poor trimming or shoeing techniques discourage a horse from performing to potential.

Every five to seven weeks, athletic horses meet with a farrier. These meetings are far more than a pedicure, or a trimming away of hoof growth. Each shoeing appointment is an opportunity for you to interact in the decision-making process that is so vital to your horse's athletic soundness. Your veterinarian and shoer should collaborate to shoe each horse to its best advantage (Photos 31a & b).

As the owner and rider of your horse, you should be very much involved in this aspect of management of your athlete. As you train your eye to recognize good shoeing practices, you can direct appropriate questions to your shoer and veterinarian. Questions encourage these professionals to include you in the process. Your interest also stimulates a greater commitment to ensuring that your horse receives appropriate foot gear.

As you train your eyes to see what is normal and abnormal, you will begin to appreciate how significant even slight problems may be if allowed to persist over the long term.

Long Toe, Low Heel Syndrome

Let's first look at an example of what happens when a horse has a long toe, low heel (LTLH) foot configuration (Photos 32 & 33). This is probably one of the most common problems seen in any horse, and it is one that is often created by poor shoeing practices.

Both a low heel and long toe cause the hoof to assume a more sloping (acute) angle relative to a steeper appearing pastern. The pastern stands in a

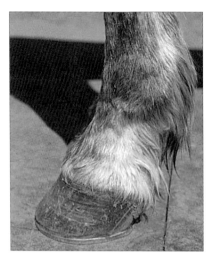

Photo 31a *A well-trimmed hoof with correct hoof-pastern alignment and fairly well-shod although the rear branches of the shoe could be about a half inch longer.*

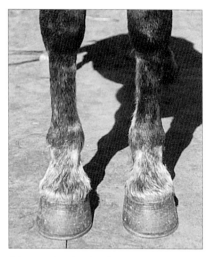

Photo 31b *A pair of well-shod hooves. Note that the coronary bands are symmetrical, there is an equal amount of hoof on either side of the pastern columns, the toes are squared back, and there are no flares to the hoof walls.*

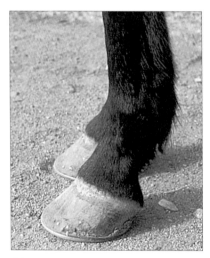

Photo 32 *A foot with a broken hoof/ pastern axis demonstrating the "long toe, low heel syndrome." (A line drawn from front and top of pastern to the tip of the toe should be straight.) This photo was taken after the horse's hooves had gone untrimmed for ten weeks.*

Photo 33 *A hoof model cross-section exhibiting an internal view of a long toe, which is the noticably excessive length of hoof wall sticking out in front of the coffin bone.*

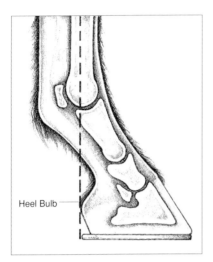

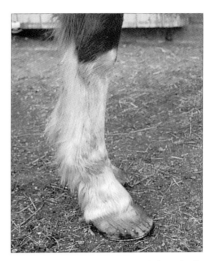

Figure 10 Viewed from the side, the heel bulbs should fall directly beneath an imaginary line drawn through the center of the cannon bone. This is good hoof alignment.

Photo 34 Despite this horse being shod only two weeks prior to this photograph, it still has a long toe and low heel because the farrier neglected to correct the problem.

more upright position than normal. The effect is to create a *broken-back* hoof-pastern axis. Ideally, the front of the hoof wall should be parallel to the slope of the pastern. To properly evaluate the alignment of the hoof and pastern, place your horse on a flat, level surface and square him up as much as possible.

Viewing the horse from the side, we would like to see the heel bulbs fall directly beneath an imaginary line drawn through the center of the cannon bone (Figure 10). The heel should have a slope similar to the front face of the hoof wall. A horse is considered to have an under-run heel if the heel bulbs fall in front of the ideal line bisecting the cannon bone, and/or if the slope of the heels is more acute than the front hoof face.

Long Toe, Low Heel Effects on Performance

How do a broken-back axis, a long toe, and a low heel affect the performance of an equine athlete?

A long-toed, low-heeled foot is at a mechanical disadvantage both in leaving the ground, and in the way it impacts the ground (Photo 34). Let's first discuss the concept of *breakover*, the period of time measured from the time the heel leaves the ground until the toe leaves the ground. A horse's limb pivots

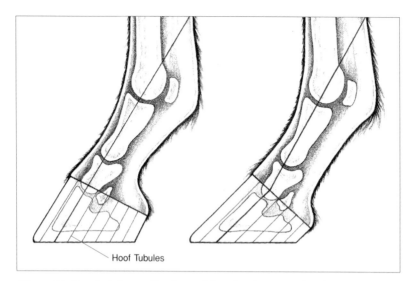

Hoof Tubules

Figure 11 On the left, a well-trimmed foot showing properly aligned hoof tubules (represented by the angled lines drawn on the hoof surface). On the right, a foot with a long toe and low heel. Note the hoof tubules extended in a more horizontal direction and sloping angle.

over its toe. The length of the toe determines the length of this *lever arm*. Most of us as horse owners spend a considerable amount of time pushing around a wheelbarrow, so let's use this as an analogy that you can well relate to. Consider trying to dump a full wheelbarrow that has a long bucket: it takes considerable effort for you to tip that kind of wheelbarrow to dump its contents. Now, what does it feel like to tip a barrow with a shorter bucket? It goes over easily with far less effort on your part. The same principle applies to the effort required for a horse to lift its foot. A long toe creates a longer lever arm (like the longer wheel barrow bucket), causing a delay in breakover (or tipping of the barrow) (Figure 11).

Prolonged breakover causes the heel to remain on the ground for a longer time than normal. This becomes significant when you ask your horse to go faster. One of the primary means a horse has to increase its speed is to minimize the amount of time the hoof remains in contact with the ground. Since an acute hoof angle increases the duration of the *stance phase* (the period when the foot is in contact with the ground) by delaying breakover, the horse will slow down. Or, at the very least, the horse is not able to increase its speed to seemingly "fly" across the ground. This is not conducive to optimal performance of the competitive athlete.

With delayed breakover, a horse's body also continues to move forward over his leg before the foot starts to lift and the leg is able to advance. The horse slows down, and takes shorter steps. Because it is harder for the horse to "dump its load" or lift its foot to advance the forelimb, the back legs also must slow so they won't hit the forelimbs. In effect, the stride shortens, and the horse's speed slows. The horse is less able to engage its haunches to use them to push himself forward along the trail. Remember also that the more steps a horse must take to cover ground, the greater the number of opportunities for a misstep, and the more concussion is received by the feet and the limbs.

Muscles fatigue more quickly if a horse has to take extra numbers of steps to cover the distance. Tired muscles lose their load-damping effect. The fetlock drops further with each step. Ultimately, hyperextension of the fetlock injures joint cartilage or the sesamoid bones. Also, the flexor tendons or suspensory ligaments may be overly stretched. Any strategy you can implement to allow your horse to maximize its stride will deter fatigue.

As a horse's body continues to advance over the limb that is delayed in its liftoff by its long toe, more torque is placed on the lower joints of the limb, especially the coffin and pastern joints. Additionally, the coffin, pastern, and fetlock joints flex more than usual to achieve sufficient force to move the foot. Torque and flexion forces that are greater than normal set up conditions for development of sprains, strains, or arthritis of any of these joints (See Figure 7, page 21 for a diagram of lower leg structures).

Normally during breakover there is some stretching of the deep digital flexor tendon (DDF) which attaches behind the navicular bone onto the back of the coffin bone. Some tension in the deep digital flexor tendon allows it to flex the coffin joint to lift the foot. With a delayed period of breakover and a longer lever arm created by the long toe, there is increased tension on the deep digital flexor tendon. The deep digital flexor tendon must pull harder to achieve foot lift and breakover.

The supporting ligaments of the navicular apparatus reach maximal stretch as the foot starts to breakover. In the horse with long toe, low heel syndrome, the limb advances farther forward before the foot breaks over. This creates an excessive amount of stretch on the suspensory ligaments of the navicular bone. Large arteries pass through the region of these ligaments; with excess tension, circulation may be compromised within the foot.

Excessive tension on the deep digital flexor tendon created by a long toe and delayed breakover also amplifies compression of the deep digital flexor

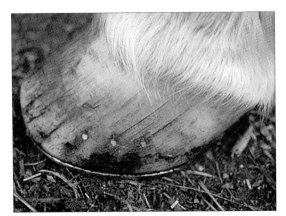

Photo 35 A hoof with a long toe, low heel configuration exhibiting brittle, dry hoof horn and sand cracks; a common result of hoof tubules being horizontally aligned and less able to retain moisture.

Photo 36 This toe was worn back naturally while this horse was barefoot. A farrier then incorrectly placed the shoe forward of the horse's natural toe length, artificially increasing it, thereby making it more difficult for the foot to breakover.

tendon against the navicular bone and bursa. This leads to fraying of the tendon and abnormal friction along the bottom surface of the navicular bone. Inflammation created by these occurrences leads to pain, shortened strides, and potential lameness.

Are you getting the picture? By now, you must realize that the effect of a long toe and a low heel on the navicular apparatus and the heel structures is dramatic. Horses with this type of foot configuration are more prone to developing heel soreness, navicular disease, and deep digital flexor tendinitis. The result to your horse is discomfort and poor performance. The result to you is lost opportunities for your horse to excel, possible lay-up time, and emotional and financial costs involved in rehabilitating a lame horse.

We're not done yet! The horse with a normal foot lands heel first 40% of the time, and flat-footed 60% of the time, but never toe first. But, a horse with a long toe and low heel lands **toe** first up to 40% of the time. This generates abnormal concussion forces all the way up the limb. Additionally, the horse is more subject to sole bruising at the toe or to bruising and injury to the coffin bone. A horse that lands with a toe-first impact also tends to stumble and trip more often than he would with a heel first or flat-footed impact, making it dangerous to himself and to you.

Internal Shock Absorbers of the Foot

Hoof tubules give strength to the hoof capsule, and act as shock absorbers for the foot. These horny tubules usually run fairly vertically within the hoof wall (Figure 11). An under-run heel is a result of "crushing" of the hoof tubules from excessive loading of the heel of the foot. The *coronary corium* (the active tissue of the coronary band that is responsible for hoof growth) of the heels is compressed by the extra load assumed in the heels. The hoof tubules will continue to grow in a more horizontal direction and heel growth slows considerably. Elongated and horizontally aligned hoof tubules lose their shock-absorbing function. Distortion of the coronary corium in the rear part of the foot adds to an unending cycle of improper hoof growth and alignment unless aggressive corrective measures are taken by a veterinarian and farrier.

In addition, more horizontally aligned hoof tubules are less able to retain natural hoof "water." This loss of moisture retention ultimately leads to dry, brittle hoof horn, with resultant sand cracks (Photo 35). Nails are less able to maintain a purchase in the weakened horn, so shoes are lost more often.

Not all afflicted horses experience an exaggerated degree of long toe, low heel syndrome. Yet even a mild case is mechanically affected by the principles just reviewed. With improper shoeing, it only takes about three months for a horse to develop under-run heels. It may take a year to return them to a more normal configuration. Half the battle of preventing a long toe, low heel problem is your ability to recognize what it looks like.

The Effects of Shoeing on Hoof Configurations

Some adverse shoeing practices are responsible for creating the long toe, low heel syndrome. The first is an attempt by a farrier to match the foot to an imaginary vision of what it **should** look like based on old-fashioned shoeing ideals (Photo 36). To create this inappropriate vision, heel is trimmed away and the toe is left long.

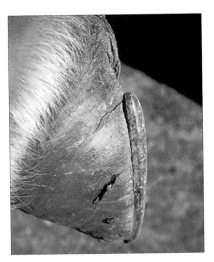

Photo 37 A short-shod hoof with a crack at the end of the shoe branch where the shoe is placing too much pressure. This is a common (but misguided) shoeing practice because farriers fear a shoe will be pulled off by a rear foot if a branch of the shoe is left protruding beyond the heel.

Another case of this syndrome is a fear that a horse that is shod with a long shoe will step on a protruding branch (the end of a shoe) and pull the shoe off with a rear foot. We'll look at this in more detail further along in our discussion.

A common error is to fit a foot with a shoe that is too small (Photo 37). In the photo, you can see that the branch of the shoe ends at the same spot as does the horse's heel. Because of the extra loading of the heels by the broken-back hoof-pastern axis (see Page 51), and because the foot receives no rear support from a properly sized shoe, an extreme amount of stress falls on the horse's heels. We see evidence of this fact from the crack that is obvious just above the end of the shoe branch. The extreme loading of the hoof wall at that point has caused it to weaken.

A low, under-run heel creates a smaller surface area to dissipate concussion from impact, so the hoof wall experiences abnormal loading, particularly at the stress point where the shoe ends. In fact, a smaller surface area amplifies concussion per square inch not only in the hoof, but also all the way up the limb.

Foot growth tends to follow the alignment of the hoof tubules. As mentioned earlier, the hoof tubules normally grow in a relatively vertical direction, and are able to absorb some of the impact force with each step. Once the heels start to grow in a more horizontal direction, the rate of heel growth slows, the feet lose their natural moisture, and weaken. Then growth of the hoof tubules continues to follow the abnormal, horizontal foot form.

The hoof wall experiences *shearing forces* from the relatively long toe, while the very short and small shoe concentrates the impact. The result is cracks or thin fissures in the hoof wall.

How Foot Lameness Develops

Normally, the hoof wall is very expandable. A shoe that is fit too narrowly limits the expansion of the foot at the quarters, causing the foot to absorb more concussion. If the shoe is too short as well as too narrow, the heels assume greater impact. In response to a restrictive shoe, the hoof grows out with low, slow-growing heels that run under more with time. The low heels cause the horse's base of support to shift forward, meaning the foot "moves" farther in front of the cannon bone.

As time and miles accumulate, the horse begins to get sore on its heels. Tension is increased on the deep digital flexor tendon and more compression is forced on the navicular apparatus in a low-heeled horse. A long toe, low heel increases the force needed to lift the hoof for breakover, so muscles fatigue more quickly and the joints and tendons must do more work.

Furthermore, the broken-back hoof-pastern axis forces the pastern into an abnormally upright position. This geometry increases the concussion to the bones and joints in the lower leg by as much as threefold. This sets up conditions for the development of degenerative joint disease or arthritis.

For each degree of change in the angle of the hoof, we see the following effects on the other joints of the lower limb:
- The fetlock joint only experiences one tenth of a degree change in its angle.
- The pastern joint experiences three tenths of a degree change in its angle.
- The coffin joint angle is altered a full degree, a similar amount to the angle change of the foot.

Lowering the heels, or breaking back the hoof-pastern axis, exerts substantial effects on the pastern joint, and particularly on the coffin joint. The angle changes due to a long toe and low heel also create the potential to develop degenerative joint disease or strain and injury to support tissues like ligaments or joint capsules.

Correct Shoeing Techniques

Now that we have looked at ways that a horse should **not** be shod, what is the preferred way to shoe a horse? The toe should be slightly trimmed if possible, and the heels left alone. Left to their own devices, the front of the toes will be

*Photo 38 Shoe branches should
extend at least one quarter inch past
the heel of the hoof. If the perfect
sized shoe is not available, it is
always best to shoe a horse with shoes
that are slightly too big rather than
too small.*

worn down, thereby moving the *breakover point* rearward. This makes it easier for the horse to "step over" the toe and lift each foot from the ground. With this in mind, in situations where a horse has not been able to go barefoot for a while the toes should be squared back considerably.

Ideally, we would like to see the shoe fit the contour of the hoof wall. The shoe should be fit to the foot, rather than the foot shaped to fit the shoe. The shoe should be about one quarter of an inch wider than the hoof at the heels to allow more expandability in the quarters. Nails should not be placed past the bend in the quarters where they might interfere with flex and elasticity in the heels.

The length of the shoe branches should extend at least one quarter of an inch past the heel of the hoof almost, but not quite, to just beneath the back of the heel bulbs (Photo 38). It is always better to use shoes that are too big or too wide than shoes that are too small.

A shoe that is long enough at the rear of the foot is particularly important to a trail horse, because that horse's feet encounter rough and irregular terrain, often littered with rocks. The feet must have good protection, and the lower joints of the limb must have enough support to prevent them from hyper-extending or over-flexing. The only way to achieve these ends is to shoe all four feet with shoes that have adequate length and breadth.

Improved Stride

Arabians notoriously have problems with overreaching, a phenomenon that has been blamed on an anatomical variation in the number of back vertebrae. Some Arabians have one less vertebrae, leading to a marginally shorter back as compared to other breeds. Yet, not all Arabians with short backs pull their shoes off. So this excuse is unlikely to be the only reason for pulling shoes.

A horse that is shod correctly and is given adequate support in both the front and rear of its foot will move more comfortably. The horse that is free of pain in its front end is going to move its shoulders more freely. That horse will have a more elastic stride with a longer reach. If the front end has a place to move because the horse is comfortable, then the rear limbs should not interfere with the front feet. Then, the front shoes should stay nicely in place.

Your horse's efficiency of foot *breakover* and stride length can benefit from correct shoeing practices. This depends on several factors:
- The horse must be free from lameness problems.
- The feet must receive adequate rear support from properly sized shoes with extended branches.
- The toes must not be long and the heels should not be under-run, or else long toe, low heel syndrome (described on pages 49-55) will cause a delay in foot breakover. A delay in breakover provides a greater opportunity for the rear foot to grab the branch on a front foot.
- The feet must be balanced so that both sides of the heels can impact the ground at the same moment. This prevents the horse from becoming sore in the feet or in joints due to rocking or twisting of the foot.

Foot Balance

Foot balance is a critical aspect of maintaining soundness and achieving the best performance your horse has to give. Balance implies a state of equilibrium. In mechanical terms, Webster's Dictionary defines balance as "stability produced by even distribution of weight on each side of the vertical axis." Extra pressure points created by imbalances create stone bruises, heel soreness, ligament or tendon strain, or sprained joints. Muscles compensate for uneven limb placement, resulting in injury or cramping. Over-worked muscles fatigue more quickly, and a horse ties-up, or prematurely runs out of energy.

In our quest for balance with regard to a horse's foot, the objective is to trim the foot so that each side impacts the ground simultaneously while the horse is in motion. The only way to accomplish this to perfection is by using a

Photo 39 A shoe with very uneven wear on the bottom, showing foot balance has not been achieved in shoeing. Note that the outside heel bulb is also pushed up due to uneven pressure on the foot when it makes contact with the ground.

treadmill and a video camera. A little bit of hoof is then trimmed away according to slow motion analysis of each foot strike until the foot lands perfectly level. With this specialized equipment, it is possible to balance each foot of a horse regardless of its conformation.

You probably don't have the luxury of such fine-tuning tools, but your horse's hooves will provide a visual record of deviations from perfect balance. If you study your horse's feet carefully, you can detect inconsistencies before serious problems develop.

Over time, uneven wearing patterns accumulate stress in certain portions of the limb, for both humans and horses alike. For a marathon runner or an endurance horse, uneven loading on the joints and ligaments will exact a toll in structures further up the leg and on into the back.

The Bottom of the Feet as Indicators of Balance

Up until now we have been looking at the foot from the side and analyzing the various effects of a long toe, low heel configuration. Now let's evaluate the feet from the front, the bottom, and from behind.

To illustrate this point, pick up a couple different pairs of your own shoes, and examine the bottoms to see how you may wear one side of the shoe more than another. You know better than anyone how you stand and walk. From that knowledge you must have an appreciation of how your shoes came to be worn unevenly.

Examine the bottom of your horse's shoes for uneven wear patterns. The first tip-off may be seen if the nail heads on one side of the shoe are worn more than the other side (Photo 39). Is the *breakover point* at the toe wearing to the side of center? This would indicate that the foot is twisting slightly as it leaves the ground. Is one side of the shoe worn more than another?

On a smooth, level surface (preferably concrete or asphalt) watch each foot as your horse is walked away from you and then back toward you. Does one side of a foot land sooner or harder than the other side? Try the same analysis at a trot.

The untrained or unassisted eye often has trouble visualizing uneven foot strikes at "real" time, but slow motion videography makes them more obvious. If you can, get a camcorder to videotape your horse's footfalls at both a walk and a trot, then play the tape on slow motion or single frame to see just exactly how each foot lands. It is best to have the horse led in a straight line directly toward and directly away from you, with the handler leading off to the side of the horse so as not to obscure your view. Squat down and aim the camera at the horse's feet, or better yet, place your camera on the ground so the recorded image will not be distorted. In this fashion, you can pick up inconsistencies in foot balance, and avert long-standing problems by pointing these things out to your farrier.

Foot Growth Contributing to Imbalances

Not all foot imbalances are attributed to inappropriate trimming. Many horses grow one side of the foot more quickly then the other side between shoeing intervals. This is particularly true of the side of the foot that receives slightly more impact. If shoes are left on the feet too long, very minor variations in hoof growth develop into more obvious imbalances.

Because the equine hoof is elastic and remodels in response to impact and weight-bearing stresses, it will assume a shape directly reflective of those stresses. The side of the hoof wall that receives more concentrated impact will compress, and develop a steeper appearance to the hoof wall. The rate of growth on that side speeds up relative to the other side. The portion of the hoof that receives less stress will expand, developing a flare on that side. A flare in the hoof wall stimulates the horse to breakover on the side with the steeper slope (the side opposite the flare). This perpetuates the flare by further concentrating the weight-bearing load on the side of the hoof with the steeper wall.

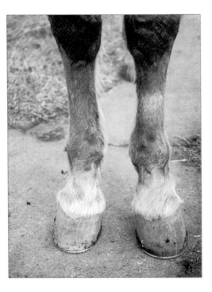

Photo 40 An example of asymmetric coronary bands on both legs. The bands should look the same on both sides of the hoof. This horse also suffers from poor leg conformation and faulty shoeing, which contributes to his uneven impact with the ground, which causes this asymmetry in the coronary bands.

Effects of Balance on the Coronary Bands

More impact on one side of the hoof ultimately results in an upward movement of the heel and/or coronary band. Ideally, lines that extend across the foot through the coronary bands should be parallel to the ground surface. The coronary band should also be similarly perpendicular to the vertical axis of the leg, only slightly dropping away toward the quarters of the heels. If impact has been concentrated on one portion of the foot, the coronary band will be "driven" upward on that heavily loaded side, causing the coronary band to slope at an angle to the ground surface (Photo 40). Similar asymmetric loading forces experienced by the foot are felt throughout the limb.

As a horse lands on each foreleg, loading forces come down the limb over a very concentrated area considering the weight of a horse and the relatively thin skeletal column that assumes his massive load. The greater the surface area over which this load can be diffused, the less chance that support structures will be over-stressed. If the foot can land equally side-to-side, then a greater surface area absorbs the impact more equally in all parts of the limb. Alternatively, if one side of the foot hits the ground before the other side, then not only is concussion assumed by a reduced area of the limb, but there will also be twisting forces exerted on the leg. With each repetitive foot fall, one side of the foot and leg takes more punishment until eventually ligament, bone, joint, or the structures within the foot fail.

Photo 41 Sheared heels are a sign of abnormal loading impact on the foot. When one side of the foot (in this instance, the left side) constantly hits the ground harder than the other, the heel bulb eventually is driven upward. This horse's heels contracted as a result of him protecting the foot due to chronic pain created by the imbalanced foot and sheared heels.

Effects of Balance on the Heel Bulbs

Another sign of abnormally accumulated loading impact on the foot may be apparent as you examine the heel bulbs. If one side of the foot constantly hits the ground harder than the other, then eventually that heel bulb will be driven upward relative to the other. This phenomenon is known as *sheared heels* (Photo 41). If allowed to persist long enough, the heels become very unstable, and can even be displaced with pressure from your hands. This will result in pain and lameness. The side of the foot (and limb) that receives added concussion can develop quarter cracks, sidebone, or navicular disease.

Imagine how running would feel if you had to first land on the inside of your foot and then shift your weight over to the outside of your foot. The inside foot structures would become very bruised, and the rotational forces experienced with each footstep would accumulate over the miles. Your ankles would be sore, and your inclination to run would diminish with each step.

As with many problems creating foot imbalances, the correction for sheared heels depends on leveling and balancing both sides of the foot equally. Over time, the heel bulbs will return to a normal orientation, and your horse will move with greater comfort.

The Visual Record of the Entire Foot

The long-distance equine athlete depends on exquisite foot balance to perform to potential, mile after mile. Accumulated asymmetrical stresses on the

Photo 42 A hoof shod with an egg bar shoe and pad.

feet and joints due to imbalanced trimming practices hasten "wear and tear," particularly on the joints. Watch for signs of asymmetrical foot shape (steep walls and flares), for sloping coronary bands, and for uneven heel bulbs.

You have now gathered a list of visual clues to monitor in your quest for the balanced foot. They include:

- hoof flares or very steep hoof walls
- stress cracks where the hoof is overloaded
- asymmetrical slopes to the coronary bands
- one heel bulb higher than the other
- unequal wear on the shoe bottom or nail heads
- *breakover point* not central at the toe

Types of Shoes

The diversity of equine foot gear that is currently available can be somewhat overwhelming to the rider who tries to stay abreast of the latest developments. Shoes now come in various designs and are composed of steel, synthetic plastics, or a blend of the two. As you puzzle over which shoes are best for your horse, don't forget that the principles of balanced trimming will have more to do with your horse's performance than the style of shoe does.

Egg Bar Shoes

Of the variety of shoe configurations we have to choose from, I'd like to discuss here the benefits of using an egg bar shoe for the long-distance horse (Photo 42). **Many** horses competing today in endurance sports would not be as able (if at all) were it not for wearing egg bar shoes. We have investigated the risks of a broken-back hoof-pastern axis and the detriment of a long toe, low heel foot. Historically, an egg bar shoe has been applied to these kinds of problem feet as a therapy to correct an already existing problem. An egg bar shoe can also be used to **prevent** these syndromes from developing in the first place. And, egg bar shoes provide stability to limbs with less than perfect conformation. For the horse with many miles on the campaign trail, egg bar shoes help protect joints that suffer from mild degenerative arthritis. The support offered by egg bar shoes also relieves stress on the suspensory ligaments and other support ligaments of the fetlocks and pasterns.

How does an egg bar shoe help support your horse's feet? First, let's look at this from the point of view of what happens when a standard type steel plate is placed on the foot, with the shoe just barely covering the bearing surface of the hoof wall (see Photo 37, page 56). The shoe in question does not have an extended branch or a bar, and provides no extra support for the foot. In fact, this type of shoe (which is one that is commonly placed on a horse's foot) actually reduces the surface area with which the hoof contacts the ground. A horse that goes barefoot would have a greater surface area of ground contact. Barefoot is obviously not an option for a long-distance equine athlete.

A reduced ground surface created by a "just-barely-fits" shoe has several negative effects on the foot and the rest of the limb. The impact energy of the foot hitting the ground is intensified onto a smaller area of the foot. We have already seen how this results in hoof cracks at the point of extreme loading. Such concentrated impact also magnifies concussion in unbalanced and un-supported areas of the foot, creating "hot spots" and leading to persistent lameness. For feet shod in this fashion, it is difficult to resolve corns, bruised heels, or a bruised sole unless the inciting problem is corrected: the length and breadth of the shoe applied to the foot.

Our goal in managing long-distance horses is to minimize "wear-and-tear" diseases of the musculoskeletal structures. A shoe that reduces the ground surface is counterproductive to that end because it increases rotational stresses on the joints. With each step, the ankles sink; more stress is placed on the front surfaces of the fetlock joints, on support ligaments, and on the sesamoid bones. Such stress on the lower limb structures is particularly harmful when a horse is already fatigued from a difficult or lengthy exertion. It is not just the fetlock joints that succumb to abnormal rotational forces. The coffin joints also experience extra flexion when the foot has a reduced surface area of contact with the ground. To compound the problem, extra rotational forces on the joints amplify the work effort necessary to lift and advance each foot, wearing the horse down more quickly during training and competition. Musculoskeletal fatigue overtaxes a horse's metabolic system and threatens further injury to the legs.

How can egg bar shoes help support your horse's feet and joints? Think of the shoes in your closet. A dress shoe tends to be narrow with less bottom to it than your hiking boot. Dress shoes may nicely fit your feet and be comfy enough to wear in a friend's living room or at a restaurant. Yet, when you scramble along hiking trails and over rocks, would you be as comfortable or feel as secure wearing dress shoes instead of the wide treads provided by your hiking boots? No contest.

An egg bar shoe provides a similar kind of support for a horse's foot. The oval shape and extended branch inherent to an egg bar shoe increase the surface area for weight distribution as the horse loads the limb. With the bar extended back to just under the heel bulbs, the total surface contact with the ground is increased by as much as 30-40% by the rear foot support! Remember, the larger the surface area that the foot contacts with the ground, the better the energy of impact is diffused through the entire foot and on up the limb.

Egg bar shoes protect the heels and frogs from bruising, particularly on terrain with rough going, like rocks, ruts, dirt clods, and gravel. A horse that is prone to heel soreness benefits from egg bar shoes because they stabilize the foot by adding some rigidity to the heels. Contrary to what you might think, an egg bar shoe does **not** cause feet to contract over time. In fact, by making it more comfortable for a horse to bear weight on previously sore feet, the feet will grow out with more spread to them. A horse with under-run heels will see correction of this problem over a six to nine month period as the hoof tubules (see Figure 11, page 52) grow more vertically in response to rear foot support. The most efficient means of gaining rear foot support for under-run heels is afforded by the "egg bar" of the shoe.

A horse that needs the protection of pads because of severely rocky terrain or because of a flat-footed conformation can also benefit from egg bars. In the same way that the bar protects the heels and frog, the bar will reinforce a pad so it is not as likely to deform over miles of pounding.

As a support for the hind legs, egg bars again have a role. The push by the hocks as a horse climbs a mountainside underscores the impressive load assumed by the joints of the hind end. Hours of trotting along winding roads and irregular trails requires that a horse push evenly with its hindquarters, and place its hocks squarely under its body. Guess what! Egg bar shoes again give the rear end the needed stability each time the horse plants its leg. The ankles won't twist as readily as they would without the support, and the hocks experience less twisting forces with hind feet shod with egg bars.

Not all horses need egg bar shoes for optimal performance. Some instances where egg bar shoes may not be appropriate include the following:

- Egg bars on the front feet may be cumbersome for sand work or very deep footing because the lift and advance of the limb that mires in sticky ground may be slowed further by these shoes.

- It can be argued that the extra weight of an egg bar shoe may hasten fatigue. However, if this is a concern, there are plastic or aluminum forms of egg bar shoes that are light yet offer heel support. Typically, the advantages of egg bar shoes so outweigh any concerns created by a slightly heavier shoe that this is not a real issue.

- An egg bar shoe that is incorrectly fitted, especially too wide on the inside of the foot, could lead to interference injuries of the opposite leg. This, of course, is true of any shoe.

- Finally, egg bar shoes can be a nuisance or even a hazard in a wintry climate. Snow and ice packed in the foot potentially bruises the sole through pressure points. High heels created by snowballs abnormally elevate the foot and increase rotation on all joints of the lower limb. Snowballs packed in the feet also create a dangerously slippery surface. This problem is overcome to some degree with the use of pads.

The use of egg bar shoes will vary depending on your geographic location, the terrain over which you ride, and your horse's special needs. The ideal situations that promote use of egg bar shoes include riding over hard packed or rocky terrain that has no cushion to the ground surface. Application of a specific synthetic horseshoe like Equithotics would automatically provide a bar shoe type design, providing rear foot support and anti-concussion damping at the same time.

There is no reason not to apply an egg bar type shoe when training or competing over rigorous terrain and then changing the shoes back to regular plates in more forgiving ground. Sometimes the only way to tell if your horse is more comfortable in an egg bar shoe is to try out a set and see how he moves. Then you can make a decision whether to continue with that shoeing strategy, or not.

Egg bar shoes are hardly a new invention. In one book entitled *Horseshoeing* that was written in 1884 for the Royal Veterinary College in Dresden, Germany, it states that "By using a bar shoe, we can either gain a more extensive bearing-surface of the hoof, or can make it easier for the surface that bears the weight to do the work." Egg bar shoes are a great tool to providing our horses with a support system for longevity along the trail.

Alternative Horseshoes

Until just recently, we haven't had much in the way of choices in equine foot gear. There have been metal shoes with bars or without bars, choices between aluminum or steel, a potpourri of pads, but not much in the shock-absorption department. Concern with musculoskeletal longevity has now carried over into the manufacturing arena of horseshoes. Today we have plenty of choices in synthetic horseshoes. What we will examine here are some advantages to using synthetic shoes over steel.

A barefoot hoof is relatively soft and elastic as compared to a hoof shod with steel. In its normal state, the equine hoof and internal structures "deform" with impact. With each step, a horse tends to land heel first, then rocks forward onto the rest of the bearing surface of the hoof wall. As barefoot heels hit, they flex outward slightly due to their inherent elastic properties. The horn tubules within the hoof wall act like shock-absorbing springs, while the digital cushion with its network of fluid-filled lymphatic vessels acts like a hydraulic shock to absorb impact energy. The collateral cartilages, the frog, the bars of the foot, and the flexor tendons all contribute to maintaining pressure in the digital cushion while the limb is loaded. This creates a "spring system" within the hoof that effectively transfers strain and dampens concussion. The energy of impact is slowed as the soft tissues deform and rebound with each contact of the hoof with the ground.

The Effects of Steel Horseshoes

What happens when you place a steel shoe on your horse's foot? Several phenomena change:

1. The foot now has added weight, thereby altering the mechanics of foot flight and increasing the muscular effort to move each leg.
2. Research has shown that the rate of heel expansion is accelerated by a steel shoe, resulting in a greater and more rapid transmission of impact energy to the more forward structures of the foot. Concussion is increased dramatically over that experienced by an unshod hoof, by as much as 400%! In addition, with a steel shoe shock is transmitted through the rest of the limb, rather than being absorbed primarily by

the bare hoof's spring system.

3. Nails affixing the shoe to the hoof alter the "entry" and transmission of impact energy, causing it to rebound through the entire foot and up the limb into joints and tendons.

4. The heels wear more quickly as a result of the increase in concussion forces due to the use of steel shoes. Excessively lowered heels (created by increased wear or improper trimming) are even less capable of reducing concussion strain. A long toe, low heel foot configuration adversely affects the ability of the hoof tubules to dampen concussion.

How does this affect your long-distance horse? With many miles and faster speeds, more strain is accumulated in all structures in the limb. Natural concussion-damping actions by the tissues cannot keep pace with repeated trauma to the musculoskeletal structures. Vibrations created by repeated strikes of shod hooves against the ground are transmitted through the hoof and up the entire skeletal column. Joints absorb far more concussion than they were designed to take, tendon and ligament fibers are continually exposed to these impact vibrations, and the hoof tissues experience persistent trauma. It is no wonder that a distance horse is at risk of chronic lameness. At the very least, performance suffers due to subtle but persistent pain generated by these shock waves.

We have discussed the critical importance of a balanced foot and adequate shoe support to minimize uneven loading of each hoof and limb. Other strategies to minimize musculoskeletal damage include lightening the weight of a shoe by using aluminum or titanium or plastic materials rather than steel.

Synthetic Horseshoes

For a synthetic shoe to absorb energy, it must be able to "deform," preferably in a manner similar to that of an unshod hoof. As the shoe impacts the ground, the less rigid the shoe material, the more it is able to absorb energy. As an example, leather makes a fine material for absorbing the energy of impact, but it quickly wears away and provides limited foot protection. Many of the synthetic shoes incorporate polyurethane or flexible rubber to achieve concussion dampening. These materials are more elastic and deformable than steel, and wear for an acceptable period (Photos 43 & 44).

The faster a horse goes, the more quickly and more often each hoof strikes the ground. Faster speeds exacerbate the trauma generated by steel shoes. Consider the analogy of the strike of a hammer on a nail: the more quickly one strikes the nail with an iron hammer, the further the nail is driven into wood. The rapid impact time of a forceful blow generates great energy. However, if

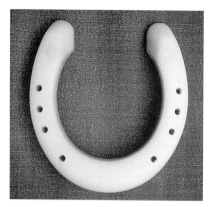

Photo 43 A "Mustad Nail Shu."
A popular type of synthetic shoe, this is
an aluminum shoe that is coated with
shock–absorbing polyurethane.

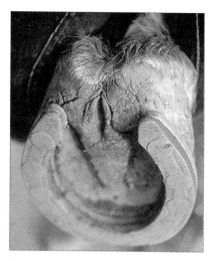

Photo 44 A Slypner synthetic shoe,
showing the polyurethane insert that
is used in conjunction with the shoe
that is nailed to the horse's hoof.

you use a rubber hammer to drive the nail with the same force, the nail is not driven as far into the wood. The rubber dampens the impact by **prolonging** the impact time of the blow. This results in a reduction in concussive energy transmitted to the nail. If you apply this analogy to the forces felt by a hoof shod with polyurethane horseshoes, you can see that such synthetic material may well dampen concussive forces on the foot and all limb structures.

The Horse's Attempt at Comfort

High speed cinematography has demonstrated that to compensate for the concussion incurred by a steel shoe, a horse will modify the way its hooves strike the ground. In an instinctive attempt to prolong the impact time, a horse will skid its hooves on a hard surface. By lengthening the impact time, much as in the rubber hammer analogy, the energy of impact is reduced within the hoof. However, to coordinate each of the other limbs with such a skidding strategy makes it difficult for a horse to maintain a comfortable stride rhythm. Inadvertently, his muscles must exert a greater effort to move him down the trail as he tries to soften the blow with each step. Fatigue is accelerated in the course of training or competition, and compensatory injuries are more likely to occur.

Consider also that to increase speed, a horse's hooves must spend less time contacting the ground, not more. Skidding the foot even slightly slows the horse and creates a less efficient stride. Since our goal with our long-distance horses is to improve locomotive efficiency and reduce muscular effort, it would seem we are doing a disservice by working our horses in steel shoes. Synthetic shoes tend to have greater traction on hard surfaces, thereby reducing the slip and slide of the foot. This improves your horse's push-off and acceleration, so you can move down the trail more efficiently.

Disadvantages of Synthetic Horseshoes

As with most things in life, the issues are not always black and white. Synthetic shoes are not perfect in all situations. In some terrain conditions, synthetic shoes may actually lessen your horse's traction. Specifically, a horse wearing synthetic shoes in mud, or while working on a sideways slope, may have more difficulty keeping his feet under him. A slightly moist surface, particularly if slanted, forces your horse to try to keep his feet level. Although you may slow your pace to allow your horse's muscles to "rest," his muscles may in fact work a lot harder than you realize just trying to keep himself on his feet. You may not feel this while in the saddle, particularly if your horse is quite athletic. But, if you follow behind another horse who is fighting the poor traction created by synthetic shoes on slick surfaces, the problem will be evident. Wet grass or grass coated with a light layer of snow especially amplifies the slippage problem.

The trick is to anticipate this as a problem if such footing arises at a competition. You may be able to apply studs or borium nails in some synthetic shoes to help reduce slippage, or you may need to adjust your speed accordingly for the conditions. In certain situations, it may be worthwhile to reshoe with steel shoes for a particular ride.

Other Advantages of Synthetic Horseshoes

Plastic shoes add another advantage that may not be instantly apparent. Because the material is softer than steel, it wears somewhat more quickly, particularly if a horse is landing unevenly. This provides you with interesting diagnostic information about how your horse's hooves impact the ground. You can follow the wear patterns as the tread abrades away. This enables you and your veterinarian to better understand your horse's gaits. It may shed some light on subtle lameness issues, while inspiring strategies to help prevent chronic pain problems.

Perhaps even more importantly, if your horse has been shod unevenly, or if your horse prefers to *breakover* off center due to conformational peculiarities, he can wear the synthetic tread to accommodate his preferred movement pattern. We all do this with the rubber soles of our shoes. Pick up some of your hiking shoes and examine the bottoms. Just because one side is worn more than another doesn't necessarily mean you have a locomotor problem. It just means your body has learned to move that way and your musculoskeletal system has compensated for your lack of symmetry. The same is true of our horses — they don't always want to land on their feet the way we and our farriers try to force them to. Synthetic materials wear down more quickly in small increments that may favorably affect your horse's comfort while in motion.

Your horse will tell you if he doesn't like his "high tech" shoes. His stride length will change if he is uncomfortable or not as confident in his new foot gear. Sometimes you will immediately recognize a shortened stride, a choppier gait, or a slowing down on the hills. Other times, the alteration in gait is more subtle, and you may need to measure foot imprints by trotting your horse on a soft ground surface and measuring the distance between front and rear steps. Compare this to your horse's previous way-of-going in steel shoes.

In most cases, an owner comments that the horse "loves" his new synthetic shoes, and is traveling with a more extended stride and a nicer bounce in his step.

Synthetic shoes generally are a great help to the older horse and to the long-term campaigner. The less resilient the bones, joints, tendons, and ligamentous tissues in the aging horse, the more important it is for the horse to be equipped with good shock-absorption footwear. The synthetic materials are also a real advantage to those horses that tend to bruise their feet quite easily or who suffer from inflammation of the coffin bone (*pedal osteitis*). But remember to continue to respect the footing even though your horse is equipped with shock-absorbing shoes.

4 Intelligent Nutrition

For the last couple of decades, our society has reminded us that "you are what you eat." It would seem on a superficial level that being an herbivore, a horse doesn't have many choices in nutritional fare that would influence his performance output. This is quite far from the truth.

The subject of nutrition of the equine athlete actually has two important components. The first is the availability of adequate energy and nutrients to fuel locomotion; the second is the promotion of intestinal health and the horse's overall well-being. If you understand these essential elements, you can more easily customize a feeding program to accommodate your horse's individual needs while using local feed sources to advantage.

On a simplistic level, a horse eats plant fibers (grass and hay) or grains to maintain body condition. Yet, the diversity in selection of each of these foodstuffs has a dramatic influence on muscle metabolism and *endocrine* balances in the body. Let's take a look at the basic components of horse food and follow each substance through the digestive process.

Carbohydrates

Your horse's need for energy during the intense exertion required by prolonged endurance exercise is more than double the usual maintenance requirements. You will need to tailor his diet to supply these additional needs.

A primary energy source for horses is obtained from complex carbohydrates, or starch. This is found in the stem and leaves of plants (hay or *roughage*) and seed heads (grains). Once in the small intestine, all carbohydrates (grass, hay, alfalfa, and grains) are converted to glucose. Glucose that is not used immediately to supply the brain and nervous tissue is then assimilated by liver and muscle cells and converted to its storage form: *glycogen*. Further surpluses are stored as fat.

Often more energy is needed for muscular work than can be supplied by glucose that is circulating in the bloodstream. In these instances, muscle cells transform stored glycogen into a chemical form of usable energy known as *adenosine triphosphate (ATP)*. Adenosine triphosphate is made of protein molecules that are connected by high energy bonds. When these bonds are divided during the process of metabolism, energy is released. ATP is essential to all reactions in the body, including the most basic functions of breathing, the beating of the heart, and those reactions that extract energy from food. All physiological functions depend on availability of ATP. Think of ATP as the energy currency of the body that drives every cellular function from the most microscopic of levels to the obvious muscular contraction that you see as a horse powers himself down the trail. ATP is our life force, what makes us more than inanimate objects. The more energy efficient the metabolic process, the less fuel is consumed to generate ATP and the longer work can be done.

The most productive metabolic process is called *aerobic metabolism*, when oxygen is available in the muscle cells. This normally occurs with low to moderate intensity exercise at walk and trot speeds. *Mitochondria* are energy factories within the muscle cells that function in the presence of oxygen to metabolize glucose to carbon dioxide and water with the production of 36-38 ATP molecules. Carbon dioxide and water are innocuous by-products and don't harm the muscle cells. As you will see, aerobic metabolism is exceedingly more efficient at generating energy (ATP) than is its alternative.

High intensity exercise, like sprinting, often demands active muscular work more rapidly than the muscle tissues can receive oxygen from the circulation. In the absence of oxygen in the muscle tissues, the conversion of glycogen to glucose is called *anaerobic metabolism*. For each molecule of glucose generated by anaerobic metabolism, only two energy molecules (ATP) are produced as compared to 36-38 ATP generated by aerobic metabolism. A by-product of anaerobic metabolism is *lactic acid* which is toxic to the cells if it accumulates in the tissues. This form of metabolism makes it possible for a horse to sprint, climb mountains, jump obstacles, or execute any intense athletic effort for a short period, but certainly not for a long period of time.

With this in mind, you can appreciate that an endurance athlete benefits by optimizing its ability to do aerobic work, also referred to as *submaximal exercise*.

A word of warning: feeding excess carbohydrate in the form of grain results in increased glycogen levels in the muscles with the potential for greater production of lactic acid. In order to avoid the toxicity of lactic acid accumulation in the bloodstream, it is therefore prudent not to overfeed grain supplements to the endurance athlete. (For more details on lactic acid, please refer to Chapter 5.)

Fortunately for the long-distance athlete, there is another form of carbohydrate that resides in plant leaves as fiber, often known as *roughage*. Fiber reaches the large colon and cecum in a relatively unchanged form. Resident bacteria within the large colon and cecum produce enzymes capable of converting plant cellulose into *volatile fatty acids (VFAs)*. Volatile fatty acids are organic acids that are the end product of digestion of soluble carbohydrates derived from the diet. Not only do volatile fatty acids supply at least 25% of the energy required to maintain a horse at rest, but they are an essential energy source for the long distance horse. These fatty acids are well absorbed from the large intestine and used as energy for aerobic work. If you supply adequate roughage in your horse's diet, the large intestine then serves as a reservoir to continually supply the muscles with energy sources for protracted exercise.

Fats

Fats in the form of liquid oils or powdered supplements, are an excellent energy source for aerobic muscle contraction. Fat deposits are stored in tissue located between individual muscle cells and are also available as energy from volatile fatty acids that are generated by bacterial fermentation in the large intestine as described above. Fatty acids (from either triglycerides or volatile fatty acids) travel a metabolic pathway similar to that of glucose molecules: all these energy forms are metabolized within energy factories (*mitochondria*) of muscle cells in the presence of oxygen. Once fat is broken down in the small intestine, its mobilization and transport to the muscle tissues is relatively slow as compared to the more immediate availability of glycogen in the muscles. This limits the usefulness of fat as an energy source when a horse works at a higher intensity that demands immediate fuel, like the efforts required by sprinting or steep climbs.

The more conditioned the horse, the more he is able to rely on fat metabolism to move him down the trail, because his muscles predominantly work in the presence of oxygen, aerobically. Feeding fat to the horse has been proven as an excellent source of energy with minimal side effects. During *aerobic* exercise, a horse's metabolism burns fat first, thereby sparing glycogen reserves in the muscles and liver for later use in the competitive event. In addition, fatty acids cannot be used *anaerobically*, so there is little chance of forming lactic acid that hastens the onset of fatigue (see page 97). Using aerobic energy sources such as fat also delays the onset of fatigue that accompanies glycogen depletion. A high fat diet improves a horse's tolerance to exercise in hot weather since metabolism of fatty acids generates 30% less heat than does metabolism of high protein diets. A high fat diet also increases your horse's calorie intake without increasing the volume he must eat. Fat as a concentrated form of calories reduces your horse's intestinal fill so he can consume more roughage.

Feeding fat as a dietary supplement reduces the amount of grain that must be fed, thereby reducing the risk of colic, *tying-up syndrome*, or laminitis. As much as 10% of the total diet can be in the form of fat. This means you can feed as much as one cup of vegetable oil **twice** a day, with excellent results. Oil should be introduced gradually into the feed so your horse becomes accustomed to the taste, and so that diarrhea doesn't develop from a sudden feed change. Start with about one-third cup twice a day, building up to your goal over a two week period. Too much oil is unpalatable, and it may interfere with mineral absorption.

Fat contains 2.25 times more energy than an equal weight of grain. A cup of vegetable oil (240 grams of fat) is equivalent in caloric value to 1.2 pounds of corn, 1.5 pounds of oats, or 1 pound of sweet feed. You can substitute vegetable oils for some grain, but it's best not to feed more than two cups of oil per day to the 1000 pound horse.

Oil is more than 85% digestible, particularly if you feed any of the long-chain unsaturated fats such as corn, soybean, coconut, peanut, canola, or sunflower oil. Animal fat is also a valuable energy source and is easier to handle than vegetable oil when it comes in a powdered form; this product is 80% crude fat in a sugar base. All fat supplements are prone to going rancid, so they should be stored in a cool, dark place. Vitamin E (400-1000 IU/day) should be supplemented as well to improve the utilization of fat.

Rice bran is another popular feed product to supplement energy for the hard-working horse. On average, horses are fed two pounds of rice bran per day as a supplement. This product is 20% fat as compared to the 100% fat of oils, so you'll need to feed five times more rice bran to supply calories equivalent to that obtained from oil.

Comparison of Carbohydrate vs. Fatty Acid Benefits

A horse's blood glucose peaks about four hours after consuming a generous feeding of grain. This high circulating glucose level does not go directly to fuel muscle work; instead it must be converted through the described metabolic pathways which require ample blood flow to the intestines. The hard-working equine athlete needs to have 85% of its blood flow through the muscles; digestive processes detract from routing of blood to the muscles.

Within 30-60 minutes of eating a large grain meal, insulin surges through

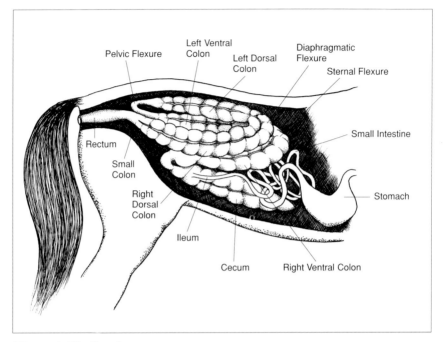

Figure 12 The digestive system.

the blood. Both glucose and insulin peak about two to four hours after feeding. One of the functions of insulin is to drive glucose into the cells, in this case making less glucose available in the bloodstream for muscles. Because of this phenomenon, known as *rebound hypoglycemia*, it is best not to feed a heavy grain meal within four hours of competition.

On the other hand, *roughage* does **not** influence glucose production, since its energy form is produced as *volatile fatty acids*, which pass directly into pathways for aerobic energy production. In most endurance endeavors, fatigue is a result of glycogen or triglyceride depletion from aerobic metabolism rather than lactic acid accumulation. By feeding ample roughage and fat, you maximize your horse's energy sources by providing efficient energy sources for aerobic exercise.

Roughage also keeps the intestines working efficiently, and roughage serves as a fluid and *electrolyte* reservoir to be tapped during time of need during long-distance work. One study demonstrated that horses fed only hay and salt had 73% more water in the digestive tract after exercise and 33% more available electrolytes as compared to horses fed a low roughage diet. Not only does plant fiber have the capacity to hold water in the intestinal reservoir, but a high roughage diet encourages horses to drink more. Safe feeding practices include roughage comprising at least 50% of the diet; concentrates such as grain or pellets should be restricted to **less than** 50% of the diet by weight. Up to 10% of the total diet can be replaced with fat to gain calories and a useful energy source. Remember, you can safely feed your horse two cups of oil per day to provide a source of fat, and it should be fed daily so your horse's body "learns" to use it as an energy source. This strategy should be started at least several weeks prior to competition.

Protein

The protein requirement of the mature horse, including the endurance athlete, is only about 10% of total food intake. Sources of protein include alfalfa and other legume hays, soybean and linseed products; protein is present in variable amounts in other hays and grains. Although protein can be used for energy, it is metabolically expensive. Its breakdown in the liver results in increased urinary excretion to rid the body of nitrogen that results from protein metabolism. Horses on high protein diets, like alfalfa, urinate more than horses fed grass hay or pasture. This may make a significant difference in competition where a horse needs to retain as much fluid as possible, while counterproductively urinating it away if fed high protein levels. In addition, high protein diets generate more body heat, which is detrimental to a working horse. Finally, an accumulation of the by-products of protein metabolism, such as ammonia and urea, stimulate irritability of the nervous system. In a stall environment, these substances are also irritating to the respiratory tract.

Rarely does a horse need to use protein for energy unless on a carbohydrate-restricted diet. Such a situation is rarely encountered in a performance horse, so a rule of thumb is to feed a diet of around 10% protein *total digestible nutrients (TDN)*.

Body Condition

It is important to manage your equine athlete's body weight at an optimal level. You don't want too much flesh covering his frame since fat impedes dissipation of body heat during exercise, and extra weight adds stress to the musculoskeletal structures. If your horse is too lean, on the other hand, then he won't have reserves to draw on during prolonged exercise.

Ideally, you'd like to just barely be able to feel the last two ribs as you lightly run your hand across the side of his body. You shouldn't have to hunt for

Photo 45 A horse in perfect body condition. Neither too fat nor thin with appropriate muscling for long distance work.

Photo 46 A horse in poor body condition for competition, underweight and tucked-up (dehydrated-looking).

the ribs with firm pressure. Likewise, you don't want to be able to feel every rib, and you certainly don't want to see every rib (Photos 45 & 46).

Horses tend to lose weight during competition for a variety of reasons. Water losses, muscle metabolism, the stress of transport to and from rides, and adjusting to a new environment at a competition all contribute to weight loss in the competitive horse. Your goal should be to maintain your horse in a peak body condition so that some loss of body weight subsequent to a competition will not affect your horse's performance and stamina.

Water

Water is one of the most critical ingredients to a healthy horse's diet, and particularly to an equine athlete. An idle horse needs five to seven gallons of water per day to process food and maintain physiologic health. However, an active horse engaged in training and competition may drink 15-20 gallons of water each day to replenish fluid losses from sweat and muscular metabolism. Clean, fresh water should be available at all times and the horse given every opportunity to drink.

Vitamins and Minerals

Usually a balanced diet and a healthy functioning digestive system provide a horse with all necessary vitamin requirements. However, the stressed endurance competitor may benefit from vitamin B and C supplementation to compensate for stress-related effects on bowel function and nutrient absorption. Also, in areas where the soil is deficient in specific mineral nutrients, these substances may need to be supplemented. For example, selenium is very important to adequate muscle function; a horse on a selenium-deficient diet is prone to *tying-up* syndrome. Before you supplement with selenium, have your feed analyzed since selenium is toxic if fed in excess. (If there is a concern about potentially excessive dietary selenium from hay or pasture, it is helpful to analyze the selenium level of your horse's blood, tail or mane.) Vitamin E (one to four grams daily) should be supplemented along with a selenium additive.

Most electrolytes are available in a normal ration, with the exception of one electrolyte which bears mentioning: sodium. Sodium is not available in forage or grains, so a horse must have access to a supplementary salt source, either as a salt block or as an additive to the grain.

Read the directions on supplements carefully and request the advice of your veterinarian so you do not over-supplement vitamins and minerals, since too much stimulates a horse to urinate more. This could add to fluid losses during competition.

Nutraceuticals

Nutraceuticals are food additive supplements that allegedly alter the function or structure of your horse's body. Although their efficacy remains unsubstantiated, they may give a horse an unfair advantage over another. In many cases, nutraceuticals are components of naturally occurring substances in the body or may be a concentrated component found in standard food. These products are not considered drugs and therefore are not regulated by the Food and Drug Administration (FDA). Examples include products such as MSM (methylsulfonylmethane), DMG (N-Dimethylglycine), or oral formulations containing glycosaminoglycans that supposedly improve metabolism and nutritional health of muscles and joints, and reduce inflammation. Other food additives include biotin or DL-methionine to improve hoof growth.

In endurance sports, many nutraceuticals are prohibited from use several days before and during competition. In addition, they may cause a positive result in blood drawn for drug testing at a competition.

Preventing Intestinal Upsets

As horse owners, one of the dreaded situations we all fear is colic. Horses get colic in the best of management conditions, for no apparent reason. Often, the source of a colic is grounded in human error. Recent studies have correlated an increased risk of colic whenever feeding practices have been recently **changed**. More often than not, when questioning owners of a colicky horse, I have noted that feeding practices have been modified significantly within the two week period before an event. Most commonly, riders introduce new elements to their feeding practices upon arrival at a ride site.

For people who trailer long distances, it is often difficult to transport enough hay for an extended trip, particularly for more than one horse. Then you are at the mercy of buying whatever local hay is easily available. Any sudden feed change alters intestinal bacteria in some way. Fortunately, many horses are able to adapt to an altered diet with no ill effects. Other horses have a more fragile system, falling prey to excessive fermentation in the bowels, with gas accumulation and pain.

Some guidelines to help your horse cope both at home and at a ride:

- If you normally feed grass hay and must purchase from a strange source during your travels, try to find a comparable quality of hay. Steer clear of very "stemmy," coarse hay if your horse is not used to it. Coarse hay can be irritating to the intestines, and can lead to impaction colic. A grass hay that is very leafy like alfalfa may be highly fermentable, creating similar colic problems. If you must buy or borrow from a new source of hay, initially try to blend it with your horse's normal hay, at least half and half. Save enough hay on the trip to enable you to do this for several days so your horse's intestines make an easier transition to the newer food.

- If your horse is used to being on pasture, a sudden change to dry hay can really throw his intestines into a tailspin. The stresses of transport and exercise place a greater demand on your horse for water intake. Just when your horse needs moist foods the most, you are switching him from high-water-content pasture to dried grasses (in the form of hay) while exacting tremendous physical demands at a competition. You can prepare for this by introducing grass hay at home at least a couple weeks before the ride so his intestines are accustomed to processing the drier feed. Offer hay in the pasture every day. Because it is different, your horse will probably dive into it despite the presence of good pasture.

- Conversely, a horse that is used to hay **only** should be given limited access to grazing at a ride site. Many camping areas are situated in a comfortable meadow, abundant with juicy and tempting pasture grasses. If you allow your horse to over-indulge in the native grasses, they ferment in the bowel, and may lead to painful colic.

- Don't suddenly switch from grass hay to legume hay. You may have heard that a competitive horse needs alfalfa hay at a ride to replenish rapidly the calcium that is lost in sweat. Certainly alfalfa hay provides a good source of calcium, but if your horse isn't used to it, don't overdo it! Part of a flake or a small flake offered at each vet check and at the finish is sufficient during competition. If you prefer to feed a little more alfalfa, spend at least two weeks accustoming his bowels to increasingly greater amounts, starting with about half a flake initially.

- If you feed concentrates, like pelleted feed, remember that these processed feeds require a lot of intestinal water for digestion, yet hard-working horse tends to dehydrate over the miles. In addition, blood flow is diverted away from digestive processes to the working muscles, and water is pulled from the intestinal reservoir to replace water lost in sweat. Inadequate intestinal water for digestion leads to an impaction. Any distention of the intestines causes pain, cramping, and colic. And, the potential then exists for intestinal displacements or twists.

- Before you offer large quantities of hay or grain at vet checks and at the finish line, make sure he is well cooled down (rectal temperature of less than 103°F or 40°C). If not, then blood continues to be diverted away from the intestines to the skin and muscles to dissipate heat. Reduced intestinal circulation leads to trouble. Cool him out first, and at the very least, offer water-logged feed like soupy bran mashes or even wetted hay. This is important throughout the ride and during the day or two after the ride while your horse is recovering his fluid losses.

- Don't suddenly start packing the supplements to your horse just before or during a ride if he isn't normally on such a diet. Feeding more than five pounds of grain at a single feeding overwhelms the ability of the small intestine to digest and absorb the starch. When starch bypasses the small intestine and enters the large intestine, it ferments which could cause laminitis and/or colic.
- Be conservative in your decisions on what to feed and whether or not to offer something in the first place. This includes not only grain products, but vitamins, minerals, and *nutraceuticals*. Electrolytes are an exception because you are attempting to replace those lost in sweat due to hard exercise. Electrolyte supplementation is necessary to the welfare of the long-distance athlete and is especially important in a hot, humid climate.

For several days following a competition, help replenish your horse's energy and fluid losses by feeding wetted hay and soupy gruels made from your horse's usual grain. Make sure your horse has plenty of water at all times. Find out what type of water bucket your horse prefers (plastic, rubber or galvanized) that might improve water intake.

The best way to stay out of trouble is to keep things **consistent**. Feed like you always do at home. Maintain a routine. A competition is **not** the place to experiment! Don't make sudden feed changes if at all possible. Your horse will perform better and be happier over the miles.

Feeding Summary

In summary, safe feeding practices for the endurance athlete include:

1. Provide as much quality roughage as your horse will consume. A horse should be fed at least 1 to 2% of its body weight per day as hay. That is 15-20 pounds of hay for a thousand pound horse. A hard-working athlete should have free choice hay available at all times.
2. Feed roughage (hay) or allow access to the horse's accustomed pasture as at least 50% (by weight) of the daily ration.

3. Limit grain supplements to less than 50% (by weight) of the daily ration.

4. Do not feed a heavy grain meal within four hours of competition and offer less than a couple of pounds of grain (if any) at the vet checks during competition.

5. Include up to 10% of the ration as fat (vegetable oil) as a substitute for some grain supplementation.

6. The equine athlete only needs 10% protein in its diet. Routine feeding of excess protein is detrimental to performance.

7. Do not over-supplement vitamins or minerals, but analyze your feed so you can add any substances that are deficient.

8. Supplement with electrolytes during prolonged exercise, especially in hot and/or humid climates.

5 Conditioning Principles and Training Philosophy

Systems Development

Athletic Longevity

Looking back through American Endurance Ride Conference (AERC) and North American Trail Rider's Conference (NATRC) yearbooks of 1000 mile recipients, it has become more common to see horses logging 3000 competitive miles or more in their long-distance career. In fact, by actual count in the 1995 American Endurance Ride Conference yearbook, 26 horses have competed more than 6000 miles, with four of them completing more than 11,000 competitive miles! 84 horses have competed between 4000 to 6000 miles. The horses (and their riders) that accumulate this magnitude of competitive miles deserve the greatest respect. The 1000 and 2000 mile horses are also to be commended on their achievements, and I hope they will successfully continue to log more miles for years to follow. All too often the horses that win the points and year-end awards are not the same horses that continue to compete along the trail year after year. What makes some of these veteran campaigners stay the distance?

To develop a true distance horse requires a commitment over a **long** period of time. The premier goal of conditioning a horse is to develop his structural and metabolic foundation so that he can withstand the stress of competition with minimal injury. A horse that is brought along too quickly over only a few months is destined to fail structurally. An elite endurance horse doesn't just pop out of the pasture ready to win a 50 or 100 mile race. The building of an endurance prospect is a lengthy project, requiring **years** to peak to excellence.

A wise training program focuses on the need of different body tissues to adapt over time. You should outline your personal goals and construct a conditioning strategy that takes into consideration your horse's starting point and

*Photo 47 When choosing an endurance prospect, try to select a horse that has had
plenty of pasture turnout while a youngster. This yearling is developing
musculoskeletal strength and neuromuscular coordination as he plays in the field.*

how the different organ systems respond to training.

The Effects of Age

The age at which a horse is started toward the campaign trail influences how
effectively conditioning strategies will develop it to peak abilities. A young
horse responds well to careful conditioning since his tissues are still growing
and developing. The organ systems of a five-year-old that is faced with conditioning stress will improve, whereas the tissues of a mature horse in his teens
have, to some degree, lost the inherent ability to remodel.

In choosing an endurance prospect, try to select a horse that has at least
had the opportunity of pasture turnout while a youngster. A confined young
horse never appropriately explores his own athletic agility and coordination
(Photo 47). Refer to Chapter 1 for more detail on this issue.

The starting of any young horse that has not previously performed in any
athletic career may take up to three years to adequately condition for endurance events. More mature horses that have been regularly trained and exer-
cised in some athletic endeavor can be expected to work conservatively at their

first 50 mile endurance or competitive ride within six months, assuming the horse has not experienced previous musculoskeletal injuries.

Cardiovascular System

Each tissue in the body is endowed with a varied blood supply; those tissues (especially muscles) with the greatest blood supply respond and adapt most quickly to conditioning strategies.

The *cardiovascular system (C-V)* includes the heart, arteries, veins, and capillary beds that deliver oxygen and nutrients throughout the body. The lungs can be considered as part of this system since they are intimately involved with oxygen and carbon dioxide exchange with the bloodstream. The time required to bring the cardiovascular system to an efficient peak is only about three months.

The cardiovascular system and muscle tissues respond to conditioning by improving oxygen delivery to the tissues. This occurs due to development of an expanded network of blood vessels and capillary beds along with more efficient utilization of oxygen by muscle cells. The heart improves in its pumping efficiency by increasing its strength of contraction to send more blood to the tissues with each beat. For a given level of exercise, the heart rate decreases as compared to its rate at the start of a conditioning program.

With conditioning, more red blood cells circulate through the blood vessels and more are stored in the spleen to be tapped in time of need. *Hemoglobin* increases to carry more oxygen to the tissues. Hemoglobin is a protein within red blood cells that binds oxygen for transport to the tissues. Because the endurance athlete is limited by fuel supplies and oxygen availability to the tissues, cardiovascular adaptation is an essential part of building a foundation that will be further developed in subsequent months.

Muscles

In general, muscle tissue is well infiltrated with an ample blood supply. In addition to improvements in oxygen and nutrient perfusion of the muscle tissue, muscle cells must modify reactions of enzymes which are catalysts to drive biochemical pathways for energy production, and muscle fibers must learn to contract with efficiency.

Development of the cardiovascular system forms the basis of metabolic conditioning. As the network of blood flow throughout the body improves, more oxygen is taken in, transported, and delivered to the working muscles. The muscles improve in their ability to utilize oxygen which is so critical to maintaining *aerobic* work of the endurance athlete. Muscles are more efficient in locomotion if they are better able to convert fuels to energy in the presence of oxygen. As muscles strengthen and work more efficiently, your horse has to work less hard than before at the same task.

Because a great amount of heat is generated as a by-product of muscular work, an extensive blood and capillary vessel supply within the muscles and skin improves heat transfer out of the horse's body. All these conditioning adaptations maximize the time before muscular fatigue. (For an in-depth discussion, refer to Chapter 8.)

In addition to cardiovascular conditioning, strength training is an essential part of the conditioning process for muscular work. An example of a strength-training exercise would be a hill climb where the muscles work against the resistance of gravity as the horse pushes its own mass (and yours) up the hill. This type of work effort is similar to exercises performed by human body builders. Muscle responds quickly to training, but nonetheless requires **at least** three to six months to mature in response to training stress.

Muscles should also be trained in dressage and gymnastic exercises to improve flexibility and suppleness. Stiff muscles are prone to injury. Dressage training teaches your horse to move in balance with a steady rhythm that improves metabolic efficiency.

As you train your endurance prospect, you will notice that heart rate recovery improves rapidly after just a couple of months of training, and muscles start to tone up and become more defined. But relying on heart and respiratory recovery as a measure of preparedness for sustained long distance work can lead to a false sense of your horse's true fitness. Other tissues in the body, like tendons, ligaments, joints, bones, and feet require even longer periods of time to withstand the concussive stress of both training and competition.

Support Tissues

Support tissues, like ligaments, tendons, joint capsules, and hoof tissues have a relatively limited blood supply. You should plan at least six to twelve months for these structures to gain a strengthening response to conditioning. Support tissues must improve in elasticity and stretch, and in their ability to withstand the strain of speed and difficult terrain. Too much work on support tissues early in the conditioning process invites injury.

After each workout, be sure to monitor your horse for any signs of swelling, heat, stiffness, or lameness. Also check signs of stress before you begin the next exercise period. What can you monitor to determine if you are pushing your horse too fast for the load the support tissues can sustain? Any puffiness in the ankles or tendon sheaths certainly points to too much stress. Gentle squeezing with your fingers along the flexor tendons and suspensory ligaments behind the cannon bone may pick out a tender area where there has been mild strain from excessive work. Filling along the cannon bones indicates tendon or suspensory ligament strain of potentially serious consequences. A lessening of forward impulsion or reluctance to move out, particularly on downhill inclines, may point to sore muscles, sore back, strained tendons, or bruised feet.

Bone

Because bone has a very limited blood supply, its development involves a **minimum** of one to two years to attain its peak strength. Bone is unique in its ability to remodel to accommodate the stresses placed on it by exercise. The conditioning process stimulates bone to increase in its mineral density, making it less susceptible to microfractures or splints that lead to lameness.

Bone is the framework for the muscles and support tissues. A horse's quality of movement is dictated by its conformation, described by how the bones are put together. A horse that has some conformational weakness such as a crooked leg or pasterns that are too long may need even more time than the standard recommendations to prepare support tissues and bone for the rigors of long-distance exercise.

Once a horse's basic structural foundation has been developed over the first year of athletic exertion, bone needs some stress at a faster speed to achieve a greater conditioning response. The work of speed play (*fartleks*) or *interval training (IT)* contributes to bone strengthening. Bone does not receive sufficient stress to increase in density until it receives the stimulus of speed work. Speed work cannot be introduced until the horse has a strong underlying foundation of *long slow distance (LSD)* work. The cardiovascular, muscular, and support tissues must be developed first so they can adequately dissipate concussion forces before exercise intensity or speed is amplified. This foundation takes at least a year to adequately develop in any age horse. (For more detail, see pages 90-96 of this chapter.)

Building on the Foundation

Each horse must be treated as an individual, and a conditioning strategy should be prepared that is tailored to your horse's particular needs. Like building blocks, each organ system must be prepared before the next can be developed. Simultaneous adaptations do occur, but the only sure way to minimize musculoskeletal injury is to allow **time** to be the main ingredient in your conditioning recipe. The amount of consistent training time that you are able to pursue with your horse is an important factor in determining when your horse is really able to **compete**. If a solid foundation is developed, there is no reason a horse can't be started slowly at a competition during its second athletic season. The event should be viewed as another training ride; it is also an opportunity to develop you and your horse's ability to rate your speed in the commotion of a pack of horses.

Trotting along at the middle or back of the pack for a season or two ultimately develops stamina and structural strength in your horse. Then, you can ask for more. As you progress along the distance and speed trail with your prepared horse, you can sadly watch the "flash-in-the-pan" horses fall apart in front of you. More than one race has been won by a solid horse maintaining an honest working effort, as those "speed demons" in front are pulled for lameness or metabolic problems.

Remember to look at your long-term goals, be patient, and enjoy the entire conditioning process. Years spent developing your horse's metabolic and structural abilities will give you great satisfaction as your horse logs thousands of miles and continues to campaign along the endurance trail.

Conditioning Principles

Conditioning Log

As you start into a conscientious conditioning program, it is invaluable to maintain a written log documenting each work effort (Figure 13). Notes should include time, distance, speed, working heart rate, recovery rates, the horse's mental state and physical response to the exertion. It is also helpful to note the weather and terrain conditions. A log enables you to track a horse's progress, and to follow trends that might point to a musculoskeletal problem or fatigue due to overtraining.

Intelligent Application of Stress

With each workout, a horse's tissues experience some mild "damage" due to stress. Within hours and days, this transient damage should repair while the tissue adapts to a slightly advanced intensity of work. This continuous process of progressive adaptation eventually leads to a well-conditioned athlete, provided each subsequent stress is applied gradually over time.

During each recuperative time period, enzyme systems are rebuilding, toxic by-products are removed by the circulation, and stretched muscles, ligaments,

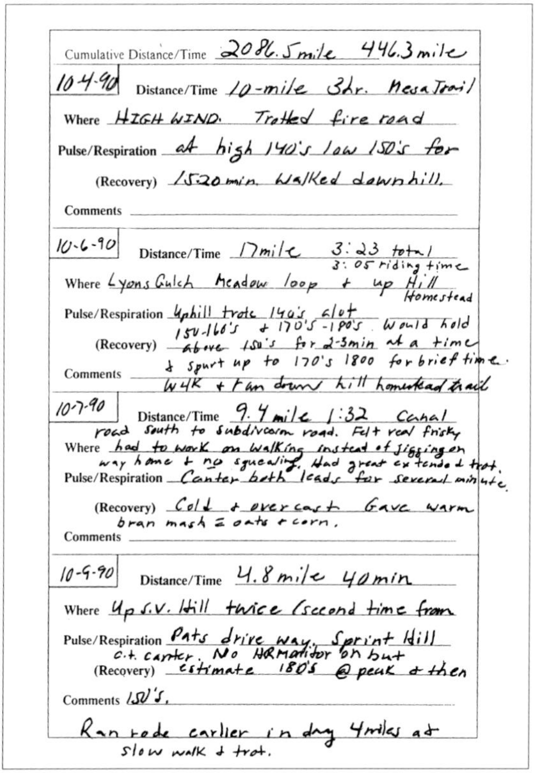
Cumulative Distance/Time 2086.5 mile 446.3 mile

10-4-90 Distance/Time 10-mile 3hr. Mesa Trail
Where HIGH WIND. Trotted fire road
Pulse/Respiration at high 140's low 150's for
(Recovery) 15-20 min. Walked downhill.
Comments

10-6-90 Distance/Time 17 mile 3:23 total 3:05 riding time
Where Lyons Gulch Meadow loop + up Hill Homestead
Pulse/Respiration Uphill trots 140's clot 150-160's + 170's-180's. Would hold
(Recovery) above 150's for 2-3 min at a time + spurt up to 170's 1800 for brief time.
Comments W4K + ran down hill homestead trail

10-7-90 Distance/Time 9.4 mile 1:32 Canal road south to subdivision road. Felt real frisky
Where had to work on walking instead of jigging on way home + no squealing. Had great extended trot.
Pulse/Respiration Canter both leads for several minute.
(Recovery) Cold + overcast Gave warm bran mash = oats + corn.
Comments

10-9-90 Distance/Time 4.8 mile 40 min
Where Up S.V. Hill twice (second time from
Pulse/Respiration Pats drive way. Sprint Hill c.t. carter. No HR Monitor on but
(Recovery) estimate 180's @ peak + then
Comments 150's.
Ran rode earlier in day 4 miles at slow walk + trot.

Figure 13 A sample conditioning log.

and tendons repair themselves. Nutrients (glucose, fluids, and electrolytes) are replenished. Without stress, none of the tissues will improve in elasticity or strength. Without stress, capillary beds won't develop to improve blood circulation in the tissues. Enzyme systems would remain at a baseline level that is inappropriate for the rapid energy production required by demanding work.

It is important to balance the stress periods with sufficient repair time for the body to rebuild. If you don't allow enough time, then stressed tissues are predisposed to serious injury. A horse can continue to recover while being worked lightly; just provide a day or two between strenuous workouts.

Long Slow Distance Training

The career of any equine athlete is built upon a foundation of *long slow distance training*. The objective of long slow distance training is to improve a horse's *aerobic* capacity while mildly stressing all the structural and cardiovascular tis-

sues. Generally, most horses work within an aerobic range at heart rates between 120-150 *bpm* (beats per minute). This correlates with an easy working
trot over relatively level ground. Prepare your horse for training with a few
weeks of legging-up at a walk. To initially gain a long slow distance training
effect, a horse must be maintained in an aerobic working state of this heart rate
intensity for about an hour, or four to six miles a day, at least every other day.

This first phase of the conditioning process focuses on conditioning the
cardiovascular system with mild stress to the musculoskeletal structures. This
is accomplished by a process of progressive loading which is created by increasing **either** the duration or the speed, but **never** both at the same time. Slowly
increase the duration of the training periods at a low intensity of exercise; then
maintain or decrease the duration while gradually increasing the intensity.
Adjustments are made on a weekly basis so your horse has a chance to accommodate each new level of effort. As a rule of thumb, first slowly increase time,
then slowly add intensity.

Strength Training

Once the cardiovascular system has improved its oxygen delivery systems over
the preliminary three months of long slow distance training, your horse's muscles
and support tissues must be strengthened to withstand the stress of strenuous
exercise. A limitation to continued equine performance is the development of
musculoskeletal injuries. In humans it has been demonstrated that strength
training can reduce the incidence of musculoskeletal injuries by 50%. Any strategy you can apply to minimize structural damage will improve the longevity of
your distance horse's career.

For muscular **endurance**, you want to develop a horse's ability to perform
muscular work without fatigue. The best way to achieve this is by applying
many repetitions of low to moderate intensity work, maintaining the working
heart rate at less than 150 bpm. (Moderate exertion includes flat work, trotting
speeds of four to seven mph, and occasional mild hills of short distances.) In
essence, this is what you will have accomplished in your long slow distance
work. Once a horse handles these tasks with relative ease, the next step involves muscle strengthening.

Strength training is accomplished by progressively increasing the intensity
or the number of repetitions of a particular drill. For example, to increase the
intensity, work your horse on a steep hill, or increase the speed of ascent up a
moderate climb. If you increase the number of repetitions, don't also ask for a
steeper climb, or a faster climb. Make incremental adjustments on a weekly

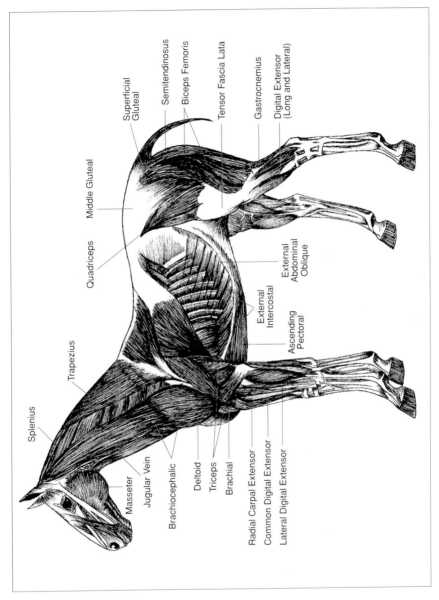

Figure 14 The muscular system.

basis by adding no more than a 20% increase in **either** duration or difficulty.

Examples of valuable strengthening exercises include developing dressage skills, working in deeper footing, and introducing hill work. As an example, the effort of intensity that a horse must put out in deep sand is 50% greater than the effort expended on a firm surface. This increases the load on the musculoskeletal system as well as on the cardiovascular system. Hilly terrain also provides an excellent opportunity to strengthen and fine-tune the musculoskeletal and the cardiovascular system, as well as neuromuscular coordination. Much like the effect of weight-lifting in humans, hill work develops a horse's shoulder muscles, hip extensors, and the gluteal and quadriceps muscles that power the hindquarters (Figure 14). Asking your horse to negotiate hilly terrain increases the resistance on all the muscles as the horse must move its own mass up a hill, as well as carry the combined weight of you and your tack.

You don't want to develop too much muscle bulk and mass since that is counterproductive to efficient muscle metabolism and cooling mechanisms of the endurance horse. Yet, hills allow steady development of the cardiovascular system while also strengthening muscles, tendons, ligaments, and joints. Hill training also simulates terrain conditions often encountered in competition. Uphill climbs accelerate the heart rate, and if applied correctly can bump a horse up against its *anaerobic threshold* (the point where lactic acid begins to accumulate in the bloodstream and muscles). In the face of this stimulus, enzyme systems and energy utilization in muscle tissues are continuously improved.

When doing hill work, remember to save your horse on the downhills to minimize wear and tear on joints and suspensory ligaments. If you climb a steep uphill at a walk, then walk down it. If you canter a gradient, allow a period to walk down of the same duration used to canter up it; this allows sufficient time for recovery. In competition, you may need to trot or canter down hills to gain time, so some faster downhill work is necessary to train your horse's neuromuscular coordination and balance, but limit downhill **speed** work to competitive situations when possible. If you expect to compete at higher speeds down hills, you will need to train your horse periodically to accommodate such an effort.

Include strength training exercises on a schedule of two to three times per week, but don't do them two days in a row. This should be adequate to improve both cardiovascular condition and strength training. Once a horse has reached the desired level of fitness, once or twice a week suffices to maintain him at that level.

Speed Play

With the introduction of speed play (*fartleks*), you can superimpose faster bursts of effort over a foundation of long slow distance work. A fartlek consists of a short sprint of a few moments or an energetic climb. Initially, these fartleks are brief and infrequent. As a horse gains in condition, longer gallops or faster hill climbs teach the horse's muscles and metabolism to briefly bump against the *anaerobic threshold*. Then the horse is quickly returned to the aerobic work of long slow distance exercise — walk, trot, slow canter — for rapid recovery.

Fartleks are an intermediate form of cardiovascular conditioning, rated somewhere between long slow distance work and more intensive *interval training* techniques. Fartleks enable you to achieve solid cardiovascular conditioning without the wear and tear created by continuous miles of long slow distance work. In addition to being useful as part of the conditioning process, speed play is an excellent method for priming a horse in the last month prior to competition. It allows the horse to peak on the day of competition without over-indulging in speed or miles prior to the event.

Interval Training

Once your horse has developed at least five to six months of long slow distance background or a solid first season, it is appropriate to introduce interval training. The objective of interval training is to teach a horse's tissues to tolerate *anaerobic* work. To accomplish this end, exercise your horse at a high enough intensity to drive the heart rate over 180 bpm, even to 200 bpm or beyond. This can be achieved with flat gallops or trots and canters up grades. Your horse is then quickly returned to a recovery effort of less than 150-160 bpm by returning to slower gaits or more level terrain. By initially implementing these high intensity stress periods for two to three minutes duration, your horse gains the advantage of metabolic and structural development without the risk of structural damage that is normally incurred with continuous high intensity work.

The first hill climbs you introduce to your horse represent a form of interval training for *aerobic* conditioning (working heart rates of less than 150-160 bpm). Allow the time spent in the "recovery" phase to be the same as or twice as long as the time you spend executing the hard exertion. To apply interval training to anaerobic conditioning (working heart rates greater than 160 bpm) or strength training, allow rest periods that are five to six times as long as each intense work period. For example, if you gallop for two minutes, then work your horse at a slow to moderate pace for ten to twelve minutes before asking for another hard gallop.

These recovery periods minimize fatigue by flushing the *lactic acid* from the tissues. Any oxygen debt in the tissues is repaid during the recovery periods, readying your horse for the next work cycle. Meanwhile, the work periods challenge muscle cells to adapt to a low oxygen environment. This is critical to staying the distance over a 50 to 100 mile event. See Chapter 6 for more details on interval training and fartleks.

Energy Demands of the Equine Athelete

There is probably no other equine sport that asks a horse to perform as rigorously as what is required of a long-distance horse. No other discipline asks a horse to remain in continuous motion for as long, and over rugged terrain.

With each movement a horse makes, muscles are doing work. How much work a horse must do is determined by a number of factors: speed, terrain difficulty, the weight of the rider, and the horse's level of conditioning.

To perform work, muscles need energy fuels. As we saw in Chapter 4, the most efficient muscular use of energy involves access to oxygen, or aerobic work. The muscles must also be able to eliminate waste products generated from the metabolic burning of fuels. A good circulatory system is essential to the equine athlete, since it delivers oxygen and nutrients to the muscle tissues and flushes away metabolic by-products.

The health and efficiency of the cardiovascular system is the limiting factor to excellence, for without a steady supply of oxygen to working muscles, an endurance athlete cannot continue to perform. If muscle energy needs exceed oxygen-carrying system capacity, the muscle cells turn to less efficient energy pathways. This results in an accumulation of fatigue-producing lactic acid. Improving the efficiency with which muscles convert energy sources to fuel is one of the adaptive responses achieved by conditioning.

Muscle Fiber Types

Slow twitch (ST) muscle fibers are surrounded by abundant blood vessels that supply them with ample oxygen and fuel (glucose, *glycogen*, and fat) to perform work. In the presence of oxygen (aerobic metabolism) these energy sources are burned to produce *adenosine triphosphate* energy molecules plus carbon dioxide and water. These by-products are innocuous and are easily flushed from the tissues by circulating blood.

Fast twitch (FT) fibers, on the other hand, are not supplied with abundant blood vessels. In the absence of oxygen (anaerobic metabolism), fast twitch fibers burn glycogen to produce rapid bursts of power and speed. However, the by-product of this type of metabolism is lactic acid, which is toxic to the muscle cells.

Lactic Acid

Some lactate is always present in a small amount in both muscle and blood. Lactic acid begins to increase slightly as exercise intensity increases, and will accumulate in the muscles of an unconditioned horse. Training alters the tendency to accumulate lactic acid with aerobic exercise, thereby delaying the onset of fatigue.

Regardless of conditioning, intense work efforts involving the need for power or speed will generate more lactic acid than the muscles or liver can neutralize. Lactic acid causes muscle pH to fall, and it interferes with energy-producing metabolism within the muscles. The force of muscle contractions diminishes. During intense exercise, glycogen stores are depleted. In addition, the horse runs out of energy fuel because of limited conversion of glycogen to adenosine triphosphate. At this point a horse's performance suffers greatly and may cease altogether.

Generally, with low intensity exercise of long duration, fat is the predominant fuel source. With a greater intensity of effort such as hill climbs or sprints, glycogen contributes more than 90% of the fuel for energy production. By definition, endurance exercise is considered *submaximal*, operating in the aerobic range if possible. Conditioning improves a horse's use of fat during aerobic work. Yet, with longer distances and duration on the trail, even a fit horse may be forced to do anaerobic work as terrain becomes more difficult, as speed accelerates, or as a horse starts to fatigue due to energy depletion.

The horse that experiences intense anaerobic work will breathe deeply and rapidly once stopped in order to repay the extreme oxygen debt of the tissues and to remove the carbon dioxide in the bloodstream. The heart rate accelerates to assist in circulating blood to deliver needed oxygen, and to remove lactic acid and large quantities of heat from the muscles.

As lactic acid is removed from the tissues, the heart rate gradually declines toward resting or recovery. But after an extremely intense work effort, all horses, including the elite endurance horse, do develop circulating lactic acid in the blood stream sufficient to create fatigue. High blood lactic acid concentrations delay heart rate recovery significantly. The threshold to reach this point is different for each horse, but one of your goals is to train your horse to work for periods of time at an anaerobic intensity.

MINIMIZING LACTIC ACID ACCUMULATION

Interval training at heart rates greater than 200 bpm moves the *anaerobic threshold* to a higher level, so that your horse is able to work longer at a higher intensity before beginning to accumulate lactic acid in the bloodstream. Nonetheless, heart rates greater than 180 bpm generally correlate with some lactic acid accumulation.

One suggestion is to train your horse to carry more weight during conditioning periods than he will carry in competition. The added weight places a greater burden on the heart, which the horse's muscles and metabolism "learn" to accommodate. Then in competition, with less load to carry, the horse moves along the trail with greater ease. Consider that even a well-conditioned horse can only work anaerobically for about four minutes before lapsing into a fatigue state due to accumulated lactic acid levels in the bloodstream. After an intense effort, if the horse is brought back to aerobic working levels, some of the toxins will be removed from the bloodstream, but the horse has lost a leading edge on forestalling fatigue. If a horse's level of condition is not used to that intense work effort, or if the horse literally runs out of energy reserves, it may be pulled from competition due to veterinary observation of a fatigue state. The horse's heart rate and respiration will remain elevated and the *cardiac recovery index* will be unacceptable. These may be additional signs of exhaustion syndrome that make it impractical and dangerous for the horse to continue the competition. (For details on cardiac recovery, see Chapter 6.)

Conditioning Program Strategy

Now that you have the working principles in hand, let's consider how to start your distance horse on its way to a successful career. Please note that your horse should be at least four years old before initiating an intense conditioning program.

First Season

During the first season of training, your intention is to build a solid foundation of long slow distance. The best way to do this is to keep most work within a heart rate of 100-140 bpm. Initially, start with an every-other-day schedule, alternately walking and trotting during each working period. Ride for about one hour or for five to six miles. This type of mild stress provides ample time for tissue repair and strengthening during the rest days, while still achieving a cardiovascular conditioning effect.

To increase progressive loading on your horse, slowly increase the mileage.

Aim toward a total working distance of no more than 30 miles each week for this first season. Once the horse is accustomed to a steady distance and duration, you can gradually ask for more intensity by adding more trotting time and/or by introducing some slow canter work (one to five minute periods). The heart rate can be briefly elevated to 170 bpm by incorporating some mild hills into a training session. If the intensity is more demanding, then do not simultaneously increase the distance. In fact, it is best to work over a shorter distance as you intensify the horse's exertion.

During these initial months of development, it is important for you to evaluate when your horse is ready to accept an increased work load. One means of estimating this is accomplished by tracking the *heart rate recovery* times. Pay particular attention to the horse's heart rate after a 10 minute rest. As a rule of thumb, if the heart rate reliably returns to 60 bpm or less, then it is safe to ask for slightly more intensity. A heart rate of 60-70 bpm suggests that you should maintain the horse's current level of intensity. A rate of 80 bpm or more indicates that your horse is being pushed too quickly, and is not accommodating the stress very well. In this case, the distance or speed, or both, should be decreased.

Some individual horses have genetic capacities that allow for rapid adaptation to metabolic stress. Although the metabolic recoveries hint that the novice horse is ready to progress to a higher level of work intensity, remember that the musculoskeletal system needs at least two to three months of slow, steady work. This ensures that tendons, ligaments, and joints are not prematurely stressed.

As the first season progresses, you should have the horse safely working at 8 mph over fairly level terrain three to four days per week. Then it is time to start planning workouts based on a two week cycle. Implement a schedule of five workouts per two week period. Four of these exercise periods will be fairly short in duration (up to one hour), and average about 10 mph. The horse's heart rate should be maintained between 110-150 bpm. Some *fartlek* work can be mixed in to elevate the heart rate to 170 bpm during occasional gallops. The fifth ride (and not necessarily in that order) in the two week period is a long ride at a slower speed. Initially start at 10 miles or less, and over the next two months increase the distance of the long ride to 18 miles.

Once this solid conditioning base is formed in the first season, slightly diminish the horse's work during the wintertime. You need only ride two to three times per week for about five to ten miles to maintain the fitness developed thus far.

Second Season

As you start into your second season, gradually return to the more intensive work schedule that you followed prior to the reduced winter ride routine. Your horse may need six to eight weeks of long slow distance work to return to the level of fitness at which you ended the first season. Again, you will plan your training schedule based on a two week cycle.

This season's strategy consists of three to four short rides plus one long ride during a two week period. The distance of the short rides will be slightly longer than the first season, and the speed slightly faster. Cover about 10 miles at a speed of 10-12 mph, working at heart rates between 120-150 bpm. Include some fartleks and long uphill climbs to drive the working heart rate up to 170-180 bpm. This higher intensity work bumps the horse against its *anaerobic threshold* to improve its aerobic capacity.

The long ride can start with 15-20 miles, gradually increasing to 30 miles over the next few months for a progressive loading effect. When the terrain is fairly level, you can work at about 8 mph. Exercise various muscle groups by using walk, trot and canter gaits according to what the terrain will allow.

Third Season

The workouts will be similar to the second season, with four short rides and one long ride every two weeks. The short rides will cover 10-18 miles, while the long ride covers 30-36 miles. Limit your horse to no more than 90-100 miles of work every two weeks to protect against musculoskeletal wear and tear. In difficult terrain you may want to limit your mileage to less than 60 miles in a two week period.

Preparing for Competition Day

The essence of any conditioning program prepares a horse to reach its peak on the day of each competition. A horse's work load should be tapered to one-third to one-half of the normal routine workouts about 10-14 days prior to competition so the horse has ample glycogen stores and minimal lactic acid residues in the muscles. Tapering strategies allow musculoskeletal tissues to have healed completely from prior workouts, and to be sufficiently strong so the horse is ready to give his all on competition day.

Following each competition, allow a solid rest period of at least one day for every 10 miles of competition; then reduce your horse's exercise demand by at least 20% for the first half of the time interval between events. Then, slowly and progressively increase the work load to bring the horse to its peak on the next race day. Fartleks are useful for maintaining high intensity practice that reminds the muscles and energy pathways how to operate near the anaerobic threshold. While allowing a reduction in mileage for about two weeks prior to an event, fartleks continue to stimulate a conditioning response.

Training Philosophy

Implementing Training into a Conditioning Program

For all the miles you and your horse will share as you develop a fit equine athlete, it is important to develop all aspects of his education. While you condition his physique and strengthen his body to the distance task, you can work on limbering his muscles, teaching him trail skills, and improving his mental concentration.

Suppling and Improving Flexibility

The use of suppling exercises is an important and useful format to combine with a conditioning program for the distance athlete. Athletic demands are stressful to your horse, whether it be negotiating a difficult trail or coping with the excitement of a competitive event. Stress takes its toll on your horse by creating muscular tension and accelerating fatigue. A stiff and tense horse is especially prone to injury. The more elastic the tissues, the more they are protected against strain. This is an important issue for the horse who must perform well over miles and miles of difficult terrain.

There are many techniques you can apply to minimize the tension your horse feels while performing. Time and experience improve your horse's ability to adapt more easily to new places and events. Just as importantly, improving your riding skills also makes life a lot easier on your horse.

Trail riding tends to stiffen a horse's carriage. A working road trot actually tightens muscles, particularly those along the topline (the horse's neck, back, and croup). A trail horse that is never asked to do anything but move forward down the trail never learns to bend (Photo 48). These horses lose a lot of flexibility over time. You can help supple your horse's muscles by doing some homework during your conditioning program.

WARM-UP AND STRETCHING

Before you start any workout, be sure to warm up your horse for 10-15 minutes. You can achieve this warm-up with an energetic walk and some light

Photo 48 A horse in a hollow, tense frame.

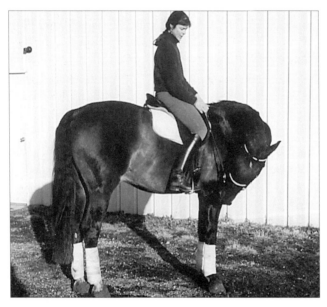

Photo 49 Suppling exercises help the distance horse warm up. Here this horse is being asked to bend his neck, bringing his nose to the shoulder.

trotting either on the longe or while riding. Initially, with movement, heat produced by working muscles remains within the body tissues until the circulatory system cranks up enough to dissipate the heat. Some mild tissue temperature elevation (about 1.8°F or 1°C) improves the efficiency of muscular work. A slightly elevated temperature raises the heart rate and improves enzyme function and metabolic reactions to more effectively produce energy.

Warmed support tissues, like tendons and ligaments, improve in stretch and elasticity. Circulation is improved to the muscles and joints. Warm-up exercises dramatically reduce the risk of musculoskeletal injury. This is especially important for a nervous or tense horse.

Once your horse is warmed up with improved blood and oxygen circulation, and the tissue temperature has risen, stretching exercises increase the range of motion of all tissue components.

DYNAMIC SUPPLING EXERCISES

After working your horse lightly on the longe or under saddle for 10-15 minutes of walking and trotting, then you can begin dynamic suppling exercises under saddle. These exercises stretch soft tissues and joints while the muscles are contracting or the horse is in motion and the legs are assuming the load of the horse's own weight. While mounted, incorporate some bending exercises to increase suppleness in the joints and spine. These include bending the head and neck toward each shoulder, then asking your horse's nose to touch your toes (Photo 49). Encourage your horse to stretch long and low through his back and neck, even asking him to yield to bit contact and stretch his head and neck down toward his chest. Asking him to move in small circles encourages his torso to bend around your leg. Practice leg yields and shoulder-fore exercises to further increase suppleness before you ask for harder exertions (Photo 50 & Figure 15). Examples of dynamic suppling exercises include: bending of the neck side-to-side, downward flexion of the neck, turns, circles, lateral exercises like leg-yield or side-pass, and cavalletti work. If you are not familiar with these kinds of dressage exercises, it would be a good idea to take a few basic lessons from a dressage instructor.

This form of suppling stimulates rapid contraction of the muscles. You achieve a temporary increase in tissue length and stretch so that while your horse is working, the soft tissues are less prone to injury. These stretching exercises also minimize muscle soreness that tends to develop after a lengthy workout.

Photo 50 Practice a riding suppling exercise like leg-yielding to further increase flexibility before requesting harder muscular work. This horse is leg-yielding to the right by stepping over with his left legs in answer to the rider's left leg aid.

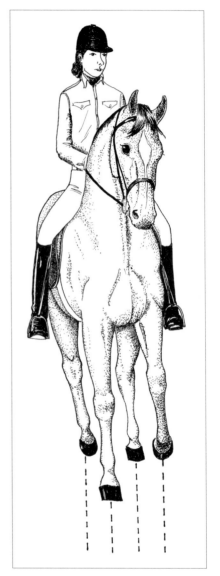

Figure 15 Shoulder-fore is another excellent suppling as well as a straightening exercise. This horse is bent around the rider's inside leg and his shoulders and forelegs are brought slightly to the inside. His legs move in four distinct tracks.

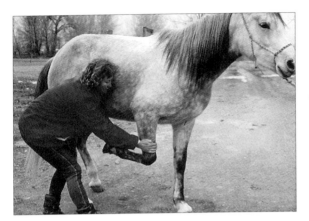

Photo 51a Begin passive suppling exercises by picking up one of your horse's front legs near the knee, then gently stretch the leg back underneath the horse and hold for 20–30 seconds.

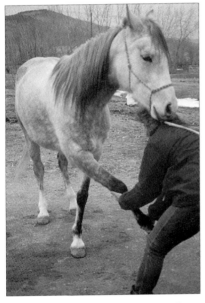

Photo 51b Still supporting the foreleg at the knee, stretch the leg out in front of the horse as shown and hold for 20–30 seconds. Remember to do an equal number of stretches on the opposite leg.

Photo 52 Stretch the hindlegs, too. Pick up the leg while supporting the hock, then gently stretch the leg forward and hold, then backward and hold. Remember to be very careful while working around the hindlegs since even horses that are not known to kick may be surprised or made uncomfortable by this new exercise.

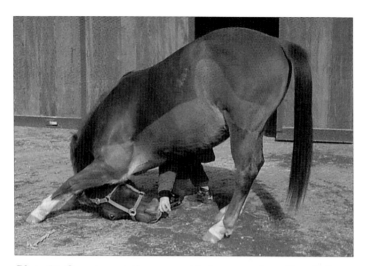

Photo 53 Carrots or apples are great inducements for asking the horse to stretch. Here is a horse performing a deep stretch between his legs to reach the treat. It may take a few tries before your horse catches on to this exercise. Don't expect such a deep stretch the first time.

PASSIVE SUPPLING EXERCISES

Another type of stretching can be incorporated into the cool-down period to more permanently improve elastic stretch of your horse's soft tissues while increasing range-of-motion in the joints. This is done by performing **passive** suppling exercises (Photos 51a & b, 52). With you on the ground, pick up one of your horse's legs near the knee or hock. Gently stretch the leg in the direction you are guiding it, and hold this stretch for 20-30 seconds. Pull slowly as you stretch, rather than jerking the leg in an unnatural position. If you pull too quickly, your horse will pull back and thwart your efforts. As an example, the front leg should be pulled directly in front of the horse and held in this position for half a minute. Then the leg is gently pulled across the horse's chest toward the opposite leg, and held. Then the leg is pulled back toward his back leg, held, and then pulled out to the side, and the stretch held as before. Each leg is stretched in a similar fashion. Be sure to prop your arm on your knee so you don't inadvertently pull a muscle in your back.

You can also lift up on your horse's abdomen with your flattened palms to stretch his back. Gentle finger pressure over the muscles along his spine stimulates him to stretch his back in the opposite direction. Carrots and apples are great inducements for asking your horse to reach his head and neck to the side,

Photo 54 A horse pushing himself efficiently up a hill. Hill climbs have strengthened and helped teach this horse to engage his hindquarters well under his body.

stretch between his legs, upward, and forward. (Photo 53). By applying these exercises each time you ride, you vastly improve your horse's flexibility, making him less prone to injury. You also counteract the tension produced by long-distance trail work. A greater freedom of movement in his joints will lengthen his stride so he covers more ground with each step. Attention to these details improve his athletic agility and abilities over the years.

Cross-Training

Versatility makes for a better horse and an exceptional rider. An important adjunct to conditioning and teaching your horse trail skills is the use of cross-training. A good trail horse should be schooled in dressage to teach his body to bend, to improve the mobility and range-of-motion of the hip and shoulder joints, and to improve flexibility through the spine and back. Dressage exercises strengthen rear end and abdominal muscles that are necessary for efficient propulsion along the trail. Exercises that promote engagement of the hindquarters enable your horse to push himself up a hill (Photo 54). A horse that pulls with his front end rather than pushes with his hindquarters up a

Photo 55 A horse with a tense, hollow frame that leads to shortened strides and fatigue.

grade tires more quickly and is unable to cover ground efficiently.

In addition, dressage training teaches your horse to move in a steady rhythm. This is a great energy-saving technique for the distance horse. If you can find a steady pace and maintain it through the miles, your horse fatigues less quickly. Think how much more gas your car uses when you are forced to drive erratically in city traffic. The same is true of your horse. Speeding up and slowing down consume a great deal of energy. Meanwhile, like your car moving at constant speed on the open highway, a horse moving steadily down the trail uses considerably less fuel.

Another useful exercise for the distance horse includes gymnastics exercises through cavalletti and jumping grids. These exercises teach your horse to balance, to pick up his legs, to stretch through the neck and back, and to establish a steady rhythm. At the same time you achieve some conditioning response from strength training of the muscles. Besides, many horses love to jump. It is a stimulating change from the tedium of trotting down a trail day after day. It is just as important to keep a horse's mental state keen as it is to condition his body for distance exertion.

Photo 56 A horse that has been cross-trained with dressage exercises moves with a supple, relaxed back, as this horse is doing. A relaxed back permits a horse to step under himself with the hindquarters, which allows for longer strides and less wear and tear over the miles.

Cross-training teaches your horse to relax through his back. A stiff back leads to shortened strides (Photos 55 & 56). A shorter stride means more wear and tear on the limbs because the horse is forced to take more steps to cover the distance. One study has shown that the number of steps can increase by as much as 20%. Over a 100 mile course this becomes a lot of extra steps.

While your horse gains immensely from dressage work, this training method helps you learn to ride more effectively and in better balance. Your horse offers a more shining performance if he is trained to respond to leg aids, rather than being steered around by the head to turn or negotiate an obstacle. Very slight pressure on or behind the girth should stimulate your horse to move away from your leg. This becomes extremely handy when you ask him to negotiate a tricky obstacle on the trail. Immediate yielding to leg pressure ensures that your horse moves forward when asked, and his obedience shows your horsemanship skills to advantage. It becomes apparent that your horse trusts you, and that you have invested the time in developing his manners. This is important in competition, but is also essential when you are faced with a dangerous situation on the trail. If you find yourself on a narrow trail on a steep hillside and suddenly need to turn around, you'd like your horse to do a quiet turn on the haunches without debate. It is hazardous if he backs up, tosses his head, or refuses to move away from your leg. Good manners are essential in a good trail horse.

Incorporating cross-training strategies into your training program focuses your horse's attention on you. Then in a competitive situation he is not distracted when you need his attention the most. Better horsemanship skills make your horse's job easier when asked to climb and descend mountains, cross obstacles, and carry you upon his back for many miles.

6 Methods of Evaluating Fitness

Heart Rate

To track a horse's progress, it is important to routinely check his ability to perform the required work without physical or metabolic hazard. One reliable method used to track metabolic development is the use of a cardiotachometer or heart rate monitor (Photo 57).

This simple little piece of technology, assists in our quest to understand how well our horses are coping with exercise stress. The world of electronics has become an integral part of conditioning the equine athlete. The sport of long-distance riding as we know it today has seen some remarkable changes in performance capabilities of our horses. There is no question that without the use of heart rate monitors, riders would continue to be unaware of their horses' heart rates while riding them, trying to find a balance between safety and how far to push their horses.

What can this device do for us? Your conditioning program can be based on a scientific approach rather than haphazard guesswork when you know exactly what your horse's working heart rate is in beats per minute *(bpm)*. You are more logically able to push his limits to stimulate a training response, and at competitions you are able to keep your horse within an *aerobic* working rate and thereby delay fatigue. Finally, you can track recovery rate to determine if your horse is responding appropriately to the exercise demands or if instead a problem is lurking behind your horse's incredible will to try.

The Resting Heart Rate

You can find a resting heart rate by placing a stethoscope just behind the point of your horse's left elbow against the body wall before you begin a workout session. You should hear a "ba-boom" rhythm (equivalent to one beat), similar to your own heart sounds. With your fingers, you also can feel strong pulses under the lower jaw or along the back of the fetlocks. Count the beats for 15

Photo 57 A heart rate monitor in place on a saddle with the digital watch ready for the rider to strap on for a ride. The watch can read out the pulse rate up to three feet away from the horse.

seconds, then multiply by four to get the rate in beats per minute (bpm). Normal resting rates in horses range from 24-48 bpm with an average rate of 32-42 bpm.

The Working Heart Rate

This is where the heart rate monitor is indispensable. As your horse exercises, his muscles demand more oxygen. This demand is answered by an increased heart rate, which bathes the working muscles with more blood. At rest, only 15% of the blood volume circulates to the muscles, while during exercise, blood flow to the muscles increases to 85%. The faster your horse goes or the more difficult the exertion, the more quickly his heart beats to deliver precious oxygen and nutrients. This rapid circulation of blood also removes metabolic waste products and heat from the tissues.

To give you an idea of the range of work a horse's heart can perform as a pump, consider that at rest (32-42 bpm) the cardiac output is 10.5 gallons per minute (30-45 liters per minute). At a working trot of about 9 mph, a heart rate of 132-142 bpm produces a cardiac output of 35.5 gallons per minute (140 liters per minute). A horse working at maximal heart rates of more than 200 bpm has a maximal cardiac output of 63.5 gallons per minute (240 liters per minute). What this tells us is that the heart can increase its output by more than sixfold during extreme exertion. The more blood is circulated to the tissues, then the more oxygen is supplied, and the more efficiently the muscles can do work without quickly tiring.

Ideally, we want to maintain a horse's working heart rate within a specific range. One of the great advantages in wiring your horse into this electronic monitoring gadgetry is that you get immediate information about your horse's heart rate **while working.** There is no other way to gather this important data; by the time you jump off and start to take your horse's pulse, it will have dropped by half, or be **at least** 20-50 bpm below the working heart rate.

The goal in long, slow distance conditioning and in competitions is to maintain your horse in an *aerobic* state of work for as long as possible. This generally corresponds to heart rates less than 150 bpm. Above this rate, muscles demand more oxygen than can be immediately supplied for that work effort. Many horses start to dip into *anaerobic* work at heart rates above 150-160 bpm. As outlined in Chapter 5, during anaerobic work, lactic acid is generated by the muscles faster than it is neutralized in the blood stream. The process related to the accumulation of lactic acid "poisons" the muscles so they are incapable of efficient contraction. Energy supplies are rapidly depleted and the horse "runs out of gas." To keep your horse performing well over the miles depends on staying within the aerobic range of work.

A heart rate monitor lets you track exactly what is occurring with exercise. It is difficult for you to train your horse to a certain level without being able to see his working heart rate. Similarly, without a heart rate monitor you may think your horse is not experiencing much stress when in fact certain conditions like mountain terrain or altitude drive the working heart rate up significantly.

You should use the monitor consistently to compare your horse's day-to-day performance. Keep in mind that a horse's **resting** heart rate does not change with increasing fitness. Only the working heart rate and rate of recovery continue to improve with conditioning. It is hard to interpret information if you put the monitor on only occasionally. This is also true in a competitive situation, as excitement modifies your horse's normal rate. After a few competitions you'll be better at estimating what is an appropriate heart rate under those stressful conditions. Whether you are training or at a competition, you should monitor for an elevation in your horse's working heart rate as compared to his normal rate for a similar work effort. A higher working heart rate than usual is an indicator of the beginning of fatigue. Rather than ignoring the hard, cold data displayed on your monitor, check for a reason and slow his pace. Pushing on as before could lead to *metabolic* or *musculoskeletal* problems. Metabolic problems generally refer to a departure from normal physiological function of the cardiovascular system, the neurologic system, the digestive system, the muscular system, or a combination of these. In the exercising horse these problems are usually a result of dehydration, electrolyte imbalances, energy depletion, or acid-base derangements.

There is a danger in using a heart rate monitor as you would use a tachometer. Certain terrain requires that you slow the pace considerably rather than trying to maintain within the target heart rate of 120-150 bpm. There's no sense in rushing through rocks just to keep the working heart rate up when you are all the while tearing up your horse's legs and feet. There's not much to be gained in keeping a horse in premium cardiovascular conditioning if he becomes lame as a result. Pay attention to the heart rate monitor **and** the terrain!

Most horses will find a pace that maintains their heart rate within a comfort zone. With few exceptions, horses are truly the masters of conserving their energy. Generally, an experienced horse finds that "magic" heart rate within the aerobic range and automatically adjusts his speed as terrain and footing dictate.

As a training tool, a heart rate monitor is useful for evaluating your horse's current level of fitness. A horse conditioned for a particular work effort performs that task at progressively lower heart rates as fitness improves. For example, an unconditioned horse may exercise at 120-150 bpm, whereas a fit horse covering the same terrain may work between 80-110 bpm. As you track your horse's progressive improvements, you'll tune in to when you can ask for a greater work intensity, such as the introduction of *fartleks* or *interval training*. Rather than guessing when to add longer distances and more speed to your training program, you can do so in a strategic fashion. Increase each stress in small increments. This allows your horse's cardiovascular and structural systems to respond and adapt with less risk of musculoskeletal injury.

A horse's heart has to work harder if he is carrying a heavier load. Given a choice, the combined weight of you and your tack should be less than 20% of your horse's body weight. If you are a lightweight rider, you might add a heavier saddle or use more equipment as a training tool to increase your horse's effort. The heart rate monitor enables you to experiment and figure out how much "stuff" to use to achieve a training effect.

Some horses work at a higher heart rate than others. This does not necessarily mean such a horse is less fit; only that at a certain working heart rate that horse finds a comfort zone in which his muscles efficiently propel him down the trail. Each horse should be compared to himself, and not to others. However, the lower the working heart rate, the less oxygen your horse must consume to fuel his muscles, and the less effort he expends. The lower the working heart rate, the easier it is for a horse to quickly reach recovery criteria. The **rate** of the drop is what is critical and what actually indicates fitness for an exertion.

Monitoring Heart Rate Recovery

Ideally, your horse's heart rate should recover to less than 60-64 bpm within 5-10 minutes following an aerobic workout. If the heart rate remains high, think about reasons for the delayed recovery. Too much exercise stress for your horse's current level of conditioning often causes a slow recovery rate. If this is the case, then you must slow your pace or back off the intensity of the work. During training you also have the option of riding over less hilly terrain or moving out of deep footing.

A horse's heart rate also fails to recover because of musculoskeletal pain, or because of impending metabolic problems created by fatigue or dehydration. At most endurance competitions, the criteria for *"fit to continue"* require that a horse recover to a heart rate of less than 64 bpm within 30 minutes of arrival at a vet check. A well-conditioned and strategically ridden horse should recover within two to three minutes to a heart rate of less than 64 bpm. This is true both in training and in competition. If your horse's heart rate hovers above 64 bpm more than 15 minutes after arrival at a rest stop, you are pushing too hard. Back down your pace, and let your horse rest periodically along the trail during the remainder of your ride.

By the same token, when you pull up after a conditioning workout and your horse recovers to a heart rate of less than 52 bpm within 10 minutes, you are probably not stressing your horse enough to achieve an adequate training effect. This result should be distinguished from what you find if you perform the cooldown phase along the trail as you slowly head for home. Then, it is desirable to see a recovery rate of less than 52 bpm within 10 minutes of arrival back at the barn or trailer.

Using the Heart Rate Monitor for Cardiac Recovery Index

Another means of evaluating your horse's ability to recover in the face of exercise stress is the use of the *cardiac recovery index (CRI)*. The cardiac recovery index is used extensively at endurance competitions to monitor how well a horse is responding to metabolic stress. Its use is not just limited to the competitive situation. During training, you can use your heart rate monitor to measure your horse's cardiac recovery index without even dismounting. Stop along the trail, and after your horse has recovered to between 64-80 bpm, take a "resting" heart rate. Then start your timer as you begin to trot 250 feet and halt again. At exactly one minute see what his heart rate recovers to. You don't have to measure a distance of 250 feet every time to perform a cardiac recovery index. If you know how long it takes for your horse to trot 250 feet, trot down the trail for that exact number of seconds, stop, and then check the heart rate at the minute. Periodic checks during a training period give you a handle on how well your horse is responding to the day's workout. (Please refer to Chapter 9 for further detail on the cardiac recovery index.)

If the cardiac recovery index increases by 4 bpm above his base resting rate, then your horse is not recovering as well as you'd like and you should lighten up the training effort. An 8 bpm increase over base indicates a lack of recovery. Repeat a questionable cardiac recovery index after a 10-15 minute rest period. If it remains increased, start looking for reasons. Either your horse is experiencing metabolic difficulties, or some structural body part is causing him pain, either from musculoskeletal injury or saddle sores.

Building a Foundation for Fitness

While you build your foundation of long slow distance training as described in Chapter 5, choose a "target" heart rate, such as 135-140 bpm. Work at that rate, and gradually increase the distance covered within the targeted heart rate. You will know how your horse is responding to the work stress by evaluating his speed of heart rate recovery. You don't necessarily have to stop moving to see how long it takes for his heart rate to drop. At a slower speed than what you had been maintaining, or on downhill sections of trail, as your horse continues to move forward his heart rate should drop to less than 100-110 bpm. With conditioning, his locomotor efficiency improves so he more quickly reaches an acceptable recovery. Once your horse handles this training demand with ease, start to lengthen the duration of his workout.

When you finish each conditioning period, keep a log (see Figure 13, page 91) of how that exercise period went. Note the kind of work effort performed, the weather conditions, the predominant working heart rate, the peak heart rate, how quickly your horse recovered, and his attitude during the ride.

After you have built a strong foundation over many months, you can start to ask for a greater intensity of exercise over a shorter time or distance. This prepares you for the next step in conditioning, the application of *fartlek* or *interval training* techniques that drive the heart rate up.

Interval Training

It is common to find yourself at a ride with steeper climbs, longer distance, or worse footing than what you have trained in. Sometimes the speed is faster than you'd like because of the excitement within the "herd" of competitors.

And, sometimes your horse's muscles fatigue a little faster than what either of you would like. The efficiency of his gait suffers, and the heart rate elevates because of increased muscular effort. Dehydration effects also drive a horse's heart rate up higher than normal. He may be able to compensate during the first half of a ride, but as he fatigues and becomes progressively dehydrated over the distance, his heart rate remains elevated. When your horse is confronted with any of these factors, he is forced to work *anaerobically* for at least a little while. If you expose your horse's tissues to some anaerobic work during training, he is better able to cope with abnormal stresses in the competitive situation. (For more on interval training, see pages 95-96.)

Fartleks (speed play) are a kind of interval training that push the horse's working heart rate into the range of 160-175 bpm for several minutes, allowing your horse to touch the *anaerobic threshold.* The intensity of the exercise demand is less than what you would ask in more advanced interval training. Horses love this kind of work. You might be trotting along a trail, and then let your horse out for a slow gallop for a few minutes. It breaks the tedium, exercises different muscle groups, and stimulates muscle fibers to recognize and adapt to less oxygen availability for short periods. And, it is mentally invigorating for both you and your horse.

Interval training stimulates the body to respond to higher levels of *lactic acid* in the tissues. To elicit this response, work your horse at a target heart rate (usually 180-200 bpm) for a couple of minutes, then slow down to allow his heart rate to return to 100-120 bpm before starting another interval. By conditioning at higher working heart rates, lactic acid is more rapidly cleared from the tissues. You know you are achieving your goal when your horse's heart rate immediately drops to less than 100 bpm upon slowing your speed or decreasing the exercise intensity.

Hills, mud, sand, and snow increase your horse's work effort by at least 50%. As the intensity increases, so does the working heart rate, and so does the lactic acid production by the muscles. As you crest the peak of a steep hill, your horse's heart rate should rapidly drop to less than 150 bpm. Within one minute of proceeding down the other side of the hill or reaching level ground, his heart rate should decrease to less than 110 bpm. The drop in heart rate corresponds to a return of the muscles to aerobic metabolism and continued clearing of excess lactic acid.

Conditioning in this manner elevates the threshold before lactic acid begins to accumulate in the body. Research shows that heart rates greater than 180 bpm usually result in lactic acid accumulation. *Heart rate recovery* is

delayed until lactic acid levels start to fall in the bloodstream. For an unconditioned horse, lactic acid accumulates at a lower level of work intensity, possibly
occurring at working heart rates of 150-160 bpm or even lower. Lactic acid is
generated during most exercise efforts, but the small amount produced by aerobic
work (heart rates less than 150 bpm) is quickly metabolized and does not accumulate in the bloodstream.

Fitness Tests

During the training process, you can continue to measure your horse's aerobic
capacity by conducting fitness tests. There are several ways to do this, each
method requiring the use of a heart rate monitor. We use a heart rate of 160
bpm to carry out these tests because that heart rate touches the anaerobic threshold in most horses. Heart rates of less than 120 bpm are affected by excitement,
nervousness, and fright and so do not always reflect the true working heart rate.

One method is referred to as a *standard exercise test (SET)*. In this test, you
bring your horse up to a working heart rate of 160 bpm and measure the time
it takes him to cover a set distance while keeping his heart rate working at 160
bpm. You can do this exercise along a trail or road for a distance of about one
mile. This measures your horse's velocity at a heart rate of 160 bpm, also called
the V160. As your horse's fitness improves, he travels faster at this heart rate
over that distance. An endurance horse that can cover a predetermined
distance at a heart rate of 160 bpm more quickly than it did at the onset of
conditioning has improved its aerobic capacity, and is responding well to conditioning. You can perform this test every two to four weeks to compare the
current level of performance with each previous test.

Another fitness test involves asking your horse to cover a distance of one
to three miles at a constant speed such as a working or extended trot or slow
canter. Keep his heart rate constant and measure the time it takes you to cover
this distance. Then rest, and repeat the exercise again but at a faster speed.
Repeat this once or twice more. By plotting your horse's speeds and heart rates
on a graph, you get an estimate of the V160 (Figure 16).

Since heart rate recovery is a legitimate measure of a horse's fitness, this is
another tool for estimating progressive fitness. Work your horse over a
specified distance at a set speed. Check the heart rate immediately when exercise stops; then at 1, 5, 10, and 15 minute intervals while walking quietly on
level ground. Plot these data points on a graph (heart rate vs. time) and con-
nect them in a line. Compare the graphs at monthly intervals. Ideally, you
want to see the slope of the line steepen because the heart rate drops more

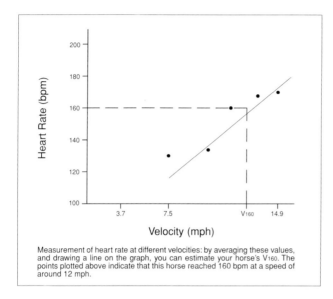

Figure 16 A good way to estimate your horse's V160, the horse's velocity at a heart rate of 160 bpm, is to plot your horse's speeds and heart rates on a graph.

quickly as fitness improves. Try to carry out this test under similar conditions each time because weather conditions affect heart rate recovery, with heat and humidity delaying the drop in heart rate.

Using the Heart Rate Monitor to Detect Pain

The stress of exercise may create an accumulated toll on your horse's structural soundness. Without some way to measure subtle indications of wear and tear, problems may be recognized too late. Your hands and eyes find swellings, lameness, and unthrifty condition after damage has occurred. A minor problem can rapidly turn into a disaster, requiring aggressive and time-consuming treatment. A heart rate monitor may help you identify an impending problem in its early stages so you can turn it around with less hazard to your horse, less expense to your pocketbook, and a quicker return to work. For example, a horse on a downhill trot should work at a low heart rate of 100 bpm or less. If the heart rate is elevated, then something probably hurts. A slow recovery, an increased heart rate of 10-20 bpm for a given work effort, or a heart rate that bounces up and down are warning signs that something is amiss. **Don't ignore the information.** Look for a musculoskeletal problem or areas of soreness created by pinching saddles or bits. This warning flag might also tell of impending colic, *tying-up syndrome*, an illness such as a viral respiratory infection, or dehydration and fatigue.

A heart rate monitor enables you to make appropriate decisions about your riding strategy. However, you should not rely entirely on the monitor to tell you if your horse is in pain. You must still use your intuition and "feel" about your horse's performance while on the trail and at rest stops. Each horse has a different pain tolerance and adrenalin will subdue some pain recognition.

The Monitor Itself

A heart rate monitor is a relatively inexpensive tool, ranging in cost from $150.00 to $500.00. For the information this device gives you, it is invaluable. There are many different models of heart rate monitors, some with "bells and whistles," and some with only a digital readout of the heart rate. Those units that have a high/low beeper are useful to alert you when your horse nears the *anaerobic threshold*. But, keep in mind that the batteries wear out slightly faster in units with a beeper. Some units have a self-contained stopwatch, while others also store up to one hour's worth of information in a memory. This can then be downloaded into a computer to create graphs of your horse's working heart rate.

Many heart rate monitors come with a wrist watch receiver that continues to track your horse's heart rate if you are standing within a range of three feet (see Photo 57, page 112). At vet checks once you have pulled your saddle and electrodes, it is still possible to monitor your horse's heart rate with the use of a belly band called a Heart Rate Belt® (see Photo 28, page 44). The transmitter is located on the bottom of a webbed surcingle which is quickly cinched round your horse. This frees up your hands to do other important things like minister to your horse at the stops while continuing to monitor heart rate recovery. However, once you present your horse to the pulse and respiration (P & R) and veterinary staff, you must turn off all heart rate monitoring devices while your horse is being examined.

When you shop for a heart rate monitor, try out a friend's if possible to check that the electrodes don't cause swellings or raw spots. One electrode is placed in the hollow below the withers beneath the saddle to act as a "ground." The other electrode is placed on the opposite side of the horse in the girth area at the level of the elbow. Any excess pressure or irritation to the skin and underlying tissue creates discomfort for your horse, which may start to move differently to protect its sore back. To get the most reliable readout, the electrodes need to make good contact with underlying skin. You accomplish this best by either clipping the hair or liberally applying electrode gel before placing the electrodes against the skin.

When electrodes do not make correct contact, you see erratic heart rate readings. Sometimes the rate is significantly lower than expected, like 60 instead of 120. Sometimes the heart rate reading jumps around with no rhyme nor reason. Occasionally, the meter gets stuck on a number and doesn't change regardless of exercise intensity. First check that the electrode wires are securely snapped into the transmitter. If they are, get off and reposition your tack and the electrodes, either adding water or electrode gel to the skin to increase electrode contact. Sometimes the girth electrode wiggles loose from under the girth. As it sits in the free air, you get really weird readings if it even reads at all. A piece of velcro® wrapped around the girth allows you to hold the electrode in place so it won't shift.

There is often a lag time between what your horse is doing and the read-out on the heart rate monitor. This happens because the meter averages electrical impulses from the heart every six beats or so. It is possible to crest a hill, start down the other side, and see the meter jump to a high rate that corresponds to the climbing effort. Yet, the rate should rapidly drop toward recovery within half a minute or so of starting down the other side. Just keep in mind that your meter may take a few seconds or even a minute to catch up to your horse's work output, particularly if the heart rate is constantly changing due to varying terrain or speed. Once you've used your monitor for a bit, you will come to understand its peculiar idiosyncrasies, and will be able to interpret the readings accordingly.

Blood Work

Routine blood work is useful for monitoring fitness improvement. Laboratory data on *packed cell volume (PCV)* or *hematocrit* to check for anemia, red blood cell counts, and hemoglobin concentration indicate how well the tissues are receiving blood and oxygen. It is best to obtain blood samples from your horse immediately after exercise. Then the results reflect the effects of red blood cell contribution from the spleen and let you know how your horse is able to respond to exercise stress. (At rest, a fit endurance horse has a packed cell volume of 30-35%, compared to resting values of unconditioned horses of 40-45%.) Also blood lactate levels measured periodically after a workout are informative. With increased fitness, the lactate level should decrease. (For more detail, see Chapter 5.)

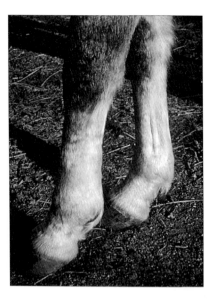

Photo 58 This left foreleg has a puffy cannon and fetlock resulting from too much strain.

Overtraining

One of the hazards of conditioning an endurance competitor is the tendency to push the horse too hard too often. Properly applied training is mildly stressful to a horse's body, and stimulates the *neuroendocrine* system to respond to increasing levels of stress. A neuroendocrine response refers to the function of the nervous system in response to hormonal substances secreted by endocrine glands. Hormones are chemical substances secreted by endocrine cells into the body fluids; these chemicals then regulate the function and metabolism of other organs and tissues in the body. Normally, the body is maintained in balance through the complex interaction between the nervous and hormonal systems.

However, overtraining alters a horse's metabolic state so that it is unable to adapt to the stress of exercise. This develops from an imbalance of the neuroendocrine function as a direct result of chronic stress. This is particularly true of the endurance horse that is not given sufficient time to recover between training and competitive periods. It can also occur when an intense competitive schedule and the stress of traveling lead to an inappropriate adaptation by the neuroendocrine system; then even a seemingly adequate recovery period does not rejuvenate the horse.

An "overtraining syndrome" develops over a period of time — weeks to many months — where the horse gradually loses ground in the conditioning program: it appears to become less fit, rather than more so as training progresses. It is incapable of tissue repair and energy restoration. Fuel sources remain unreplenished and the musculoskeletal system remains fatigued. Gastrointestinal function may suffer, with the horse prone to diarrhea or colic.

Persistent fatigue and stress further upset the neuroendocrine balance, and the horse lapses into a continual state of decline. Its coat lacks luster and shine, its appetite diminishes, while weight is shed despite free choice access to an excellent quality diet. The horse stands listless and slightly depressed. In some cases, you may see puffy joints, sensitive tendons, or sore feet resulting from too much wear and tear (Photo 58). During workouts, the horse's performance is flat and uninspired.

Signs of Overtraining

Stress stimulates heightened activity of the adrenal glands. The adrenal glands produce and release substances such as adrenalin to increase blood flow and the pumping action of the heart. As a survival mechanism, an adrenalin surge enables a horse to immediately flee from a predator or any imagined threat. A horse can run at great speed as a result of increased blood flow to the heart, lungs, brain, and skeletal muscles, coupled with immediate conversion of fuel stores in the liver and muscles to energy. Blood flow to the intestines and kidneys is diverted to organs used specifically for locomotion. For an isolated or occasional incident, such a rechanneling of energy supplies and blood flow poses little problem.

Yet, consider what would happen if such an adrenalin response persists due to the ongoing stress of intensive work. Over time, the horse would deplete all its energy supplies, including muscle protein, causing the muscles to atrophy rather than build in bulk and strength. Hormones released by nervous system impulses stimulate enzyme systems to continually convert stored energy to an immediately useful form. This occurs because the body is in a continual state of preparation for a fright and flight response. Given enough time, or enough intensity of exercise demand, the horse wears down to a fatigue state.

Initial signs are apparent in a horse experiencing a constant state of stress: its heart rate is elevated both at rest and during exercise, and its recovery rate is slow and atypical for that horse. Adrenalin suppresses a horse's appetite, so not only is it not eating with vigor, but it continues to lose weight as activated enzyme systems continue to convert fuel supplies and muscle protein into energy (Photo 59).

Photo 59 This horse, checking in before an endurance competition, exhibits a thin body condition. This is an indication of overtraining or not enough feed to support training demands.

Another more subtle form of overtraining stress may also occur in the endurance horse. Normally, the *autonomic nervous system (ANS)*, a branch of the central nervous system, involuntarily controls function of all body tissues. Two different branches of the autonomic nervous system normally balance each other, but when one of these branches is exhausted, it can no longer regulate normal function of the other system. The signs of this response to overtraining assume features that are quite different from the one described above. In this case, the heart rate slows and blood flow is diverted to the gastrointestinal tract away from the skeletal muscles. It is easy to miss the signals of an impending problem in this situation because the horse's resting and working heart rate correlate to what you would expect with a very fit athlete. Recovery rates are acceptable and even excellent. Nonetheless, the horse continues to perform poorly; it cannot respond to the demands of competition that require improved blood flow to the muscles and conversion of fuel reserves to immediate energy. A horse in this state is likely to lapse into exhaustion syndrome or shock when asked to perform on a competitive level.

Prevention of Overtraining

In essence, too much *aerobic* conditioning may result in weight loss, poor appetite, dullness, poor performance, and cumulative dehydration. Too much strength training may overload muscles with resultant injury, stiffness, and soreness. Overloaded tendons, ligaments, and joints respond with swelling, heat, and/or pain.

Besides recognizing the signs that accompany overtraining, you can prevent this syndrome by limiting your training mileage to **less** than 90-100 miles within a two week period. Also, try to vary your horse's exercises from day to day. This allows tissues that were stressed one day to have time to repair before they are stressed again.

Carefully palpate the joints and tendons for signs of heat, swelling, or tenderness before and after each ride. Make notes in your written log. Watch your heart rate monitor carefully for subtle changes that imply excessive stress and strain on your horse.

Give your horse ample rest time after a competition. Under normal circumstances it may take as long as 92 hours for a horse to completely replenish its glycogen depletion after a 100 mile competitive event. An overtrained horse fails to bounce back between training or competitive periods.

Another useful practice to conserve your horse's energy is to maintain a constant pace during the ride itself. It costs a great deal of energy for your horse to speed up and slow down. In a survey done by the University of Illinois and Kentucky Equine Research, Inc. at the 1990 Race of Champions (ROC), riders revealed that the average horse trained 7.7 hours/week at an average speed of 5.6 mph. At the Race of Champions that year, the last horse to finish the race averaged 5.4 mph. That horse may not have won, but it did complete the ride in good condition, whereas many horses that went too fast in the first several legs of the race were unable to complete the competition at all. The lessons here are simple: once a horse has a basic foundation of fitness development, there is no reason to overdo the speed component in future training. A steady pace at a moderate speed adequately prepares a horse for competition. And, a distance horse does not have to gallop through the miles to successfully complete a competition. A steady, working trot which averages 5-7 mph will get the job done, efficiently and safely. Going too fast at the beginning burns up fuel supplies, prematurely generates lactic acid, and hastens the onset of fatigue. Most competition speeds average 5-12 mph depending on the talent and fitness of the horse, and the terrain. With that in mind, it is more logical to start your horse out at his most efficient, steady pace, preferably the speeds at which you have trained, and maintain that rhythm throughout the ride.

Other Effects of Training and Competition on the Immune System

With continued stress, the adrenal glands also release high levels of *corticoster-oids* into the circulation. Circulating steroids suppress a horse's immune system. In particular, the immune defense in the lungs relies on active *alveolar macrophages* (white blood cells that scavenge bacteria, viruses, and debris), yet high blood cortisol (a form of corticosteroid) levels depress the function of these specialized white blood cells, making the horse more prone to respiratory infections and illness.

Special care must be taken for any horse that is campaigned regularly, especially if it is experiencing some physiologic changes similar to overtraining. After a long journey by trailer or airplane, the horse is particularly susceptible to viral respiratory infections. Good ventilation in the trailer and at the receiving end is essential to prevent the buildup of ammonia, viruses, or bacteria in the air the horse is breathing. (For more detail, please refer to Chapter 10.)

Enough time should be allowed for a horse to rest and recover from traveling stress before strenuous workouts are implemented. Ideally, allow one to two weeks for the muscles to rest after traveling a long way. Extended time off facilitates climatic adaptation and restores sound immune function to the lungs.

Timing Strategy Between Competitions

As a general rule of thumb, a horse should be rested one day for every 10 miles of competition. This means that after a 50 mile race, your horse should have five days off; after a 100 mile race, ten days off. During this rest period, the horse should be turned out to pasture to exercise himself. If turn-out is not available, then each day the horse should be hand-walked or ponied at a walk and slow trot for 20-30 minutes. This allows the muscles to remain supple and to continue to flush away residual toxins by encouraging blood circulation with light exercise.

This rest period is not the time to reinstate your training program. This is the time the tissues need to repair and heal, and for your horse to catch up on nutritional demands and calories lost during competition.

As a guideline for when to enter the next competition, try not to compete at 50 mile competitions more than once every three to four weeks. Ideally, you should allow six to eight weeks in between 100 mile competitions. Many horses are capable of performing more frequently than this, but subtle degradation of performance and continual abuse of the musculoskeletal structures will eventually take their toll. Besides encountering some of the aforementioned signs of overtraining, if you subject your horse to a more frequent and intensive training or competitive program, he may ultimately suffer a serious musculoskeletal injury.

7 Conditioning for Specific Terrain and Climatic Factors

Conditioning for Mountain Riding

The Mountain Challenge

Sublime poetic moments in life are often found on a mountaintop, perched above a kaleidoscope of vistas where your horizons are limited only by your imagination. To some, the mountains are both moving and inspiring. To others they represent merely a challenge to be conquered.

Whatever your motivation, there is no doubt that some of the most glorious endurance races and pleasure trail rides take place in mountainous terrain. Your horse undoubtedly does not view these rides with the same degree of wonder as do you. To the horse the uphills and downhills represent work based on sweat and sheer muscle power.

Although tempting to the robust human athlete, not many people would consider going from sea level and relatively flat terrain directly to the Rocky Mountains, donning a 60-pound pack, and climbing Long's Peak (14,255 feet high, one of the United States' highest mountains) with **no** preparation. This feat can be done, but your muscles and lungs might feel like they've been dipped in hot acid both during and after the exertion. Unlike people, horses naturally possess some physiologic adaptations that enable them to deal with mountains and altitude, which we will explore in this discussion. Yet asking your horse to climb a tall mountain requires conditioning strategies to minimize fatigue and injury. It is not uncommon for competitions in mountainous regions to accumulate at least 9,000-15,000 vertical feet of ascent over the course of a 100 mile ride. That's a lot of up and down!

There are several distinct features of mountain riding that must be addressed when preparing your horse to put in a successful performance. The first three items on this list are principles used to prepare a long-distance horse for **any** form of riding exertion. By committing to a consistent exercise plan, you will prepare your horse to tackle any mountain; by using mountain riding as part of your conditioning strategy, your horse will excel in less rigorous terrain. (What follows is a brief review of conditioning principles, please refer to Chapter 5 for more on conditioning.)

1. Conditioning of the cardiovascular system develops the oxygen-carrying systems in the body while mildly stressing the musculoskeletal structures to progressively accommodate greater demands.
2. Strength training of the musculoskeletal system is of paramount importance to improve efficiency of locomotion and energy production within the muscles.
3. *Interval training* techniques prepare the musculoskeletal system for performing intense bursts of exertion typical of steep mountain climbs or fast speeds.
4. Most mountainous terrain (particularly in the western United States) is composed of hard-packed soils littered with rocks. Toughening your horse's feet and ensuring appropriate shoeing are important features of mountain training preparation.
5. In regions of high elevations, altitude becomes a critical factor in developing and assessing the metabolic health of your horse. Altitude can also be a significant factor affecting your own performance and judgement.

The Pull of Gravity

What makes mountain riding so physically demanding?

The effort required by your horse's muscles to push him up a mountain is intense. His haunches need to develop strength and power. For maximum efficiency, your horse's neuromuscular system must learn to **push**, not pull his mass up a grade (Photos 60 & 61).

Downhills require a tremendous braking effort to keep legs and feet from tripping over each other. Soft tissue support structures of tendons and ligaments must be strong enough to complement the muscular effort involved in slowing while still propelling forward. Too much downhill on an unprepared horse, just like too much speed on any horse, tires shoulders, forearms, and backs, and risks injury to suspensory ligaments and joints.

Your body perched on top has a significant influence on a horse's balance going both up and down a mountain. The objective is for you to present as little hindrance as possible. A balanced seat, and well-fitting tack are essential.

Picking through rocks is both physically and mentally exhausting because

*Photo 60 A horse **pulling** himself up an incline, which leads to sore shoulders and fatigue.*

*Photo 61 This horse is **pushing** himself up the hill. Note how its left hindleg is well under the body and striding forward. Remember, the horse's "motor" is his powerful hindquarters.*

your horse must carefully place his feet while continually watching the trail mile after mile. This effort precludes a horse from moving on autopilot. Muscle groups work in concert, alternately opposing tension on each other. The persistent act of lifting his legs and picking his way ultimately leads to muscle fatigue in an under-prepared long-distance horse.

Weariness is evident as restricted rear end movement, or as bunching or tight muscles along the thigh or hips. With fatigue, muscle cramping (*tying-up syndrome*) may result. Other indications of weariness appear as back soreness or tentative forelimb movement. A horse with a cautious or stilted gait shows signs of fatigue that might ultimately result in lameness. If a horse is tired or sore on one side of his body, secondary problems often develop due to overcompensation in another area of the body.

The goal is to properly prepare a horse to accommodate these concerns in mountainous terrain, so he can continue to move easily down the trail with a bounce in his step.

Conditioning Strategies for Mountain Work

INITIAL PREPARATION

The key to building a durable long-distance athlete that performs well in mountainous terrain is beginning with the same basic conditioning methods that were explained in detail in Chapter 5. Miles of long slow distance training to build *aerobic* fitness and a well-developed circulatory system are essential for future work in steep terrain and higher altitudes. The efficiency of the cardiovascular system is paramount and can only be developed with a careful, dedicated conditioning program.

STRENGTH TRAINING

The principles of strength training to prepare for mountain riding are the same as described in Chapter 5.

Mountain riding amplifies the stress load on your horse's cardiovascular system without increasing the concussion impact on the *musculoskeletal* system. Walking your horse up a steep mountain achieves a cardiovascular conditioning effect similar to galloping three times the distance over level ground. This is particularly true if your horse is climbing in sandy footing or crossing deep snow or drifts while climbing. Hill work further develops your horse's aerobic capacity while it builds muscle strength.

Hill training simulates terrain conditions often encountered in competition. Uphill climbs accelerate the heart rate, and if applied correctly can bump a horse up against its *anaerobic threshold* (the point where lactic acid begins to accumulate in the blood stream and muscles). In the face of this stimulus, enzyme systems and energy utilization in the muscle tissues are continuously improved.

As you steadily improve your horse's fitness to travel in hilly or mountainous terrain, you will find that as your horse climbs a grade, his heart rate will be dropping before you reach the top. The better the horse becomes conditioned, the faster you will be able to go while still achieving similar working heart rates as what you previously had at slower speeds while climbing. If the heart rate continues to elevate as your horse climbs, then you are probably asking too much. Heart rate recovery at the top of a grade and as you head down the other side should quickly drop to less than 100 bpm.

INTERVAL TRAINING

Conditioning for mountain riding also must include interval training techniques so your horse's muscle tissues are challenged to adapt to a low oxygen environment. Steep climbs will drive heart rates beyond the aerobic limit. Muscles must be trained to tolerate anaerobic work with minimal fatigue. (For more detail, please refer to Chapter 5.)

Rocky Footing

A horse that travels in the mountains inevitably runs into a large share of rocks, ranging in size from pea-size gravel to cobbles to boulders. A horse that is confined to a stall, to a soft pasture, or to a sandy paddock is going to be at a serious disadvantage when suddenly confronted with hard-packed or rocky terrain (Photo 62). Given the opportunity, equine feet will accommodate formidable terrain over time. If possible, pasture your horse where there are at least some rocks. The feet will toughen, and your horse will learn to pick through them with better agility.

The only sure way to toughen your horse's feet is to put him to work in rocky conditions. Common sense dictates that you gradually introduce hard pack and rocks in small doses. If too much is asked for too fast, stone bruises are likely to develop.

When riding in rough footing, it is always prudent to slow down on a section of trail that is strewn with rocks. **Let the terrain dictate your speed.** Although your heart rate monitor may indicate a seemingly slow-going pace, there is no sense in tearing up your horse by going too fast over rocks. Bruised

Photo 62 A horse and rider negotiating some very rocky terrain.

feet, twisted joints, or injured tendons are the consequences of too much speed. Once the footing improves again along the trail, pick up a trot until you reach the next section of rough going. Although this strategy interferes with a horse maintaining an efficient energy-saving rhythm, slowing down in rocks is important for keeping your horse sound.

Tincture of iodine (7% strength) or copper sulfate applied to the soles of the feet a couple of times a week hardens the soles and better prepares the feet for rough going. Compounds containing bleach, formaldehyde, or turpentine soften the soles. Be sure to read the labels of hoof care products before applying them on a regular basis.

Some horses need the added protection of pads to protect flat soles from sharp rocks. You can also fit Easy Boots® over the horseshoes to accommodate particularly rocky trails.

Mountain riding demands a lot of a horse's musculoskeletal system, and the feet are the foundation to stability. Please review Chapter 3, Athletic Foot Care.

The Effects of Altitude

REDUCED ATMOSPHERIC OXYGEN

Many mountainous rides in the United States take you and your horse to elevations above 8000 feet. For example, in the Rocky Mountain region, horse trails sometimes wind up to elevations of 12,000 to 13,000 feet. It is not just the panoramic views that take your breath away. The thin air exacts a toll on both you and your horse's performance.

High altitude physiology has been well studied in humans, and some similar principles of acclimatization apply in horses. It takes three to four weeks of living at altitude for the body to adapt. The bone marrow, blood, and muscle tissues respond to the new and higher environment by improving oxygen retrieval in the body. In most cases, a horse (and rider) travel to an event, stay for just a few days, then return home to a low elevation. There is no time at all for the body to make adjustments. This will affect your horse's performance to at least some degree.

Your horse most easily accommodates altitude if he starts at a lower base camp, climbs to a high elevation one or several times, and then returns to the lower elevation of base camp. Camping above 7000 - 8000 feet elevation for several days is more difficult for both nonadapted horse and human because significant physiologic effects are not usually noticed until you attain an altitude of 7000 or 8000 feet. By the time you get to 10,000 feet, oxygen availability is approximately 10% less than what is breathed at sea level. This is not to say that a moderate altitude won't affect either you or your horse. The most noticeable effects are evident when you and the horse have to perform continuous muscular work.

RESPIRATORY RESPONSE TO LOW OXYGEN

Because less oxygen is available in the air that is breathed at higher altitudes, the lack of oxygen stimulates a more rapid and/or deeper respiratory rate. Even a well-acclimatized individual must ventilate more at high altitude than a horse performing a similar exertion at sea level. In many high altitude environments the air is dry and cold. Cold air is normally warmed in the nostrils, pharynx and trachea. In this warming process, evaporation of water from the mucous membranes lining the upper airways utilizes heat and moisture from the body tissues. An increased respiratory rate, accompanied by a need to warm incoming air, contributes to loss of both heat and "water" from the tissues. Ultimately, the airways serve to accelerate dehydration problems in the hard-working horse.

EFFECTS ON URINATION

Both the rate and depth of ventilation increase because of natural body reflexes to the reduced oxygen in the air. This over-breathing effort causes a horse to blow off excess carbon dioxide. To compensate for the lowering of carbon dioxide in the tissues, the body strives to balance the acid-base status of the bloodstream by eliminating excessive bicarbonate. The primary route for excreting bicarbonate is through the urinary tract. This means that a horse at altitude urinates more than usual. This is particularly challenging to the long-distance athlete faced with arduous exertions over many hours. Normal fluid and electrolyte losses in the sweat are further compounded by urinary and respiratory fluid losses, thereby accelerating dehydration.

EFFECTS ON THIRST AND APPETITE

Dehydration worsens the problems of altitude by thickening the blood and making it less efficient at carrying oxygen to the tissues, while also diminishing blood circulation to the muscles. It is imperative that horses working at altitude are encouraged to drink and given ample opportunities to do so.

Due to the oxygen deficit and mild dehydration effects created by elevated respiratory rates and increased urination, many horses go off their feed slightly at high altitudes. This phenomenon has significant ramifications for an endurance horse: not only does the long-distance athlete need to replenish great stores of energy while working, but the loss of body weight in terms of lost water, lost flesh, and some lost muscle mass may further weaken a horse's performance.

THE RESPONSE OF THE CARDIOVASCULAR SYSTEM TO LESS OXYGEN

Oxygen pressure is lower in high altitude atmosphere, which determines that the oxygen pressure is also lower in the alveoli of the lungs. The alveoli are clusters of tiny air sacs where oxygen is exchanged between the lungs and the blood. If less oxygen is present in each of these air sacs, then less oxygen saturates the blood. The presence of less oxygen in the blood means less oxygen in all the tissues, and especially in the working muscles.

In an attempt to deliver more oxygen through the circulation, the heart rate will elevate for the first week or so at high altitudes. This will have a profound effect on the recovery rates of an unacclimated endurance horse.

In response to limited oxygen, capillary beds expand to bring oxygen in closer proximity to each cell. The more channels blood has to run through, the more blood and oxygen will be delivered to the working muscles. Conditioning strategies promote the expansion of capillary beds in both size and number. This makes it easier for your horse to accommodate high altitude.

EFFECTS ON MUSCLE EFFICIENCY

Many enzymes that are responsible for converting muscle fuels to energy that drives muscle contraction are dependent on the presence of oxygen. These enzyme systems also must adapt to the lower oxygen availability. The abilities of both human and horse to successfully acclimate to high altitude depend on improving the effectiveness of using what little oxygen is available. Any conditioning strategies achieved to improve the capacities of muscle cells for performing *anaerobic* work such as those described on pages 94-98 are an advantage to your horse. This preparation comes partly from conditioning prior to reaching a high altitude environment. Increased numbers of *mitochondria* (energy factories within each muscle cell) develop in response to minimal oxygen whether the low oxygen is due to altitude or to conditioning. The presence of more mitochondria in the muscle cells increases the extraction from the blood of oxygen that drives *aerobic* energy pathways.

As explained earlier in Chapter 4, *adenosine triphosphate (ATP)* is the energy currency that makes all life processes happen. An ATP molecule is rapidly broken down to form *adenosine diphosphate (ADP)* plus energy. The transformation of ATP to ADP is not oxygen dependent, but the rebuilding of ATP from ADP within the mitochondria requires oxygen. Besides fueling muscle contractions, ATP is needed to resynthesize additional ATP from ADP. Rapid release of energy from the breakdown of ATP enables sudden bursts of high intensity activity, like sprinting or a short but intense hill climb. However, because of the relative scarcity of oxygen in the tissues, recovery from work is delayed at altitude relative to recovery rates seen at sea level.

Before enzyme systems and energy pathways have an opportunity to adjust to accommodate reduced oxygen availability at higher altitudes, a hard-working equine athlete depends on anaerobic energy pathways more quickly than normal and for longer periods of time. This results in premature fatigue created by *lactic acid* accumulation and depletion of *glycogen* energy stores.

An increased muscular work effort that accompanies high altitude exertions also generates more internal body heat. To dissipate this heat load from the body, a horse may sweat more than usual. Additional fluids and electrolytes are lost from this route, further contributing to dehydration and electrolyte imbalances.

SPECIAL ADAPTATIONS BY THE HORSE

Fortunately for the horse, it has a well-developed special organ that is capable of responding rapidly (within minutes) to muscular demand to drive "fright and flight" instincts. The spleen is a large muscular reservoir of red blood cells (RBCs) located on the left side of the abdomen. As much as one-third (approximately three gallons) of a horse's blood cell mass may be stored in the spleen of a resting horse. During exercise, this extra blood is put into the system to immediately increase a horse's aerobic capacity. Red blood cells contain a specialized protein called *hemoglobin* that binds oxygen and transports it to the tissues. When the spleen adds red blood cells to the blood, muscles are able to receive more oxygen to compensate for its limited availability at altitude. The added blood volume obtained from the spleen also offsets initial dehydration effects by adding more "fluid" to the circulation.

However, the contribution of red blood cells from the splenic reservoir will not carry a horse through the sustained exertions of a 100 mile competition, or even a 50 mile event. Those extra red blood cells in the circulation help for a time, and are particularly useful when a horse climbs to high altitude for brief intervals with continual returns to the more oxygen-laden air of lower elevations.

For a horse that is asked to remain and work at elevations of 7000 to 8000 feet or more for several days, the contribution of the spleen cannot accommodate a persistent and increased demand for oxygen. In addition to the changes described above, acclimatization changes over many weeks include stimulation of hemoglobin (hemoglobin holds oxygen in the red blood cells) and red blood cell formation within the bone marrow. Likewise, there is an increase in muscle myoglobin. *Myoglobin* (a protein similar to hemoglobin) binds oxygen in the muscles and quickly releases it when supply is diminished.

RIDING STRATEGIES

Consider the following when you ask your horse to give his all at altitude. Above 5000 feet elevation, the maximum work output for humans decreases by three percent for each additional 1000 feet of altitude. Although aerobic (endurance-type) work abilities improve slightly with conditioning and acclimatization, there is still a deficit at altitude compared to output at sea level.

By understanding some of the physiologic difficulties experienced by a horse working at high altitudes, you become more sensitive to subtle signs indicating the need for your horse to slow his pace. You realize that recovery rates may be delayed, indicating an oxygen debt in the tissues. Your horse's working heart rate may be elevated, as is his respiratory rate. It won't do to just continue pushing your horse as you would at sea level or low elevations. Use your heart rate monitor to adjust your horse's speed to keep him within his aerobic limits. Reduced oxygen availability in the breathed air demands that you slow your pace, and allow more rest time for your horse to eat and drink, and to re-energize. Conditioning strategies are extremely important for mountain riding to enable the muscles to accommodate the greater intensity of exertion posed by both climbs and altitude.

A note to ride management: Ride management should also consider the factor of altitude and accommodate the extra needs for competitors who travel from low altitude regions to compete in mountainous terrain. Extra veterinary checks should be included, starting early in the course of the ride (at about 12-13 miles) to allow horses to drink and refuel energy supplies often.

Conditioning for Sand

The Unique Qualities of Sand

Sand — the stuff you curl your toes around as you watch the sun set behind the surf. Sand — the stuff of which dream castles are made by little kids with rubber spades. Sand — the stuff that can destroy the dreams of the long-distance competitor if it is not respected.

There is no other footing that clutches and pulls more at your horse with each step. Mud may suck and pull, but its danger lies in its lack of traction as each foot slips and slides as it tries to gain a purchase. In contrast, sand is a "dead" footing. Your horse puts a foot down, and the ground has no give. Instead, the foot sticks as your horse's body continues to move forward over its leg. As each foot tries to lift from the ground, the sand shifts away from the hoof. To lift each foot and to propel the body forward, the horse's muscles must exert considerably more force than they do as a horse moves across a firm surface (Photo 63). Biomechanical studies have shown that sand increases the work effort of a horse by as much as 50%!

There are no magic recipes on how to condition for sand riding, but if you understand the effect it has on a horse, then you will know better how to prepare for competitive situations. Each horse is an individual, and each horse has a different training foundation. Some horses are already so strong from years of rigorous riding that they can accommodate the extra stress of sand in as little as three months. Other horses have little or no conditioning background,

*Photo 63 Sand is a very difficult terrain for horses. Here a horse and rider canter
along a beach during the 1994 World Equestrian Games in Holland.*

and sand is extremely stressful to their *musculoskeletal* systems.

At one time or another, all of us have probably taken a run along a beach.
Some of us have done this for exercise, while others of us run for the pure glee
of feeling the sand in our toes, and the surf splashing on our legs. The salt spray
is intoxicating and energizing, but can you remember how your spryness quickly
faded further down the beach. Can you remember trying to run as close to the
water as possible as your legs tired? There the footing is firmer, so the going is
easier.

A horse experiences the same effects in sand as you do as you sprint down
the beach. Muscles become weary far faster than they would if the horse were
working on solid ground. If a horse is allowed to tire from too much time or
speed spent working in the sand, he will compensate by over-using other parts
of his musculoskeletal system. The potential for tendon or joint injury is greater,
while a more rapid onset of fatigue threatens the successful completion of
an event.

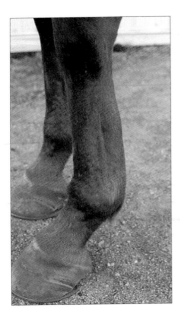

Photo 64 An old, healed bowed tendon. Bowed tendons are an injury often caused by riding in deep footing like sand or mud.

Physiologic Effects of Sand

MUSCULAR EFFORT

Not only does a horse tire more quickly in sand, but due to a more pronounced muscular effort, a horse generates more internal heat. This stimulates a greater sweat response, with the potential to lose additional electrolytes and body fluid. It is particularly important to pay attention to cooling and hydration strategies while working in sand. In addition to creating an increased work output, a sandy environment is often a hot environment. Horses should be cooled regularly with copious water applications to the head, neck, chest, and legs. If riding in a hot **and** humid environment, it may be necessary to water soak the entire body to help dissipate an intense heat load. (For more detail, refer to Chapter 8.) Encourage and permit your horse to drink at every opportunity. Administer appropriate electrolyte mixtures at each vet check and while on training rides.

SAND-INDUCED INJURIES

Muscular work, heat build-up, fluid and electrolyte losses, and energy depletion all contribute to the development of muscle cramps or *tying-up syndrome*. It is essential to warm up adequately to ensure ample circulation and oxygen supply to the muscle cells. A proper warm up also improves the elasticity of tendons, ligaments, and joints. These soft tissue structures are particularly susceptible to injury from the pull of deep sand.

One of the predominant musculoskeletal injuries associated with sand riding is injury to the flexor tendons or suspensory ligaments. More than 50% of musculoskeletal injuries sustained by performance horses working in deep sand involve injury to the superficial and/or deep digital flexor tendons (Photo 64). The risk of tendon/ligament injury is greater if the muscles fatigue too quickly. The only way you can protect your horse against strain of tendons or ligaments is to condition him adequately for the intended work. This requires many months of a conditioning program specifically applied in sandy terrain. There are no shortcuts to improving muscular strength or tendon/ligament elasticity and strength. There is no other footing that can simulate the conditions of sand. If your goal is to compete in a deep sand environment, then it is worthwhile to relocate your horse or transport him to an area with beach, dunes, or sand washes (Photo 65).

Conditioning Strategies for Sand

IMPORTANCE OF STRENGTH TRAINING

It is possible to strength train muscles to some degree over hilly or mountainous terrain to develop power in the haunches, shoulders, and back that will delay the onset of fatigue in deep sand. Hill climbs, particularly at a canter, will develop thrust in the quadriceps and gluteal muscles. Acceleration sprints can also be implemented to develop rear end power and thrust. These are accomplished with exercises of fast takeoffs from a standstill, and accelerating as a race horse would out of a starting gate. It is not so much the distance of the sprint that is integral to muscle development, but the takeoff that requires energy and power to propel a horse's mass forward from rest. For a horse to move its mass requires it to overcome *inertia*. In this way, you can strengthen your horse to also overcome the inertial "glue" of sand.

Strength training preparation is critical to enabling your horse to successfully complete a course that includes not only deep sand, but irregular terrain contours created by dunes. Dunes are wind-sculpted hills of sand, so the combined components of sand and hills further magnify a horse's work effort. Mountain and hill work help to prepare a horse for handling the ups and downs of dunes.

Photo 65 No other footing can simulate the conditions of sand. If you plan to compete in a ride that takes place in sandy terrain, you must train your horse in sand.

IMPROVING FLEXIBILITY

Just as importantly, muscles and joints must be improved in their suppleness in order to resist the straining pull of deep footing. Stretching exercises are an excellent adjunct to a conditioning program (see page 105, Photos 51 & 52). Shoulder, elbow, hip, and stifle joints become more elastic by implementing daily stretches over time. Greater freedom of movement enlarges a horse's stride, and at the same time minimizes the chance of tearing and damage to joint capsules, ligament attachments, and muscles during difficult exertions. Stretches should be applied both during warm-up and cool-down phases of a training program. Warm-up stretches improve a horse's elasticity in muscles, joints, and soft tissues, while cool-down stretches encourage continued circulation to all musculoskeletal structures. Heat and toxic by-products, like *lactic acid*, continue to be flushed from the muscles during cool-down and stretching. This improves your horse's comfort by minimizing post-exercise stiffness or cramping.

Dressage work, particularly lateral movements, further increase muscle and joint suppleness, and teach your horse to better balance its body and to work in a more efficient rhythm. A lot of energy is lost by a horse that continually speeds up or slows down. A horse that can travel in any footing condition with a regular rhythm tires less quickly than a horse that consistently speeds or slows in its pace. (More on dressage in Chapter 5.)

PACING

Another critical strategy for sand riding is to ensure that you pace your horse throughout training or competition. Don't allow your horse to expend all his fresh, vital energy in the first 20 miles of a sandy course because he will run out of gas before the end of the desired number of miles. This concept obviously applies to competition under any terrain conditions, but even more so to sand.

The use of a heart rate monitor (see Chapter 6) is instrumental to maintaining a consistent pace. During competition, try to maintain your horse's working heart rate below 150 *bpm* to encourage *aerobic* conversion of muscle fuels into energy sources. This conserves *glycogen* fuel stores for later use and prevents the accumulation of *lactic acid* in the muscles. Such conservation strategies delay the onset of fatigue. You may find that in sand your horse's speed necessarily slows in order to keep the working heart rate below 150 bpm.

AN EXAMPLE OF A CONDITIONING STRATEGY FOR SAND

To start a conditioning strategy, plan on about three to six months to adequately "leg up" your horse in sand. After this period of time, if you do your homework, tendons, joints, and muscles will be more effective at working in sandy footing at speed with less chance of injury.

As with any riding exercise, always warm up your horse for 10-15 minutes before you ask for work in difficult footing or for an intense exertion. When approaching sand, you may want to warm up your horse for half an hour to improve oxygen delivery and limberness within the muscles.

Certainly any horse can work for several miles in the sand the first time out. But in the same way that you will have "spaghetti legs" the day after a significant hike along the beach, your horse's muscles would be overused and fatigued. This does little to train the tissues to respond to the new form of stress created by sand. A gradual and progressive approach accomplishes the most conditioning, and prepares the horse for the long term.

Initially, if you have access to a beach, start your horse next to or in the water where the sand is firmest. A conservative approach starts with walking periods of only 10-15 minutes. Then move your horse off the beach onto solid ground, and exercise at the normal level of demand to which he is accustomed. Each week you can add another 10-15 minutes to each walking period, until you have built up to 45-60 minutes of walking work in the firmest sand.

You might consider ponying an undeveloped horse off a more seasoned horse, to start. By removing your body weight as a factor, you reduce the horse's work burden by as much as 30%. This gives a young or undeveloped horse a chance to develop his "sea legs," so to speak. An inexperienced horse learns to maneuver his legs and body in the sand without also having to accommodate you.

Treat your sand work periods like an *interval training* strategy. It is ideal to work on the beach or in a sand wash for 10-15 minutes, then move to firm ground or slow your speed for a period of time about three times longer than what you spent in the sand. Then return to the deep sand for another 10-15 minutes, repeating that work set two to three times during that particular conditioning day. Staggering work periods between sand and firm ground allows your horse's muscles time to recover from each exertion, yet his tissues still receive progressive loading over a cumulative time period.

Once your horse handles about 45 minutes of firm sand work at the walk without tiring, you can begin some trot work at 5-10 minute intervals. Slowly and methodically increase the stress (duration, then speed) as you did for the walking exercises. Or, to increase the stress in a different manner, move off the firm sand area onto the deeper track. Begin with walk efforts in deeper footing first, gradually building to a longer duration before you ask for more speed. Resist the impulse to initially combine work in the deeper footing with a faster speed. Either walk in the deeper sand to start, or ask for trot intervals along the firmer water line. Don't do both together at first.

Once your horse accepts the trotting intervals in the sand with minimal fatigue, start to add canter and then gallop work in a similar progressive fashion. Incorporating sand work two to three times per week along with a regular training program should sufficiently strengthen your horse. Then you can safely expect him to accept more depth and finally more speed over a three to six month period.

Monitoring for Injury

You should continuously check for signs of over-stress created by sand conditioning. Joint capsules or tendon sheaths that puff with excessive fluid indicate that your horse is under prepared for the exercise demand and you should consider backing down on duration or speed spent in sand. You may need to provide him with a rest period to allow inflamed tissues to heal. The use of ice packs for 20-30 minutes two to three times per day also minimizes the inflammatory process in tendons and joints.

A stiff gait or obviously sore muscles reflect overtraining, as well. If your horse starts to shorten his stride, he may be telling you that he is receiving excessive *musculoskeletal* stress. After each training period, your horse may be tired, but he should still move with an elastic stride with a reasonable amount of *impulsion*. A horse that is dragging or plodding when it normally bounces with enthusiasm is communicating its plight of over-stress. Decreased appetite or continual weight loss in the face of abundant food supplies are other indicators of overtraining.

As we are well aware, sand is an abrasive material. If you use leg boots when riding, you might consider removing the boots while riding in sand unless you live in cactus country. Sand gets caught in the boots, and rubs raw welts in the skin. These sores are painful, and may affect a horse's soundness. On the other hand, cacti are very hazardous to the lower legs. Some types of cactus, particularly the large barrel cacti found in the Arizona desert, have enormous spines that are toxic once embedded in the tissues. Horses ridden through cactus country should be well armored on the lower legs. If using boots, remove them periodically throughout a ride to check for accumulated grit next to the skin.

Blowing sand has a potential to sift beneath saddle pads. It is important to check under all tack during each ride. Keep saddle pads clean to prevent abrasion from sand that has adhered to mats of sweat and dirt from previous use. Always check your horse's eyes and nose for sand accumulations, and clean these areas at every opportunity.

An intense glare reflects from sandy terrain, and windy conditions are often inherent to desert or beach environments. These features are tough on your horse's eyes and on yours as well. Consider sunglasses as essential equipment for yourself to prevent eye irritation from blowing sand and to protect from the intense ultraviolet glare. Glare and wind are extremely fatiguing factors and should be considered as significant elements in a competitive event. If you tire prematurely, your judgment and sensitivity to your horse may also falter. Use sun block on your face and exposed skin, including the back of your neck, to protect against sunburn.

Foot Concerns in Sand

Persistent work in sand tends to dry out your horse's feet. This is in part a result of the abrasive nature of sand which removes the protective *periople* (soft covering encircling the top of the hoof) of the hoof wall, causing moisture loss from the feet. Over time, the hooves then become shelly and thin walled.

Your farrier and veterinarian should be consulted regularly to monitor for beginning signs of *seedy toe* or *white line disease*, both syndromes resulting from infectious processes within the white line. Sand trapped beneath the shoe can grind imperfections into the white line that separates sensitive and insensitive hoof layers. If bacteria or fungus grows within the sensitive laminae of the foot, serious lameness problems develop.

How should you shoe your horse for work in the sand? Keep in mind that sand grains find their way into the smallest places. Pads would be a poor choice for sand work for the long distance horse. Sand trapped beneath a pad applies abnormal pressure points to the sole, creating bruises or corns. Easy Boots® also collect quantities of sand, and so, too, would be a poor choice of foot gear. Sand is often trapped in the *central sulcus* of the frog between the heel bulbs, so check daily in this area of each foot.

Due to the delayed *breakover* and liftoff of hooves in sand, *egg bar shoes* may be pulled off more easily as a rear limb catches up too quickly to the retarded movement of a front hoof. However, egg bar shoes on the rear feet may increase the bearing surface of the rear feet and diminish the depth to which they sink in the sand. This might reduce the load on the muscles and allow your horse greater ease in driving himself forward. (See Chapter 3 for more on egg bar shoes.)

In general, flat steel plates are probably the best choice for the front feet when working on sand. Some sandy terrain wears steel shoes more quickly than usual, so intervals between shoeings may need to increase in frequency. Pay careful attention to preventing long toes, low heels or a *broken-back hoof-pastern axis*. Chapter 3, explains in detail the significance of these problems, which can be all the more significant when combined with the extra stress of working in sand.

Develop a Versatile Horse

Sand is a useful terrain for strength training horses for work in other rigorous terrain conditions, such as mountains or fast, flat going. But remember there really is nothing out there that can prepare a horse for sand except sand itself. Set your sights on a goal, and methodically work toward that achievement. Allow your horse to dictate how rapidly he can advance to each next stage of training. By taking the time to adequately prepare, the mirage of the finish line won't shimmer and shift out of reach.

Heat and Humidity Conditioning

The Challenge of Climate

One of the most challenging environments to train for is a hot and humid climate. Your constant enemy is the buildup of heat in your horse's body as his muscles perform extraordinary work. The average pace of most endurance and competitive rides ranges from 5 to 12 mph. This kind of work effort requires 10 to 20 times more energy expenditure than what your horse needs to maintain himself at rest. When a horse is in "idle" mode standing around the paddock, normal *metabolic heat* (heat generated from normal metabolic processes such as breathing and digestion) maintains a constant body temperature.

As your horse moves along the trail, more than 70% of the energy generated by muscle metabolism is released as heat. If your horse were unable to shed this heat from the body, his working muscles could generate enough heat to potentially raise his body temperature by 2°F (1°C) for each hour of exercise.

Obviously such mounting heat is incompatible with life. There are many times when each of us feels like we are dying a slow death in the suffocating humidity that envelops us on a hot day. But nothing compares to what it is like for a horse having to work his heart out over miles and miles and miles, carrying a person upon his back in that kind of weather. A horse has only three times the surface area of a person, while having nine times the mass. Surface area is important for radiating and dissipating heat created by the large muscle mass of a horse. Working muscles generate lots of heat. The greater the muscle mass, the more surface area of the skin is required to stay abreast of cooling.

The more muscular the horse, the harder it is for that heat to escape the muscle depths. Tack and saddle pads further reduce a horse's useful surface area for dissipating heat. All these factors make it far more difficult for a horse to eliminate heat from its body than it is for you to do so. Not to speak of the fact that you can strip down to minimal clothing if need be, while your horse continues to sport a thick hide and a relatively hairy coat (even if you do body clip him).

Fortunately, the body has developed refined systems to release the heat load generated by muscle metabolism. There are many ways you can capitalize on improving natural biologic processes to condition your horse to cope with the heat and humidity monster.

The Impact of Hot and Humid Air

HOT WEATHER

The essence of the problem is this: In a hot environment, the primary means your horse has to rid himself of an accumulating heat load is to drive the heat from his body with the use of water vapor, or sweat. Usually, heated blood is circulated from the muscles to the surface blood vessels where it drives the evaporation of water from the skin. (Think of the water vapor that evaporates off when you boil a pot of water on the stove.) With rising body temperature, more blood flow is flushed to the skin to stimulate sweating. This rids the body of heat, while also unfortunately ridding your horse of vital body water and electrolytes. In any competitive situation, the sweating process compromises the metabolic health of your horse. The good news is that for every liter of sweat lost in *evaporative cooling*, internal body heat is driven down by half a degree Fahrenheit. Normally, a horse can sweat sufficiently to dissipate heat load from working muscles, provided heat and humidity factors are not unreasonable.

HUMIDITY

Humidity adds another challenge. For evaporative cooling to be effective, sweat must evaporate off a horse's body. However, in humid conditions, evaporation is greatly diminished because the air is already saturated with moisture. Instead, a horse continues to sweat, but the sweat runs in rivulets, loosing its potential cooling value. Without an effective evaporative process, minimal heat is lost through sweating while your horse continues to shell away precious water and electrolytes. Even while sweat drips off his skin, body heat continues to rise due to incomplete evaporation. The horse sweats more since his body temperature is not coming down. Endurance horses can lose three to four gallons of fluid in sweat for each **hour** of exercise in a hot, humid climate.

INADEQUATE SWEATING

In some cases a horse's sweat glands go into an overload cycle, and the sweat glands are literally exhausted of their ability to generate "water." Such a horse ceases to sweat, either partially or completely. An observant rider may notice inadequate dampness on a horse's skin that experiences this phenomenon, known as *anhidrosis*. It is sometimes hard to determine if the skin is too dry. You might easily underestimate your horse's sweat losses if unevaporated sweat is retained within the hair coat.

A horse that stops sweating yet continues to exercise is in peril of fatal overheating. The horse in crisis fails to continue to perform as its body succumbs to the power of heat exhaustion. Like a car that is overheated, the thermostat is out of control; instead of a radiator boiling over, an overheated horse falters and potentially collapses. (For more detail, see Chapter 8.)

FLUID AND ELECTROLYTE LOSSES FROM SWEAT

More often than not, though, humidity exacts an insidious toll through its persistent assault on the hydration and electrolyte balance of the horse. Even with just a few hours of endurance exercise, dehydration begins to detract from your horse's performance. In just 20 miles, the average fluid loss approximates four gallons of "water"! Over 50 miles, a horse may lose at least ten to twelve gallons of fluid through sweat. A little more than half of that can be replaced by drinking regularly throughout the event. At the very least, your horse needs to drink a minimum of a gallon of water for each hour he is working to stay safely abreast of continued fluid losses. Heat exhaustion develops from a combination of dehydration, electrolyte imbalances, depletion of energy reserves, and an accumulated heat load in the muscles. Heat and humidity pose the ultimate challenge to your horse's metabolic capacity to cope with all these variables.

So that you understand the kind of situation you'd rather avoid, let's look at the potential hazard of serious sweat losses. Continued dehydration from sweat loss reduces the volume of blood coursing through your horse's body. Circulation to the skin diminishes during prolonged aerobic exercise as muscular demand continues to call for blood flow. A dehydrating horse must slow down to be able to accommodate the work you are asking for. If not, then as circulation to the skin is reduced, sweating slows or ceases altogether. In this situation, body temperature continues to climb, exacerbating the development of heat exhaustion.

As dehydration worsens, your horse's heart rate increases in an attempt to maintain adequate circulation to support a continued work effort. Yet circulation to the skin does not necessarily improve with an accelerated heart rate. Recovery times at vet checks are prolonged, and fatigue rears its ugly head.

Heat Index

With a crude estimation of heat and humidity factors, you can determine how hard you can push your horse on any given day. Also referred to as the *effective temperature*, the *heat index (HI)* predicts how dangerous it is for your horse to work in hot and humid conditions. The score for the heat index is found by adding together *ambient (air) temperature* (in degrees Fahrenheit) plus relative humidity (%). For example, a 70 degree day with 65% humidity has a heat index of 135.

You can apply some rules of thumb by estimating the heat index. If the heat index is less than 130, your horse should be able to cool himself effectively through natural physiologic mechanisms. At a heat index of 130-150, you probably need to assist your horse in cooling by sponging him with water. If the heat index is greater than 150, it is very difficult for your horse to shed the heat, especially if humidity contributes to more than half of this score. A heat index of 160-170 dictates that you **must** reduce your horse's speed in addition to using cooling strategies. An effective temperature greater than 180 creates an impossible situation for an exercising horse to cool itself even with supplemental cooling techniques. (Refer to Heat-Reducing Strategies in Chapter 8 for more detail.)

Strategies to Condition a Horse to Heat and Humidity

ACCLIMATIZATION

The beauty of a living body is that it is able to **adapt** to a variety of stresses, given time. This process does not happen overnight; it requires strategy and weeks to stimulate the physiologic responses of a horse to more effectively cool itself in the face of high heat and humidity. Appropriate responses to humid heat usually develop within two to three weeks of acclimatization. The issue of heat and humidity becomes more pressing to a horse that is transported to that climate from a more temperate environment. A rider who expects a horse to perform up to its normal standard is guaranteed to be disappointed. One rider revealed that in the Colorado mountains, her horse finished a very challenging 100 mile race in 12 hours. Within that same competitive season, this same experienced horse and rider team took almost 24 hours to finish a flat 100 mile course on a Texas summer day. The pace had to be slower, while recovery times at the vet checks were markedly longer than what the horse had been capable of in an arid mountain climate. Before the horse had acclimated to the heat and humidity of a Texas climate, sweat would pour off his body while standing quietly in his paddock at 3 am prior to the ride. Imagine how hot the weather must be to stimulate a resting horse to sweat in the middle of the night, and consider the volume of fluid and electrolyte loss this would exact before the horse even starts an exercise effort!

CONDITIONING STRATEGIES FOR HEAT AND HUMIDITY

To achieve the best and safest performance possible, the key is to acclimate your horse appropriately, and strategically train your horse to accommodate the gruesome weather.

As with any training strategy, your horse must be exposed to the conditions in which he will compete. It is far better to discover a horse's limitations in a more controlled training environment rather than in the "heat" of competition. Not all horses are able to perform in a hot and humid climate. Every horse is different in its tolerance to heat. It is wise to follow some good advice: if you can't safely train in that climate, then by all means, don't compete in it. To do so could endanger your horse's life. If your horse continually has problems during training, it is possible that he is incapable of adapting to the heat and humidity, at least at this stage in his career. Don't push your luck.

Although it is tempting to get up early and ride in the wee hours of the morning before the sun has started its relentless climb in the sky, by doing so you will be missing out on training opportunities. The objective is to adequately stimulate your horse's abilities to dissipate heat from the body. The sweat glands must be developed; the capillary beds and blood vessels in the skin must expand in size and number. Just as with any conditioning process, the *cardiovascular system* and muscular endurance must be improved to make your horse more efficient at increasing levels of exercise intensity during adverse heat conditions. Remember with training, a horse's *aerobic* capacity is expanded, delaying reliance on *anaerobic* energy pathways to fuel muscle work. Energy supplies are conserved, and *lactic acid* does not accumulate as rapidly.

Heart rate recoveries improve with conditioning, and the heart rate elicited from a given work effort will diminish. The easier the task, the less heat is generated from the muscle tissues. As fitness improves, the insulating fat layer disappears from your horse's frame, allowing more effective radiation of heat from the body. Training teaches a horse's body to sweat sooner as each exercise period repeatedly stimulates the body's mechanisms for dissipating heat. In particular, the responses of increased blood flow to the skin, and the activation of sweat glands are triggered more quickly. These adaptive responses delay the increase in mounting body temperature during prolonged exercise.

But, too much training in heat and humidity wears a horse down eventually. Sweat glands are overworked, and cumulative dehydration and electrolyte losses will creep up to overwhelm your horse's ability to maintain a normal physiologic state. The homework of conditioning pays off, and your horse gains a great advantage if you train at least one ride each week during the hottest and most humid part of the day. Riding your horse in the afternoon when it is 104°F (41°C) and 30% humidity stimulates an effective training response for coping with high ambient temperatures. To train for humidity, schedule a good workout some morning each week when it is only 85-90°F (30-35°C) but the air is laced with 90% humidity. Some of you may be at the point in your conditioning program where interval training is an important part of your strategy. Remember that speed work of interval training drives muscle temperature up even in cool ambient temperatures. It is safer to perform *interval training* repetitions during the coolest, least humid part of the day. If you live in a climate that tends to be relatively cool and dry even in the summer, take advantage of those pummeling hot and humid days that occasionally appear. Don't hide inside; go out and ride. This is important if you plan to compete in a hot and humid climate. Capitalize on those rare opportunities.

As part of your conditioning strategy, you **must** train your horse to drink along the trail and at every opportunity. Studies have shown that thirst is not stimulated until a horse is 2-3% dehydrated. This level of dehydration develops when a horse has lost three to four gallons of body fluid. Unless you encourage your long-distance horse to develop good drinking habits, especially early on in a ride, his performance will greatly suffer. (For more on the importance of drinking, see the section on Drinking in Chapter 8.)

8 Cooling Strategies during Training and Competition

Ways You Can Assist Your Horse's Natural Means of Cooling

Under any climatic condition, exercising muscle generates a vast amount of heat. Even in arid climates of low humidity, both warm and hot weather exact a huge demand on a horse's inherent cooling systems. Your role in assisting your horse in ridding itself of extraneous body heat is essential. Cooling techniques become even more critical to safely continue exercising your horse in a hot and humid climate.

Heat-reducing strategies make or break a successful endurance horse. If body temperature of an exercising horse is maintained within a normal range (less than 103°F or 40°C), he will recover rapidly at rest stops. Heart rate quickly drops, assuming other metabolic factors are in good working order. Any method you can employ to get a horse through an endurance vet check as quickly as possible will give you a winning edge. By the same token, many of the techniques used to improve the recovery times on a competition horse are also helpful to the horse in training or to the recreational trail horse to delay the onset of fatigue.

To effectively decrease sweat losses and result in less fluid and electrolytes lost in your distance horse, you need to find the best strategies to minimize heat buildup and improve the cooling process.

Evaporative Cooling

Evaporative cooling in the form of sweat is responsible for dissipating up to 60% of a horse's heat load, but other mechanisms are also important. You can capitalize on the principles of some of these natural mechanisms to hasten cooling in your horse. (For more detail on sweating, refer to the section on Heat and Humidity Conditioning in the Chapter 7.)

Photo 66 Steam rising off a warm horse on a cool morning. This is an example of radiational cooling.

Respiratory Cooling

Besides heat loss through sweating, *respiratory cooling* is an important avenue of heat escape. An increased respiratory rate can contribute as much as 33% to heat loss. However, in reality your horse generally dissipates about 15-20% of his heat load through faster breathing and panting. Nothing you do can influence a greater loss of heat through a horse's airways except proper preparation in conditioning to minimize heat accumulation in the first place.

Radiation

Heat is also lost from your horse's core as it radiates from the skin and muscles into the cooler surrounding air. The effectiveness of *radiation* depends on a difference in temperature between the air and the horse's skin (Photo 66). Although you are helpless to control the climate, you should seek out shady spots that reduce the sun's intensity at vet checks. Covering your horse with a minimum of tack and saddle blankets effectively improves your horse's radia-

Photo 67a You may find you need to body clip your horse if his hair coat is preventing cooling. This horse has been given a trace clip.

Photo 67b A more extensive body clip — a hunter (or blanket) clip.

tion capabilities. Cantle bags, pommel bags, large saddles, and heavy blankets eliminate a useful surface area on a horse's back for both radiation and evaporative cooling. The neck and back of a horse contain a large proportion of sweat glands. The more surface you expose, the better off your horse will be.

On this same note, use saddle pads that absorb moisture. Avoid saddle pads that don't breathe such as rubber or compressible foam materials used to cushion ill-fitting saddles. These substances intensify heat beneath them, and can lead to *heat bumps*, small welts created by excess temperature in the skin.

A thick hair coat or an excessive layer of fat under the skin insulates your horse and diminishes the effectiveness of radiation. Hair also traps sweat so it can't get to the surface for evaporation. Even an average summer hair coat retains as much as three cups of "water." Body clipping or trace clipping removes hair that is a cooling deterrent (Photos 67a & b). You achieve the best cooling effect by shaving hair away from the areas with the greatest supply of large blood vessels, such as the neck, chest, and belly regions. A fit horse doesn't pack any extra fat under the skin. In the process of conditioning, fat transforms into lean muscling and renders a horse fit.

Convection

Convection is yet another useful tool for removing internal body heat. As heated blood travels from the deep tissues to the skin, it is cooled in the superficial skin veins. Upon return to the body core, the cooler blood mixes with the warmer blood, further assisting in cooling. Heat transfer from a horse in this manner is accelerated by cool air blowing across the skin. Again, this process is dependent on a temperature differential between horse and air. Take advantage of breezy spots at stopping points. In a hot and humid climate, it is helpful to blow a battery-operated fan over a horse or to fan him with towels to increase convection currents while removing saturated air near the horse's skin.

Conduction

Conduction also transfers heat by direct contact of the skin with a cooler surface. We are all familiar with this favored method of cooling used by dogs lying on a cold stone floor or in a puddle. When you soak your horse with water to cool him down, you not only simulate evaporative cooling, but cool water serves as a conduction medium to draw heat away from hot skin. You need to continually pour water over your horse's head and neck to keep coolness in contact with warm skin. The warmed water should be scraped away, and fresh cool water applied to achieve the maximum effect (Photo 68).

Photo 68 Repeatedly sponging cool water onto a horse helps with conductive cooling as the cool water draws heat away from hot skin.

One of the big problems presented by a hot and humid climate is that often the temperature of standing water is very close to the air temperature. This applies to water that sits for a long time in a bucket. You may need to add ice to cool it to a potentially useful temperature before sponging your horse. You can cool the water by adding ice cubes, or placing frozen plastic liter water bottles ("bullets") in a bucket of water. However, this doesn't mean you should pour ice water on your horse. Using ice water on a long-distance horse is a poor idea in any situation, even in heat and humidity. If water applied to a horse's skin is **too** cold, then superficial blood vessels reflexively constrict away from the skin surface. Instead of continuing to release heat, the blood vessels pull back into the deeper confines of the muscles. The result is a rise in muscle and body temperature quite the opposite of the effect you are trying to accomplish. And worse, muscles may stiffen or cramp in response. Heart rate will remain elevated due to high body temperature and/or pain from muscle cramping. This certainly won't help you get through a vet check in good speed.

Research has evaluated the use of ice water to cool combined-training horses. The work effort of these horses involves both *aerobic* and *anaerobic* exercise. Ideally, an endurance horse works primarily in the aerobic range and at relatively slower speeds than a galloping and jumping combined-training horse. The differences in exercise intensity between the two sports may make it difficult to draw correlations from conclusions gained from combined-training research. Distance riders should be cautious in drawing conclusions from the ice water data that was directed toward the 1996 Atlanta Olympics.

Signs of Problems from Overheating

Remember that as a rider you are not working as hard as your horse. It is often difficult to recognize a horse's true work effort as you are perched quietly on his back as he negotiates a steep hill or gallops the trail. Those muscles are working and working, and the heat is building. It is critical that you be keyed into your horse's behavior and willingness to work.

Subtle Signs

There are subtle signs of fatigue, such as body posture and the look in a horse's eye at a stopping point. Do you feel you have to continually urge your horse on to maintain a steady pace? Is he drinking or eating less than he should? Listen to your horse; always listen to your horse!

Panting

Look critically at your horse when you climb off at a rest stop. One practical technique is to monitor a horse's respiratory rate. Horses pant to help rid the body of more heat load when sweating cannot keep up to the task. Up to one-third of the heat load can be dissipated from the respiratory tract by rapidly moving heat from the bloodstream, across the lungs, to be expired in exchange for cooler, incoming air. This involuntary response becomes increasingly helpful as blood flow to the skin diminishes with progressive dehydration.

A very hot horse will pant. That's okay for a short time. But a hot horse having difficulty ridding his body of heat will continue to pant. He may have been going too fast for his ability to cope, or he may be underconditioned for the task at hand. The *heat index* may exceed the ability of a horse to continue to cool itself. Panting may also indicate that a horse is not sweating sufficiently for the work load, and may be developing *anhidrosis*. Learn to read your horse's respiratory rate so you can prevent him from getting too hot.

Rise in Rectal Temperature

If a horse is able to employ successfully all these natural heat transfer mechanisms, then what is left over and stored in body tissues is about 5% of the heat load created by working muscles. This correlates with a rise in rectal temperature to bring it up to 102-103°F (39-40°C) readings at vet check points. Rectal temperatures greater than 103°F (40°C) indicate that a horse is working too hard or is unable to employ effective cooling mechanisms. If such is the case, check that your horse is sweating appropriately for the climate, and monitor his respiratory rate for prolonged panting.

Slow Heart Rate Recovery

Body temperature remains elevated in a horse that has problems coping with high heat and humidity. This significantly affects *heart rate recovery*. A horse that recovers relatively slowly, yet still meets veterinary criteria within the required time period, should be monitored closely. Assuming your horse is okay, you **must** slow down your speed once you proceed out of the vet check. (For more details, refer to Chapter 11.)

Heat-Reducing Strategies While Riding

Preparation

Let's look at some applications of heat-reducing ideas in the competitive situation. To start, even before you climb aboard, you should have prepared your horse for the event. Not only must he be a sleek, fit athlete, but you should have minimized the surface area your tack covers and should have used thin, but moisture absorbing, saddle pads. Prepare for the demands of a hot environment by body clipping and removing hair that interferes with heat dissipation.

Warm Up

As you start the ride, sufficiently warm up your horse's muscles before undertaking a stronger exertion. The slight rise in body temperature at the initiation of exercise improves the efficiency of muscular contractions and the enzyme systems in the muscles necessary to convert muscle fuel to energy. After a 10-15 minute warm-up, you can start to ask your horse to move out in a strong, working stride. If you desire, you can do your warm-up in the first few miles of a ride, unless you plan to start out racing. In that case, your horse should be well warmed up before you cross the start line.

Heart Monitor

To minimize sweat losses and heat accumulation in the working muscles, you must make use of all possible cooling strategies, including slowing down when necessary. A horse's work effort has a lot to do with how quickly and how much heat is released from the working muscles.

Use your heart rate monitor to maintain your horse's working intensity within an *aerobic*, rather than an *anaerobic* range. This usually corresponds with heart rates less than 150 bpm. Because muscles and skin compete for blood flow in a hot climate, it is far too easy to override your horse. His muscles will convert to anaerobic metabolism more quickly than they would in a cooler climate; an anaerobic work effort accelerates the onset of fatigue.

Don't use the heart monitor as a tachometer; adjust your speed for the terrain. Pay attention to the terrain over which you ride, and adjust appropriately for the difficulty, be it hill climbs, sand, mud, or rocks. Slow down your speed, especially as you ascend a hill. Better yet, get off and lead or tail your horse on hill climbs. This is not permissible in most competitive trail competitions, but is a useful strategy in training or endurance competition. The less weight your horse has to carry on his back translates to a reduced physical effort. Your horse has many miles to go during competition.

Steady Rhythm

It is important to develop strategies to save your horse's energy while in motion, particularly in a hot, humid climate. Anything you can do to limit muscular exertion will minimize the heat load. When possible, maintain as constant a pace as you can. Slowing down or speeding up wastes valuable energy, and forces muscles to work harder as they accelerate or decelerate with changing rhythms. Find an efficient working rhythm and stay there, or at least change pace gradually.

When cantering, try to maintain a constant stride rhythm since respiratory rate is directly linked with stride frequency at the canter and gallop. Your horse takes a breath each time its hind legs impact the ground, while expiring when the front legs hit the ground. This becomes very important when attempting to maintain your horse in aerobic work. A constant pace optimizes the amount of oxygen uptake and delivery to the tissues. And, with each expired breath, heat is dissipated through the respiratory tract.

Photo 69 As you move along the trail, remember to assist your horse with evaporative and conductive cooling by applying water to his skin. Continually drenching the skin with water can decrease sweat loss by half.

Skin Soak Strategies

As your horse works along the trail, find opportunities to assist with evapora-tive cooling. Applying water to your horse's skin conserves the amount of wa-ter he must provide for the sweating process. Continuous use of water drenches on the skin potentially decreases sweat losses by half (Photo 69). This trans-lates to improved hydration and *electrolyte* balance over the course of many miles. Take advantage of this strategy throughout a ride whenever you come upon creeks, streams, rivers, puddles, or stock tanks. Stop and take the time to soak your horse at every opportunity. If you use a common water source, like a stock tank or water bucket, use a separate container to pull water from the vessel. Dunking wet, sweaty sponges directly into the water fouls it as drinking water for other horses. Collapsible water buckets or cut-down plastic gallon jugs make handy and lightweight watering implements for use along the trail.

Train your horse to accept you sponging "on the fly." Using a sponge at-tached to a long string, you can repeatedly fling the sponge into the water as you cross a creek or river, and then wring it over your horse's neck. This technique saves time for the truly competitive horse and rider, while still allowing you to achieve some cooling while in motion.

Drinking

One of the **most** important ingredients of successful completion is the ability of a horse to drink well both before and during a competition. Encourage your horse to drink whenever possible (Photo 70). He should drink at least every 10 miles or every hour of exercise. A well-hydrated horse will have ample blood volume to supply both the muscles and the skin with circulation. Adequate blood flow to the skin enables effective evaporative cooling through sweat. At the same time muscles competing for blood flow are not starved for oxygen and won't have to resort to the less efficient form of anaerobic metabolism to fuel locomotion.

Try to slow down before you reach a watering spot so your horse will be relaxed enough to drink. If you come on a water source unexpectedly, give your horse a chance to "blow" and settle his respiration rate so he drinks willingly. If he doesn't drop his head right away, give him a few minutes to catch his breath. Loosen the breastplate straps so the collar doesn't pinch his chest and throat as he lowers his head.

After your horse has had a good drink, give a dose of electrolytes, even if you are on the trail. Offering water and electrolytes about two miles before arriving at a vet check gives a horse more time to absorb fluids and electrolytes from the bowel so that he is refueled by the time he leaves the vet check. It takes at least 20 minutes into a rest break for the intestines to start to absorb nutrients and electrolytes. This is especially true in hot and humid climates when the skin continues to compete for blood circulation to cool the horse. (For more detail, see section on Electrolyte Supplementation in this chapter.)

Minimizing Muscle Cramping

It is not uncommon in hot, humid climates to see a higher percentage of endurance horses develop muscle cramping than what is experienced in an arid climate because the great volume of sweat released by a horse in an effort to cool itself contributes to excessive calcium and potassium losses. The calcium loss and electrolyte imbalance can also cause *thumps (synchronous diaphragmatic flutter)*. It is possible to work a horse out of a self-limiting muscle cramp by radically slowing the pace to a walk. Slow movement allows the muscles to dissipate the accumulated heat load and to flush away *lactic acid*. Administer a

*Photo 70 Offer your horse the chance to drink at **every** opportunity. A horse should drink at least once every ten miles or every hour of exercise to stay abreast of fluid losses through sweat.*

double dose of electrolytes to a mildly crampy horse and offer alfalfa hay at the vet checks. Alfalfa is a rich source of calcium. If your horse is unaccustomed to alfalfa, offer less than a thin flake. At the vet checks, allow your horse ample time to play catch-up for the fluid and electrolyte deficits. If need be, pause along the trail and give your horse time to snack and drink. Always discuss concerns with the veterinary staff although your horse appears to have recovered from a mild crisis. (For more on this subject, refer to Chapter 9.)

Cooling Strategies at the Vet Checks

Approach to Vet Checks

Slow down as you approach a vet check, especially over the last quarter to one-half mile. If you enter the vet check still maintaining a working pace, then suddenly pull your horse up, muscle metabolism remains turned on in "work"

Photo 71 If you are on an endurance ride, dismount as you approach the vet check to decrease the burden on your horse's muscles, allowing a more rapid heart rate recovery.

mode. Heat and lactic acid continue to be released through the bloodstream. This drives the heart rate up for an unnecessary period of time.

As you slow down on approach to the check, hop out of the saddle if you are in an endurance competition to further decrease the burden on your horse's heart that comes from carrying your body weight (Photo 71). (Competitive ride rules do not allow riders to dismount and proceed forward down the trail.) Loosen the girth as you proceed down the trail toward the vet check to improve circulation in the skin along the belly and back. Be ready to quickly pull off the saddle. Removing tack increases the surface area available for evaporative cooling and radiation by exposing sweat glands and skin to the air. If you have enough water in your fanny pack bottles, pour what you have over your horse's neck as you enter the check.

Photo 72 A pressurized water sprayer is an effective tool for continually applying cool water to a horse.

Water Soaks

Before you enter the *P & R* area, start sponging your horse, paying particular attention to soaking the head, neck, chest, and lower legs. These areas contain numerous large blood vessels that conduct body heat to the cool water. A pressurized water sprayer is an effective tool for continually applying cool water to a horse (Photo 72). If the air temperature is very warm, at least over 80°F (26°C), it is probably safe to soak the entire body of your horse (Photo 73). Generally, however, unless there is high heat and humidity, it is safer to restrict water application only to areas in front of the withers. It is thought that 80% of cooling takes place on the head and neck, so sponging efforts should be addressed to these areas. Rapid chilling over large muscles in the back and rump can induce cramping. A cool breeze makes chilling more likely when those large muscles are wet, either from sweat, water soaks, or a summer drizzle. A chilled horse maintains a high heart rate. In some instances, you may need to apply a cooler over the haunches so the large muscle masses cool down slowly

Photo 73 If air temperature and humidity are high, full body soaks are a good idea. This horse is fitted with a heart rate belt so its pulse can be monitored as it is cooled.

while you continue to soak the neck and chest.

Once water has conducted body heat, it loses some of its cooling power. The hair coat can retain several liters of water. If you only apply water once and leave it there, it may actually hold heat on the horse. This means you should repeatedly apply water until your horse's chest no longer feels hot to the touch. As the skin surface cools with water application, blood that returns to the body depths is initially cooled in the superficial skin vessels. Heat within the muscles is conducted to the cooler blood and once again carried to the skin surface. Water soaking also washes away sweat and dirt from the hair follicles and sweat glands to increase the surface area for normal *evaporative cooling* mechanisms. Scrape away the warm water so you continue to cool the horse.

Another technique to pull body heat rapidly from the skin surface is to mix up a bucket of one part (no more) rubbing alcohol to four parts water (half a pint per gallon works well) and use this mixture for sponging. This is particularly helpful in heat and humidity. However, a few notes of caution: do not use alcohol near your horse's eyes; and, any alcohol that contacts small nicks, scrapes, and abrasions is bound to irritate your horse. Agitation from the stinging may cause his heart rate to fail to drop toward recovery parameters. Specifically mark the bucket with the alcohol so it is not inadvertently offered as drinking water!

Over-Cooling

It is possible to over-cool your horse if you continue to apply water to the neck and chest after the skin feels cool to the touch. Once you have accomplished your goal, **stop** soaking. It may be useful to monitor rectal temperature as you cool down the horse.

Shade

Some people believe that dark horses tend to be more affected in a hot climate than a lighter horse. Any horse will benefit if you try to find shade when possible at each stop (Photos 74 & 75). Pull off saddles and tack to increase surface area for the body to eliminate heat.

Icing the Legs

Some riders put ice boots on their horse's legs immediately upon arrival into the vet check. This effectively helps cool a horse through the process of *conduction* (Photo 76). However, consider a few things about this technique. Before the legs go numb, icing can be a fairly uncomfortable experience to the horse, and any discomfort can raise the heart rate. Icing the legs also rapidly decreases body temperature with the risk of chilling the horse. But even more importantly, ice wraps effectively stiffen the connective tissue components of tendons and ligaments, drastically reducing elasticity and stretch that were gained through warm-up and exercise. A stiff tendon is more at risk of over-stretching or tearing; resulting in tendinitis or a bowed tendon. Also, icing will numb the area of an injury, thereby masking signs of a beginning lameness problem. It is recommended, and in some cases required, that horses not be iced within 10 minutes prior to veterinary presentation.

If you do ice your horse's legs, do so gradually and intermittently; not all at once, all of a sudden. And whether you ice the legs or not, be sure to warm up your horse for a few minutes before leaving the vet check. Move him around at a brisk walk for about 5-10 minutes prior to your "out" time to circulate blood to the muscles, and to improve stretch and elasticity in the tendons and ligaments. Stretching exercises also improve lubrication and mobility within the

Photo 74 *Try to find a shady place for your horse at each stop.*

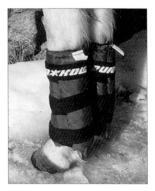

Photo 76 *A pair of ice boots applied to a horse's forelegs. Use ice boots with care since they stiffen connective tissue components of tendons and ligaments. A stiff tendon is more at risk of over-stretching and resulting in tendinitis or a bow.*

Photo 75 *Some people set up a shade tent at vet checks to be certain a horse has shade on a sunny day. This tent even has pipes in the ceiling that allow water to mist over the horse for additional cooling during very hot weather.*

joints, thereby increasing their range of motion and rendering them less susceptible to injury.

Movement

Pulling your horse to a sudden stop is counterproductive for driving the heart rate down, especially in a hot, humid climate. Although your horse has stopped moving, heat continues to accumulate in the muscles, as does lactic acid. Typically, rectal temperature decreases within 20-30 minutes once exercise is stopped. But initially, rectal temperature still climbs for 5-10 minutes as residual heat is released from the recently contracting muscles. Despite aggressive cooling strategies by you or your pit crew to soak the horse to assist evaporative cooling, a horse's body temperature remains elevated while he stands still. This results in longer heart rate recoveries than if you were to alternately walk and soak the horse at several minute intervals.

Light walking effectively reduces the load on your horse's heart by flushing heat and lactic acid from the muscles with continued circulation. The heart rate of a horse that stands still accelerates to accomplish this end, making for a longer recovery time. Additionally, intermittent walking allows tendons, ligaments, and joints to cool down at a gradual rate by maintaining circulation to these structures.

Moving from P&R to the Veterinary Presentation

Once you determine that your horse has met pulse criteria, you can present the horse to the P&R staff. In some instances, you may receive a time penalty if you prematurely present to the P&R personnel before the heart rate is down to criteria. In a competitive situation, this is certainly not to your advantage. So, it is best to intermittently walk your horse while cooling it down. With each walking bout, more heat and lactic acid is whisked away by the circulation so the heart rate progressively drops and remains dropped.

You will be released from the P&R area once your horse passes pulse criteria and the time to begin your hold is marked on your rider card. From the P&R area, you should proceed directly to the veterinarians. Often, a rider makes the mistake of allowing a horse to stand quietly for a time before presenting to the veterinarian. Sometimes this is unavoidable because of a wait to find a veterinarian who is free to examine your horse. In other instances, a rider delays going directly to the veterinarians thinking that more rest time will give the horse an improved presentation. However, as mentioned earlier, heat continues to be released in muscles that are pulled suddenly to a stop. The same is

Photo 77 You can assist a horse's circulation in flushing heat and lactic acid from the muscles by rhythmically massaging the large rump muscles.

true for lactic acid accumulation in the muscles even once exercise ceases. Water soaks may successfully bring your horse's pulse down to criteria, but then once you move your horse toward the veterinary presentation area, immediate muscular contraction flushes accumulated lactic acid into the bloodstream. In response, the horse's heart rate rapidly elevates, possibly beyond pulse criteria. The veterinarian will be less than pleased as the pulse is taken for the start of the *cardiac recovery index*. Or, the elevated pulse can affect interpretation of the cardiac recovery index.

Massage

During the periods when a horse is standing quietly, you can assist his circulation in flushing heat and lactic acid from the muscles by rhythmically massaging the large rump muscles (Photo 77). Apply hand compression at the rate of about one per second, which approximates a recovery heart rate near 60 bpm.

Temperature of Drinking Water

Your horse should be offered drinking water at every opportunity. At the vet check, offer water that is not too cold. Very cold water may divert blood flow to the intestines when it is being demanded by the muscles and skin to flush away heat and lactic acid. The sudden change in temperature in the stomach by drinking cold water not only places a demand on competing circulation, but potentially creates intestinal cramping and colic.

Offering Food to a Hot Horse

Don't allow your horse to eat until he has met pulse criteria. Be sure your horse has had a good drink before offering any dry food. It is also desirable for his rectal temperature to fall below 103°F (40°C) before you offer large quantities of food. This allows blood flow to be partially restored to the intestines. You may need to train your horse to accept the idea of standing quietly until you allow him to eat. If not used to this idea, your horse's anxiety at not being allowed to eat may keep the heart rate elevated. The rationale behind not feeding a hot horse is simple: food places a demand for circulation to be diverted to the intestines for digestion. This places an added burden on the heart and keeps the heart rate elevated. The more food the horse ingests, the greater the call for intestinal blood flow and the longer the heart rate remains high. Ideally, you should proceed through both the P&R and the veterinary presentation before you allow your horse to eat. Ride management usually makes this easy on you by requiring that you go to the veterinary presentation area directly once your pulse criteria has been met with the P&R team.

Feed wetted-down foods like sloppy gruels made from grains, bran, and water along with well-soaked hay to improve water intake. Your horse can later draw on the intestinal water reservoir to partially replenish sweat losses. If your horse consumes only dry hay, "water" is drawn into the intestines, further dehydrating his blood volume.

One thing that is particularly noticeable at rides in hot, humid climates is that horses tend to "crash and burn" much more quickly than they do in other climates. This seems to be related to the huge volume of sweat loss that compromises water and electrolyte balance in the horse. As muscles and skin compete for blood flow, blood is diverted away from the gastrointestinal tract. Based on research in lab animals, it is speculated that intestinal circulation may decrease as much as 25-40%! Reduced circulation to the intestines causes intestinal motility to shut down quickly. In an inactive intestine, food ferments rather than going through normal processes of digestion. As gas and fluid accumulate in a relatively inactive intestinal tract, colic pain results.

In a hot, humid environment, veterinary control parameters tend to be more stringent than what you might be used to in other areas of the country. Usually pulse criterion is met at 64 bpm or below, but pulse criterion is often dropped to 60 bpm or even down to 56 bpm in hot, humid weather. In many cases, veterinarians also require that a horse's rectal temperature remain below 103°F (40°C) to be able to continue. (For more detail, see Chapter 9.)

Electrolyte Supplementation

Generally for a one day race, it is good practice to give electrolytes the night before, the morning of, and at every stop during race day. Recent research has indicated that horses preloaded with electrolytes at least two hours prior to competition have fewer electrolyte and fluid deficits by 20 miles into the ride. And, horses with better hydration and electrolyte balance at 20 miles completed more quickly and in better shape than horses experiencing more profound dehydration and electrolyte losses early in the ride. In a hot, humid climate, make sure you have calcium supplementation in your electrolyte mix. It is helpful to mix the salt preparation with calcium gluconate (available from your veterinarian) rather than with water.

Make sure your horse has a good long drink before you administer electrolytes. It may actually be more advantageous to give frequent, small doses along the trail after a good drink, rather than large, single doses at each vet check. More frequent doses compensate for the lag time for absorption of the electrolytes from the intestines related to reduced intestinal blood flow during exercise.

Various homemade electrolyte supplements can be prepared in advance, and packed into two ounce increments to be given at each stop. A film canister holds just the right amount of electrolyte mixture for a single dose. One example is a mixture of two parts Lite® salt to one part calcium carbonate to one part magnesium oxide. Another commonly used electrolyte mixture is made by mixing three parts table salt to one part Lite® salt to one part calcium carbonate (an oral preparation of limestone available at feed stores). An excellent commercial mix called EnduraLites® contains a rapidly metabolized source of calcium (calcium acetate). Never give a long-distance horse any electrolytes containing bicarbonate or baking soda. This exacerbates *metabolic alkalosis* that results from the loss of chloride and potassium ions in the sweat. Read labels carefully if you are using commercial electrolyte supplements.

You can administer oral preparations of electrolytes with a syringe, or you can add the supplement to a grain and bran mash mix. Train your horse to accept syringe administration during conditioning rides at home.

One word of caution on electrolyte supplementation: it is possible that supplementing with an excessive amount of electrolytes can cause a horse to develop a soft, mushy stool. There is a potential to overload a horse with excessive electrolyte supplementation particularly on multi-day rides where the horse is given electrolytes constantly over many days. Other reasons for a soft stool also exist: blood flow to the bowels of a dehydrated horse is severely compromised; changes in intestinal microflora result from reduced intestinal motility and may create diarrhea; a nervous horse may develop diarrhea under the best of circumstances. Even knowing your horse's typical responses in this regard still makes it difficult to determine the source of a loose stool.

Body Soaks Before Leaving the Vet Check

In a very hot and humid climate, soak your horse's entire body with cool water prior to leaving the hold. This buys you some time before your horse becomes overly warm again. It is possible that in an extremely humid climate, no matter how much water you dump over your horse, you achieve limited *evaporative cooling, conduction*, or *convection*. A full body soak diminishes the amount of body water your horse must put out as sweat. Once out on the trail again, pay attention to the previously discussed cooling strategies. All these issues become more important with each progressive mile. The objective is to keep the heat load to a minimum, thereby reducing sweat losses. The elite athlete is the horse that is most capable of maintaining fluids and electrolytes throughout the course of a ride.

Mechanical Concerns of Heat and Humidity

One of the big problems with a hot, humid climate for both horse and rider is the tendency to develop chafed areas where equipment rubs tender skin. You certainly know where those places are on yourself, so these can be dealt with as you go along the trail. But it is hard to know where spots are bothering your horse until after the fact. Intense sweating occurs beneath a girth; Vaseline® or Desitin® applied in the girth area may prevent rubs and relieve raw spots (Photo 78). If you use protective boots on your horse, take them off at each check point, look for abrasions on the legs, and clean out any debris, sand, or dirt that might have worked its way beneath the boots.

At vet checks, pull off your saddle to let air onto the skin to relieve localized heat build-up and to prevent *heat bumps* from occurring. As mentioned, removing tack also helps heat to more rapidly dissipate from the body.

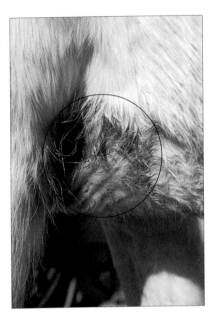

Photo 78 Chafed areas can be caused by equipment rubs and intense sweating. At each vet check the horse should be thoroughly looked over for any irritated areas to possibly prevent a girth gall before it's too late. The horse pictured has a nasty sore spot behind his left elbow.

The Rider's Needs

Although you may not be working as hard as your horse, an oppressive climate still affects you. You need to maintain sound judgement throughout the day in order to properly monitor and pace your equine partner. Be sure to attend to your own fluid and electrolyte needs. It is vitally important that you continue to drink, even though you don't think you are thirsty. This sounds like common sense advice, but often competitors forget to do this very thing. You may be losing as much as one to two quarts of fluid per hour of intense exercise, particularly if you get off and run with your horse. Drinks with caffeine or alcohol stimulate urination and tend to dehydrate you more quickly. Load your water flasks with a "sport drink" that contains salts and carbohydrates. Undiluted fruit juices are too high in carbohydrates and are not absorbed as quickly as a fruit juice that is diluted with an equal amount of water. Stick to drinks that contain less than 6-8% carbohydrates by weight. Make sure you have plenty of energy-rich food to nurse your mind and body through a competition. Just as for horses, energy stimulates the uptake of water and electrolytes from the intestines, helping both of you to endure the competition.

9 Evaluation of Metabolic Health and Soundness

Rider Recognition of Vital Signs

When we partner ourselves with a horse, we assume a responsibility unique to any other form of competitive sports. Not only must we look after our own body and needs, but we must attend to the basic requirements of our mount. Attention to small details enables a horse to give you its utmost performance.

A horse speaks in a very fundamental language. Every nuance of excitement or exhaustion is transmitted to us in a horse's body posture and attitude if we look carefully. With time and experience, a rider is able to anticipate and respond to a horse's individual quirks, and to shape events to favor the outcome. This ability comes from seeking information, and from miles spent riding the trail. A very basic understanding of the inner workings of the long-distance equine athlete allows you to read your horse throughout an event, giving you a real competitive edge. Your role, as a team player, is to develop your recognition skills. Not only must you carefully monitor your horse's demeanor, but you should always bring concerns to the attention of a ride veterinarian. Maintaining a dialogue with the veterinary staff brings together a team capable of making sound medical decisions to protect your horse. If questions pop up during training, promptly contact your local veterinarian rather than letting things simmer until they burst out of control.

At a competition, a veterinary team needs your participation, since you know your horse better than anyone. You can appreciate changes in attitude, posture, and behavior once a horse is removed from the excitatory stimulus of a vet check. An understanding of what a veterinarian is evaluating at the veterinary presentations allows you to ask important questions and be part of the decision-making process of *"fit to continue."* As you read on, you will learn a lot about what is written on your rider card, and its significance to your horse's well-being. Likewise, as you educate yourself to assess some of these parameters during training and competition, you can use these tools to evaluate your horse along the trail, and make these journeys safer for your horse.

Veterinary Evaluation of Vital Signs

Historical Overview

As we look back along an historical time line of endurance riding events, it is no secret that in the early years the sport of endurance **racing** had a terrible reputation of destroying horses by literally riding them into the ground. The shame of such horse abuse catalyzed a desire to create more safety protocols to protect the welfare of the horses. New organizations sprang up, including many competitive trail factions, in an effort to remove the element of speed. Over the last decade, stringent veterinary controls have become an integral part of any endurance or competitive trail event. Dedicated veterinarians have become well versed in the specialized needs of an equine endurance athlete. This passion for more knowledge has paid great dividends for the horses as well as for the image of endurance sports. More horses successfully finish an event in good health, and far fewer horses suffer life-threatening problems. More than ever before, horses are logging thousands of miles into their competitive records, able to go the distance again and again.

Whenever you present your horse to the veterinary staff, you may wonder exactly what kind of information a veterinarian can gather in an exam of only a few moments. Just what exactly are the veterinarians looking for to determine the stability of your horse's metabolic health?

Heart Rate Recovery

Your horse's performance hinges on the ability of his heart to pump blood effectively. A key parameter we use to determine how well your horse is accommodating the stress of exercise is by evaluation of *heart rate recovery*. Working muscles have a tremendous demand for blood and oxygen, and a need to get rid of heat and metabolic waste products through the bloodstream. During exercise, the heart beats more quickly to circulate blood to the demanding muscles. Once your horse stops moving, the heart rate should drop quickly, returning closer to his resting rate. Metabolic stability is estimated by the rapidity with which the heart rate drops to an expected recovery.

Everything that makes an endurance athlete able to perform protracted work hour after hour is dependent on a horse's ability to do *aerobic* work. As you have learned in previous chapters, aerobic exercise means that muscle tissue is able to convert fuels to energy for locomotion **in the presence of oxygen**. The amount of oxygen your horse can take into his body and deliver to the tissues is directly proportional to the speed he is traveling. In the case of a trail horse, the intensity of his work effort is not only determined by his speed, but it also depends on the difficulty of the terrain. Deep footing (mud, snow, sand) or hill climbing accelerate a horse's heart rate even at slower speeds to compensate for tougher going. The intensity of muscular work necessary to overcome deep footing or to climb a hill is comparable to a horse galloping on a flat, firm surface. As speed or work intensity increases, your horse's heart rate will correspondingly increase. Simply said, heart rate is directly proportional to oxygen consumption.

The longer an endurance athlete can work in the aerobic range, the less toxic by-products (like *lactic acid*) will be generated by muscle metabolism and the less internal heat will be retained in the muscles. In short, the longer you can maintain your horse in aerobic work, the longer you will delay the onset of fatigue.

At most endurance competitions, we expect a horse's heart rate to rapidly recover to less than 64 bpm, indicating adequate blood circulation and oxygenation of the tissues. A fit horse that is ridden appropriately for the terrain and climatic conditions usually recovers to 64 bpm within 2-10 minutes of arriving at a vet check. In very hot and humid climates, veterinary controls may require that a horse must recover to 56 or 60 bpm **and** have a rectal temperature of less than 103°F (40°C).

Competitive trail events measure heart rate recovery a little differently. A heart rate is taken after a 10 minute hold. A rate greater than 44 or 48 bpm receives point penalties depending on the competitive trail organization. A maximum pulse criterion is still set by the ride veterinarian, generally at 60-64 bpm. If the horse's heart rate exceeds this value, he is held for 10 additional minutes and extra penalties assessed on the rider card. The horse is permitted to continue in competition only if he recovers after that additional 10 minute rest period.

Under current rules for both endurance and competitive trail competitions, any horse that has not met pulse criteria within a specified time after arrival at a vet check is not permitted to continue on the trail. In endurance, that time is usually 30 minutes; in competitive trail, a horse must recover within 20 minutes.

A horse with a persistently elevated heart rate is exhibiting warning signs of significant problems:

- fatigue
- dehydration and electrolyte imbalances
- an inability to rid the body of excess heat generated by working muscles
- an indication that the horse has been ridden too hard for the environmental conditions or for that horse's level of fitness.

It would be foolish to send a nonrecovering horse down the trail since a metabolic crisis would surely develop further on. Even a decade ago, horses were considered recovered if the heart rate fell to 72 bpm or less. With that criterion, we found ourselves treating *exhaustion syndrome* in considerably more horses than we do today.

Cardiac Recovery Index

At endurance events, the continued health of your horse's circulatory system is monitored in another way with the *cardiac recovery index (CRI)*. The cardiac recovery index provides us with an excellent tool to estimate a horse's ability to recover in the face of prolonged exertions. A cardiac recovery index is performed at all vet checks at endurance rides; it is a tool you can also use during training to assess your horse's metabolic status. (See Chapter 6 for training uses.)

The procedure is simple. When you present to the veterinary staff, a resting heart rate is taken. Then the horse is trotted 125 feet out and 125 feet back. At exactly one minute from the time the horse **started** the 250 foot trot out, the heart rate is taken again. (Most horses will finish the trot out within 25-30 seconds, allowing the horse to stand quietly for the remainder of the minute.) If your horse is showing adequate metabolic compensation for the miles already traveled, he will recover to the same resting heart rate taken before the 250 foot trot out or 4 bpm less.

Historically, it has been acceptable for the heart rate to be 4 bpm more than the starting rate, **provided there are no other indications of fatigue**. With more data derived from use of the cardiac recovery index over the years, it would appear that our goal would be a return to the same heart rate as resting, and ideally to a rate of 4 bpm below resting. If your horse's heart rate elevates to 8 bpm or higher than the starting rate, the examining veterinarian will be looking diligently for a reason for the jump in heart rate. Often an elevated cardiac recovery index is an early indication of fatigue or musculoskeletal pain from muscle cramping or lameness.

A horse with a heart rate that has jumped more than 10% (4 – 20 bpm) at the one minute count will be re-presented in 10 minutes to see if there has been some improvement. A poor cardiac recovery index is only one parameter that is used to eliminate a horse from competition; the entire clinical picture is used to corroborate the ability of a horse to continue down the trail. As a monitoring tool while you condition, you can use the cardiac recovery index to determine if your horse is ready for the next phase of training intensity.

It is true that many horses with impending problems do pass through the cardiac recovery index check with no elevation in heart rate. Some horses just refuse to read the book! Likewise, some horses exhibit a small increase in the cardiac recovery index, yet because everything else falls within safe parameters, the horse is let back out on the trail to successfully finish the ride. The veterinarians will be looking for that horse to show a progressive recovery throughout the rest of the ride. There are no hard and fast rules, but many times the cardiac recovery index is the single indicator of a problem long before a problem becomes evident. As a tool to enable the veterinarians to monitor your horse's metabolic stability, it has proven to be invaluable.

Respiratory Rate

In the early years of veterinary control at endurance rides, the respiratory rate was used to determine if a horse had met recovery (pulse **and** respiration) criteria. As the years went by, experience has shown us that within reason, respiratory rate no longer holds as great a significance for allowing a horse to continue down the trail. Different climatic situations will induce a horse to breathe rapidly, particularly hot and humid weather. The respiratory tract can contribute as much as 33% of a horse's ability to cool the body. This is significant in very hot and very humid conditions, and it is not uncommon to see a horse panting once forward movement stops. Heavily muscled breeds have greater difficulty in ridding their bodies of internal heat, and so tend to pant.

What is of greater importance is the character of the respirations. Shallow and rapid respirations define the panting horse. The animal is attempting to dispel internal body heat by rushing hot blood across the lungs to be expired as hot air, while breathing in cooler air as rapidly as possible. If rectal temperature remains below 103°F (40°C), there is usually minimal risk in allowing a panting horse to begin its hold time, provided *heart rate recovery* and other vital signs are fine. With rest and cooling strategies applied during the hold time at a vet check, the panting should stop within a few minutes. (For more details, refer to Chapter 8.)

On the other hand, a horse that is gasping with deep and frequent breaths is suffering from an oxygen debt. In an attempt to fill its lungs with air and oxygen, an oxygen-deprived horse takes very obvious gulping breaths. The horse's body posture is usually somewhat "deflated" as he stretches his neck to maximize air flow into his lungs (Photo 79).

In competitive trail competitions, respiratory rate is counted after a 10 minute rest period. If your horse has a higher respiratory rate than specified, penalty points will be deducted from your rider card.

Hydration Factors

Over the miles, your horse potentially loses more body fluid than he can replace, especially if he is working in a hot and humid environment. Oxygen and water — these are two essential elements that fuel progress of your horse along the trail. With demanding muscular work, your horse sweats. In the sweat he loses gallons of precious body water and electrolytes.

Hydration of the tissues is evaluated in many ways (Photo 80). Heart rate recovery and the cardiac recovery index give us a glimpse at efficiency of the heart and circulation. A horse that is only minimally dehydrated has plenty of blood volume to permit adequate blood flow (with oxygen and nutrients) to the muscles, the skin, and the intestinal tract. A normally hydrated and fit horse can perform a given work effort at a heart rate of 140 bpm, but with moderate dehydration, the heart rate elevates to 160 bpm. With severe dehydration, the heart rate climbs to 190 bpm.

Evaluation of the mucous membranes, *capillary refill time*, and skin elasticity provide additional information about tissue hydration and circulatory health. The mucous membranes of the gums give you a wealth of data about how quickly blood is able to perfuse the tissues. Although you can also examine mucous membranes lining the eye or the vulva of a mare, you gain the quickest and safest information by examining your horse's gums. Presence of saliva on the gums often indicates sufficient body water. Pressing a fingertip to the gums pushes out the blood from that spot, and you can easily note how quickly blood returns to the blanched area. This is called the capillary refill time (Photo 81). Normal circulation returns a pink color to the gums within two seconds because of adequate blood pressure and circulating blood volume. The pink of normal gum color resembles that seen under your fingernails. A color that appears an injected, bright red or has a bluish cast around the gum margins indicates trouble. Occasionally, your horse might show a slight yellowish tinge to the gums which could be normal. This is more commonly seen if you feed legume hay or own an Appaloosa, for example.

Pale membranes, a delayed return of pink to the blanched gum (more than three seconds), or dry, tacky gums indicate that the horse's circulatory system is

Photo 79 A horse exhibiting deflated body posture, indicating fatigue.

Photo 80 A "tucked-up" abdomen often indicates that a horse is suffering from dehydration.

Photo 81 To test capillary refill time, press a fingertip to the gum, pushing out the blood from that spot; you can easily note how quickly blood returns to the blanched area.

not working at its best. In the distance horse metabolic problems generally arise due to the cumulative effects of dehydration.

Jugular refill time also reflects blood volume and the efficiency of the heart at pumping blood. Normally your horse's jugular vein distends with blood within two to three seconds of light finger pressure on the vein near the base of the neck (Photo 82).

Pinching the skin on the shoulder gives a rough estimation of the amount of water present in the tissues, rather than directly testing for adequacy of a horse's circulating blood volume. A high water content in the skin cells imparts elasticity to the skin. As body fluid is lost in sweat, cells slowly dehydrate. As skin cells lose water, they wrinkle very easily when pinched between your fingers. Instead of instantly rebounding to a flat position, the skin of a dehydrated horse remains "tented" (Photos 83a & b).

In some horses, skin remains tented for reasons other than dehydration. If you have done your homework, your very fit horse has less fat in the subcutaneous tissues, making the skin less elastic. An older horse often has thinner and less elastic skin. Water or sweat-soaked skin also remains tented for longer than usual, particularly if the skin is cool to the touch.

To gain the most reliable information from the *skin pinch test*, squeeze the skin over the point of the shoulder or on the upper eyelid, rather than pinching the skin on the neck. We have found time and again that there are limitations to relying on the skin pinch test to tell you if your horse is moderately dehydrated. For one thing, a horse must be considerably dehydrated (more than 5%) before the skin loses sufficient elasticity to remain tented. The response of the skin pinch test in a horse that is 2-3% dehydrated often gives you no clue as to true dehydration, but even this seemingly low level of fluid loss adversely affects the performance of a long-distance horse.

A thousand pound horse that is 5% dehydrated has lost six gallons (25 liters) of fluid, and probably will show sluggish skin elasticity. If a moderately dehydrated horse continues to work and sweat, continued fluid losses could seriously threaten the horse's metabolic health. Dehydration approaching 10-12% is life threatening (Photo 84).

Sweat

A hard-working horse sweats, and his continued ability to sweat depends on his circulating blood volume. More often than not, sweat and its residue are washed away by you or the pit crew during attempts to assist his cooling by sponging the skin. However, you should carefully note the quantity and char-

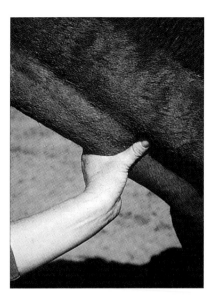

Photo 82 To test jugular refill time, lightly press a finger on the jugular vein near the base of the neck. Normally, the vein should distend with blood within two to three seconds after being depressed.

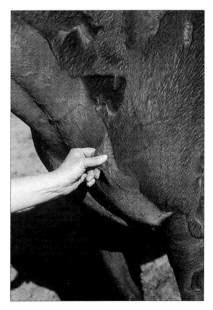

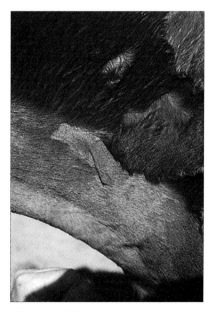

Photo 83a Pinching the skin on the shoulder gives a rough estimation of the amount of "water" present in the tissues. If the horse is well hydrated the skin possesses an elastic quality and quickly rebounds to a flat position.

Photo 83b When a horse has sweated away body fluid, the skin wrinkles easily and when pinched between your fingers remains "tented" rather than returning to a flat position.

acter (watery vs. foamy) of sweat before you sponge it away. Report your find-
ings to the veterinarian. (For more on the significance of sweat losses, refer to
the section on Heat and Humidity Conditioning in Chapter 7.)

Intestinal Sounds and Appetite

Your horse's intestinal health is critical to his well-being. Normally, waves of
intestinal movement (peristalsis) are accompanied by noises heard through a
stethoscope placed over the flanks (Photo 85). These sounds indicate that intestinal contents are being mixed and moved along the intestinal tract in a
timely fashion. The noises sound much like those your stomach makes when
you are hungry. It is not just the presence of sounds that is important, but the
character and frequency of the rumbles.

The muscles of an exercising horse place a great demand on the circulatory system, causing a diversion of blood flow away from the intestines. This
causes a slight diminishment of intestinal activity, yet sounds should still be
audible with a stethoscope on all quadrants of the flanks. Problems develop
when there is an absence of intestinal noise and activity. A stagnant intestinal
tract promotes fermentation of feed, rather than normal digestion. This encourages gas and fluids to accumulate in the bowel, leading to colic, intestinal
displacement or twists, or laminitis. Each of these conditions is life-threatening to the horse.

Called an *ileus*, an absence of intestinal activity is often a direct result of
dehydration and/or electrolyte imbalances. With diminished intestinal activity, a horse is less able to absorb water, electrolytes, or energy from the bowel.
Dehydration then escalates, endangering the metabolic health of the horse.

As is true of most things in life, often the situation is not black and white,
or easy to read. No matter how bright a horse looks, or how greedy its appetite,
depressed bowel sounds are a cause for caution and concern. A horse that does
not improve in its intestinal activity within 30 minutes of arrival at a vet check
is likely to be pulled from competition. A horse that does not want to eat,
whether or not intestinal sounds are adequate, may also be pulled from competition.

From the minute you arrive at a competition and throughout the event,
pay close attention to the quantity and consistency of your horse's bowel
movements. If he isn't making the normal number or size of "road apple" piles,
pay attention. If fecal balls persistently appear dry and firm, his body is telling
you he is becoming increasingly dehydrated. A nervous horse may have
intermittent diarrhea. You should monitor such a horse very carefully.

Photo 84 A horse receiving intravenous fluid treatment for severe dehydration.

Photo 85 Regular intestinal movement is vital. "Gut sounds" should be monitored with a stethoscope placed over the flanks.

Anal Tone

When the anus is touched with a fingertip, anal sphincter tone should be perky. This reflex is part of the *autonomic nervous system* that also controls the sweat glands, the heart, and intestinal smooth muscle. Delayed anal response to a finger touch, or an anus that stands gaping, warns of depression of the autonomic nervous system (Photo 86). If this vital sign is ignored, there is a potential for failure of other organ systems critical to metabolic safety of your horse.

Muscle Tone

The tone of the muscles is another useful hydration parameter reflective of blood and oxygen flow to all tissues, including the muscles. Your horse's muscles should feel flexible and pliable, much like a pencil eraser. Your horse should not resent touch or gentle kneading of the muscles. Fatigue causes muscles to tremble or twitch, as do fluid and electrolyte imbalances. Muscles can begin to cramp if they are cooled down suddenly by a cold wind or if you inappropriately apply water to large muscle groups.

It is not uncommon for large hindquarter muscles to cramp during an endurance event for a variety of different reasons, causing a horse to trot out too lame to continue on the trail. *Tying-up syndrome* is potentially a life-threatening condition as muscle proteins (*myoglobin*) are released from spasming muscle tissue. Myoglobin makes its way to the kidneys where it can eventually plug up the filtration channels within the kidneys, leading to kidney failure and death. Caught in its early stages, muscle cramping is easily resolved with anti-inflammatory medications, warm packs, and massage (Photo 87). The more quickly the cramping subsides, the less discomfort or danger there is for your horse.

Urination

At long-distance events, it is with great interest that we watch our horses urinate. We gain a little comfort from the fact that a horse is passing urine (Photo 88) because it implies that the horse must be well enough hydrated that his body is not trying to hang on to every drop of fluid. However, if he only delivers a small quantity of urine, or the urine appears very concentrated (dark yellow and of small volume), you are seeing a warning signal of increasing levels of dehydration. Also, the color of the urine is important for evaluating the status of the muscles. Normal horse urine is yellowish and slightly cloudy due to calcium carbonate crystals dissolved in the urine. A horse experiencing some muscle damage or *myositis* passes urine with a reddish cast. The reddish tinge

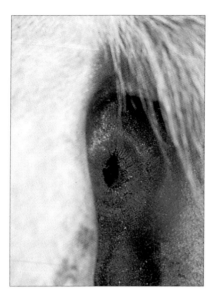

Photo 86 Flaccid anal sphincter tone like this is a serious warning sign that a horse's metabolic safety is at risk.

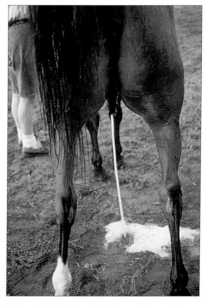

Photo 87 It is common for the large hindquarter muscles to cramp during a long distance event. Hot water bottles placed against specific cramping muscles can be an immense help.

Photo 88 Urination is a welcomed occurrence with a distance horse. It implies that the horse is well enough hydrated and his body is not hanging on to every drop of body fluid.

Photo 89 This horse looks to be in good form with a bright, alert eye and erect ears. This is a good indication that it is handling the exercise stress well.

Photo 90 In contrast to the horse in the previous photograph, this horse appears droopy, with a dull, half-closed eye. The wrinkled lips and anxious facial expression signal discomfort. It is likely this horse is suffering from dehydration leading to exhaustion.

indicates that myoglobin is being filtered through the urinary tract. Should you see any sign of a very concentrated urine or of a reddish color in your horse's urine, be sure to advise the veterinary staff at once. Dark red urine is a warning sign that a horse needs supplemental treatment with fluids and electrolytes and should be pulled from competition.

Physical Appearance

Your horse's body stance and posture gives you loads of information about how he is handling the exercise stress. He should be alert, with a bright eye, and preferably eating with enthusiasm (Photo 89).

A dehydrated horse appears droopy, with a dull eye, sunken eyeballs, and eyelids at half-mast (Photo 90). As dehydration and exhaustion continue, a horse loses interest in its surroundings, and its appetite and thirst vanish. The veterinarian takes in all this information during the exam, but artificial excitement created as the horse is moved around may obscure a beginning problem. You know your horse better than anyone, so communicate any concerns with the veterinarian. An experienced campaigner may relax completely at a vet check, and stand quietly while rechanneling its energy for the continued work ahead. Sometimes it is hard to distinguish a laid-back individual from a depressed horse that is fatigued or hovers near metabolic failure.

Fatigue and its Problems

A horse can develop fatigue without suffering any long-lasting consequences. However, sometimes the system spirals out of control, and fatigue is only the tip of the iceberg. Other syndromes appear, some with life-threatening complications. The reason for close attendance to your horse's vital signs throughout an event is to prevent a tired horse from tipping over the edge into metabolic failure.

All our monitoring efforts are dedicated to preventing the following:
- *tying-up syndrome*
- *thumps*
- heat prostration
- *exhaustion syndrome*
- kidney failure
- *laminitis*

Tying-up Syndrome

Muscle cramping, myositis, or tying-up syndrome, causes your horse to move with a stiff, stilted gait, or to refuse to move at all (Photo 91). This syndrome usually occurs in a distance horse after he has been exercising for a period of time and is experiencing electrolyte disturbances and dehydration. Horses that are fed a high grain ration, a high protein ration, or an imbalanced calcium ration seem to be more prone to developing tying-up syndrome. Selenium deficiencies also contribute to tying-up syndrome.

Occasionally, a competitive horse develops cramping muscles within the first few minutes of exercise. This may be due to endocrine influences or defects in muscle metabolism that have nothing to do with exercise stress, but may have more to do with nutritional influences (too much grain) or anxiety. Or, your horse is suffering from dehydration effects from transport to the competition. You should return your horse immediately to the trailer or barn, don't move the horse around, and call for veterinary attention.

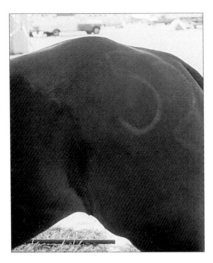

Photo 91 A horse with cramping gluteal muscles (on top of croup) experiencing tying-up syndrome.

If you are out on the trail and your horse starts to cramp, slow down immediately. Muscles often cramp due to heat buildup and inadequate blood flow in the tissues, as well as to electrolyte imbalances. Walking usually improves a horse that is just starting to cramp. He may be able to continue to exercise once circulation is restored to the muscles and heat is quickly dissipated. A horse that does not rapidly improve within 10-15 minutes may worsen with forced movement. If dehydration and electrolyte disturbances are extreme, then the horse may need veterinary treatment to gain improvement. The horse should be moved minimally until a veterinarian arrives.

Thumps

As electrolytes are depleted in the sweat, calcium, potassium, and magnesium losses alter nerve sensitivity. In the horse, nerves become hyper-irritable, particularly the phrenic nerve as it crosses the heart on its path to the diaphragm. Each time the heart beats, the diaphragm also contracts, hence the name *synchronous diaphragmatic flutter (SDF)*. This thumping is visualized or felt as a contraction of the abdominal muscles in synchrony with the heart beat. Place your hand on the horse's flanks to check for a flutter. Thumps are a warning flag of significant electrolyte derangements and dehydration that could lead to more serious problems if the horse continued to exercise.

Other signs to watch out for that can precede or be concurrent with an episode of thumps are a stiff gait, tense facial structures, a drooping third eyelid, twitching, or quivering muscles.

Exhausted Horse Syndrome

Although a veterinary staff takes great pains to prevent it, *exhausted horse syndrome (EHS)* does occur at competitive events. Exhausted horse syndrome is the end result of the combined effects of dehydration, electrolyte losses, energy depletion, and acid-base imbalances. Signs range from subtle to obvious:

- poor heart rate recovery
- erratic heart rate
- loss of impulsion/shortened stride
- lethargic
- dull eye/depressed posture
- increased skin tenting
- increased *jugular refill time*
- delayed *capillary refill time*
- diminished intestinal sounds
- lack of adequate urine production
- elevated rectal temperature
- loss of appetite
- loss of thirst (due to depletion of electrolytes)

As exhausted horse syndrome progresses, other critical metabolic systems deteriorate with the development of synchronous diaphragmatic flutter (thumps), tying-up syndrome, colic, or total collapse. The kidneys rely on continuous blood flow for maximal function. Dehydration reduces circulation within all the tissues, including the kidneys. Kidney failure can result in collapse and death, either immediately or within a week after a competition.

Typically, if an exhausted horse receives fluids and electrolytes by stomach tube and/or intravenously, the horse will perk up and begin to drink and eat on its own. The trick to preventing fatal consequences of exhausted horse syndrome is to recognize when the horse is nearing a crisis, to remove it immediately from competition, and to provide it with necessary veterinary treatment.

Musculoskeletal Injury

A tired horse is at risk of musculoskeletal injury. His coordination falters, with stumbling and unsteadiness as initial signs. Tired muscles lose their damping function so tendons assume excessive load. This potentially leads to serious tendon strain. Fatigued tendons and muscles allow abnormal stress to concentrate on bones and joints, with the possibility of cartilage damage or bone fracture.

Metabolic fatigue creates conditions for the development of a lameness. Conversely, musculoskeletal pain may cause a horse to fatigue more quickly.

Photo 92 This horse looks to be in great shape as it is presented to the veterinary staff.

Photo 93 In order to present your horse in the most favorable way, train him to be responsive to your commands and trot alongside you. This horse and rider are moving on a good straight line with proper lead rope length and position.

Gait Analysis and Mechanical Factors

Presenting the Horse

When you present your horse to the veterinary staff at a trot-out, it is your opportunity to show your horse to his best advantage (Photo 92). You want to give an impression that your horse is full of boundless energy and has unsurpassed movement. From a veterinarian's point of view, the trot-out provides an opportunity to assess your horse's movement in order to detect beginning soundness problems. This is part of a philosophy all of us pride ourselves on in long-distance sports: the horse's safety comes first.

For your horse to give the most favorable picture, train him at home to lead properly in hand, and to longe in circles. Your horse should focus his attention on you and be responsive to your commands.

Strike off confidently while asking your horse to trot alongside you (Photo 93). Many endurance horses are used to following directly behind a rider on a narrow trail. When your horse does that, all the veterinarian sees are your legs but hardly a speck of your horse that shadows directly behind you. In your straight line trot-out, think straight, don't weave! Give your horse a long enough length of lead so you don't restrict his head. If you hold the lead line too tightly near the halter, you restrict his head so he can't move as naturally as possible. The harder you tug, the harder your horse will tug back, with the end result of losing forward momentum. This leads to frustration and breathlessness as you are asked to trot out again. It also gives the impression that your horse is tired, just the opposite of what you'd like the veterinarians to think. Ideally, hold the lead about two feet from the halter snap. Your horse will have enough freedom to trot well, while you still retain control of him.

At certain times at a ride, namely the pre-ride veterinary check-in and at the finish exam, you will be asked to circle your horse. The pattern in which you lead your horse greatly influences his presentation. Here is a suggestion: Trot straight out. Stop. Make a full circle or two in one direction. Stop. Make a full circle or two in the other direction. Stop. Then trot straight back toward the veterinarian.

Always look straight ahead in the direction you are going, not at the ground or at your horse. Jog out confidently and your horse will follow. Pick your path with your eyes looking ahead! The biggest mistake people make is to shortcut the circle so that the runner jogs as enthusiastically as possible while the horse walks behind, neck outstretched to counter the tug on the lead line. Jog in a circle path that is big enough to force your horse to trot alongside you. This usually requires a circle of 15-20 meters. Think circle — not pear, not square, not triangle!

Longeing your horse is often preferable to jogging a horse in hand on a circle. Most horses move more freely on a longe line, showing good impulsion. By standing in the middle of the longe circle, you no longer interfere with the veterinarian's view of your horse as you would if you jogged next to the horse. The longe circle needs to be at least 15-20 meters in diameter. A circle that is too tight makes your horse look "off" as his shoulder falls in on the small circle. In addition, a circle that is too small does not encourage your horse to move in an even rhythm, which is an important element in evaluating soundness.

Quality of Movement

While you trot your horse out for the *cardiac recovery index* at the veterinary presentation, careful attention is paid to his gait. Your horse's *impulsion* (willingness to move forward), elasticity of movement, and the energy and length of stride with which he moves are all considered as part of his energy level. A fatigued horse depleted of fuel stores often loses *neuromuscular* coordination. Generalized muscle fatigue causes a horse to refuse to trot forward, even pulling back hard on the lead line. His outstretched head moves because it must, but his body isn't really following. Like a dead weight, his movements appear leaden. Fatigue also causes muscles to twitch involuntarily, often referred to by the veterinarians as *fasciculations*.

Soundness

The horse's soundness is carefully evaluated. Any horse with a lameness that is **consistently** visible on a straight line trot will be pulled from competition. Based on a scale devised by the American Association of Equine Practitioners, a lameness that is consistently observable at a trot under all circumstances is considered a Grade 3 lameness. Because of the rules governing endurance and competitive trail events, a Grade 3 horse will be disqualified from competition. The veterinarian may ask to see the horse trot in circles in both directions if there is only a hint of a problem on a straight line trot. Any horse that is consistently lame in a circle but not on a straight line is experiencing a Grade 2 lameness. Further limb evaluation will determine if it is prudent and safe for the horse to continue down the trail without risk of a more serious injury. Comments are made on the rider card about a subtle, inconsistent (Grade 1) lameness or a Grade 2 lameness. Then, at each subsequent veterinary presentation the lameness is compared in severity to the previous vet check. In the

Photo 94 An unusual body stance can often signify a lameness problem. This horse is "camped out" in front, indicating possible pain in the front feet.

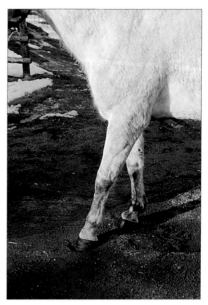

Photo 95 Pointing with a front limb, as this horse is doing, indicates severe pain in that foot or leg.

best interest of the horse, a lameness that is worsening dictates that the horse is unfit to continue (Photos 94 & 95).

Limb Palpation

After your horse has been seen in motion, if there is a question or concern about soundness, a veterinarian may feel and gently squeeze the flexor tendons and suspensory ligaments along the length of the cannon bone (Photo 96). These structures are most commonly at risk on a long-distance horse. Tendons, ligaments, and joints are checked for heat, pain, or swelling that denotes excessive strain or injury.

Tack and Equipment

Tack and equipment problems increase the potential for a horse to fatigue or develop a lameness, so these areas are also scrutinized carefully (Photo 97). Overreach wounds and interference wounds may be caused by faulty conformation, poor shoeing, or by fatigue. Some leg wounds may be caused by natural trail hazards like branches, cacti,

Photo 96 During a veterinary exam, the veterinarian will often choose to palpate the flexor tendons to check for heat or swelling.

Photo 97 A veterinarian will palpate a horse's back during an exam to check for any soreness created by improperly fitted tack or poor rider technique.

rocks, and so forth. Girth galls, saddle rubs, sore back and withers are created by improperly fitted tack, by poor rider technique, and also by horse and/or rider fatigue. If your horse pulls on your arms, and you pull back, sores may develop in the sides of the mouth or along the tongue. Bit injuries may cause a horse to hold its back and neck in abnormal positions, leading to muscle soreness and fatigue. During the exam, horseshoes are checked for their presence and condition, with the veterinarian noting if shoes or nails are twisted or bent.

Grading and Interpretation of Findings

Since we all went to school, we are most comfortable with the use of a scale of A to D. Pluses or minuses are often included to fine-tune the range of critique.

A = superior
B = satisfactory
C = acceptable (barely)
D = eliminated

A veterinarian is not looking for anything specific at the start of an exam; ideally, the veterinarian's mind is open and searching for any abnormality that appears during the course of the exam. A veterinarian uses a mental picture of a normal horse as a basis for making a comparison, and by which your horse is determined to be "fit to continue."

Normal describes a horse that is unstressed by exercise, terrain, or climatic conditions. A "normal" horse is operating within normal physiological parameters without hazard to its metabolic health or physical soundness. Your horse may exhibit parameters that fall slightly outside of the normal zone. That is the reason for B scores on your rider card — not perfect, but certainly satisfactory for continued performance. This is to be expected in any competitive long-distance event, particularly over 50 to 100 miles.

The data obtained during the veterinary exam paints an overall impression of how a horse is responding to its performance stress. At subsequent vet checks the same picture is recreated, with each horse compared to its **own** previous metabolic and physical state. In some cases, the evidence is overwhelming that a horse is failing to recover from exercise stress. In other instances, a horse just seems a little off in subtle ways. An experienced endurance veterinarian weighs the significance of persistent or progressive deterioration of various vital signs and decides if your horse should be allowed to progress down the trail.

As a rule of thumb, if a horse's metabolic status is questionable, the horse is pulled. If its soundness is questionable, then a veterinarian may permit the horse to proceed towards the next vet check, allowing the trail to sort out a borderline lameness. You, the rider, are certainly capable of pulling your horse from competition if there is any lameness present at all or any suspicion of metabolic instability. A veterinarian only has a few minutes to evaluate your horse while you have hours in the saddle to critique and consider your horse's performance. If you are unsure of how your horse is acting, slow your pace to separate yourselves from a buddy horse or another excited animal. Without artificial stimulation of your horse's adrenaline response, you will be better able to read those subtle signs. Discuss your intuitive feelings with the veterinarians at each vet check. Your insights are often invaluable. If in doubt, consider that there will always be another ride, and another day for glory.

Photo 98 A vet check station set up for the arrival of horses. Signs clearly mark the important spots a horse will pass through during the vet check.

Protocol at Veterinary Checks

At Endurance Rides

Most endurance competitions in North America and Europe use the concept of a "gate into a hold." You arrive at the vet check (like entering a "gate") (Photo 98). You proceed to the P&R area where your horse's heart rate will be taken when you feel it meets criteria. At the moment the P&R person records the time at which criteria are met, your "hold" time begins. A horse's hold time does not start until meeting a predetermined heart rate criterion, usually 60-64 *bpm*. All horses should meet heart rate (pulse) criteria within 30 minutes of arrival at the vet check. If not, then the horse is disqualified and treated if necessary. Most horses that are capable of continuing the event meet *recovery parameters* within 5-15 minutes of arrival at the vet check. A heart rate that remains elevated for longer than 30 minutes indicates fatigue, electrolyte and fluid derangements, or pain (tying-up syndrome, colic, or musculoskeletal injury).

Once the heart rate criteria are met, the horse must remain at the vet check for a specified time period. This is the "hold" time. Every horse in the endurance competition remains at the vet check for the same length of hold time. During the hold period the horse must pass through the veterinary exam within 30 minutes of reaching the pulse criteria.

Hold times vary between 15 and 60 minutes. These times are predetermined by ride management, taking into account the distance the horses have traveled along the course, the logistics and facilities at each vet check station, and the weather conditions. The hold periods allow your horse time to eat and drink while giving the rider and the pit crew an opportunity to cool the horse down and straighten out tack and equipment problems. Over a 100 mile course, horses are usually allotted a total of three hours of hold time, split between five to seven vet checks.

The "gate into a hold" process provides a distinct advantage to a more metabolically fit horse. He recovers more quickly and is then able to begin the timed rest period sooner than a less fit horse. A fit horse then leaves the vet check earlier than those horses not dealing as well with exercise stress. This process separates out horses that may try to stay apace with the leaders due to excitement and the boost of adrenalin but not due to inherent fitness. Horses are released from vet checks at a time appropriate to their individual fitness level. Use of this method prevents "hyper" horses from being run into the ground.

A "gate into a hold" also provides veterinarians enough time to assess horses without a long line developing from congestion at the vet check. This works to your advantage so you and your horse are not delayed from leaving at your scheduled departure time. The hope is that the bulk of the horses are separated at reasonable intervals based on their recovery times.

Endurance Check Procedure

Let's look at an example of a fit horse as it goes through the vet check procedure. The horse arrives at 8:57am (Figure 17). He is cooled down and presents to the P&R personnel at 9am and passes criteria. His hold time is noted on the rider card (Figure 18) and starts at 9am. From the P&R station, the horse proceeds directly to the veterinarians where he will receive a metabolic and soundness exam.

Once he passes the veterinary exam, the horse leaves the vetting area to be fed, watered, and cooled more if necessary. Any concerns a veterinarian may have will be brought to your attention. If the horse should be asked to return for re-evaluation of a metabolic or lameness concern, you must do so within the allowed hold time. At this fictitious check, the hold is 30 minutes, so you can return to the trail at 9:30 A.M. once your horse has received the go-ahead from the veterinarian.

At Competitive Trail Rides

In competitive trail events, all horses come into the P&R check, and stand

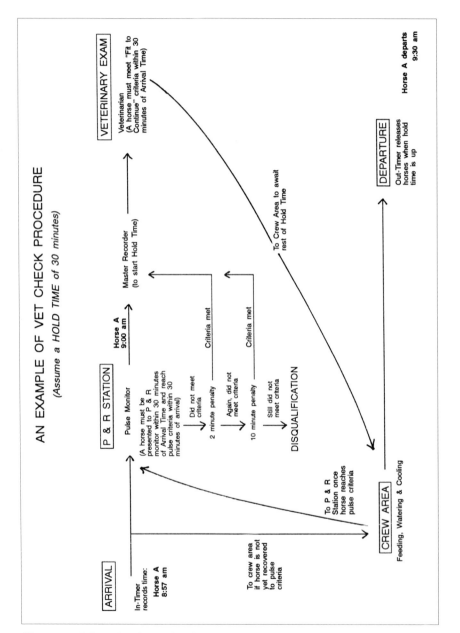

Figure 17 A chart showing a plausible progression through an endurance vet check with a hold time of thirty minutes.

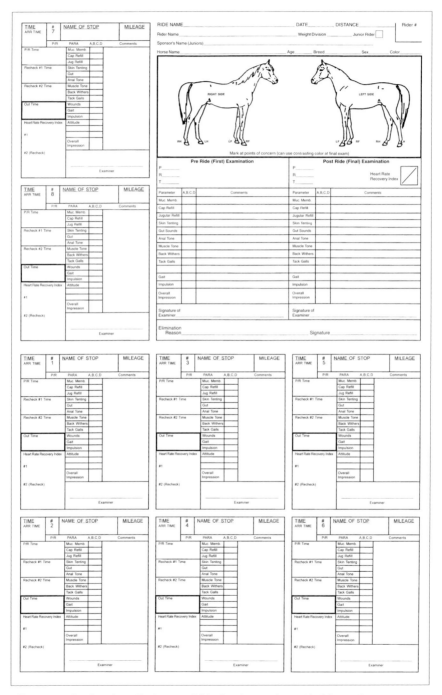

Figure 18 An American Endurance Ride Conference (AERC) rider card.

quietly in a line or in a group. Every horse has a pulse and respiration count taken at exactly 10 minutes of arrival at the stop. If your horse meets pulse criteria (usually set at 60 or 64 bpm) and respiration criteria (determined by the veterinary judge for that day), your horse is allowed to proceed along the trail. Penalty points are assessed for values greater than 48 bpm heart rate and 28 bpm respiratory rate for the North American Trail Ride Conference (NATRC), or 44 bpm heart rate and 24 respiratory rate for the Eastern Competitive Trail Ride Association (ECTRA) (Figures 19 & 20).

Some check points are stationed immediately after a forced trot, or are preceded by a steep climb. These extra stresses help separate the fitter horses from others. To gain the best P&R scores, let your horse relax. You'll have plenty of time later to rearrange equipment. So as not to disturb other competitors during your timed hold, don't walk your horse around or offer him food or water. Feed and water can be offered once you have been cleared to continue by a P&R person or at a rest stop along the trail.

Best Condition Judging

In endurance events, one of the most valued awards is given to the horse that is considered to be in the best condition at the end of the ride (Figure 22). This is the horse any of us would like to hop on and take for another lap around the course. Great pride is felt when you receive this accolade. It means that you not only have prepared your horse well for the competition, but you have ridden him appropriately for the conditions.

A horse may be presented to the veterinary staff for completion within 10-15 minutes of crossing the finish line. However, the first ten horses to finish are examined at one hour after crossing the finish line if the rider opts to show for Best Condition. The veterinary score takes into consideration all of the above described vital signs and soundness factors. Because the horse's physical condition is so important to the judging, the veterinary score carries the greatest number of points. A horse that is Grade 3 lame at the time of Best Condition judging is not eligible for Best Condition as it is not *"fit to continue."* (It is possible that one hour after crossing the finish line, soundness will have deteriorated.)

Of a possible 800 points in the Best Condition scoring, the veterinary score can award a maximum of 500 points to a superior horse. Weight and speed are also considered as part of Best Condition scoring because a heavier rider has placed a greater burden on the horse, and a faster pace also taxes a

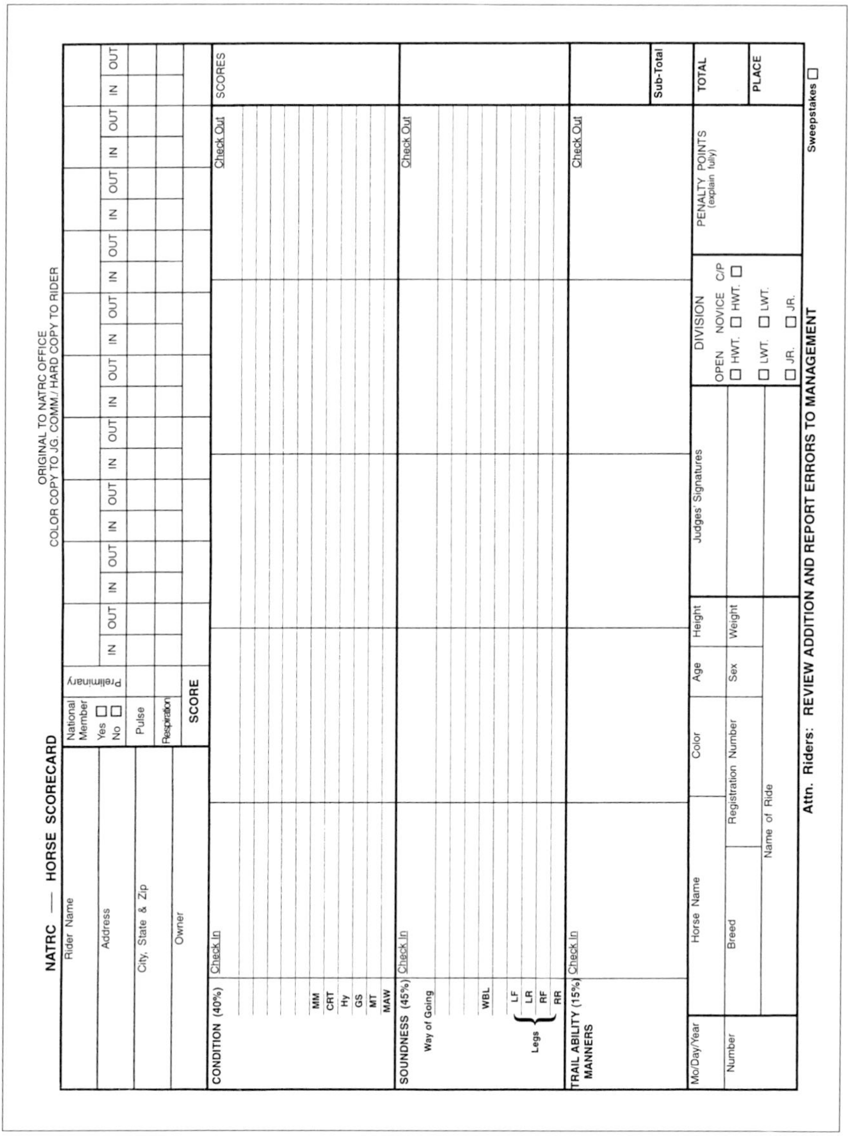
NATRC — HORSE SCORECARD
ORIGINAL TO NATRC OFFICE
COLOR COPY TO JG. COMM./ HARD COPY TO RIDER
Rider Name
National Member Yes ☐ No ☐
Preliminary
IN OUT IN OUT IN OUT IN OUT IN OUT IN OUT IN OUT IN OUT IN OUT IN OUT
Address
City, State & Zip
Pulse
Owner
Respiration
SCORE
CONDITION (40%) Check In Check Out
MM CRT Hy GS MT MAW
SCORES
SOUNDNESS (45%) Check In Check Out
Way of Going
WBL
Legs LF LR RF RR
TRAIL ABILITY (15%) MANNERS Check In Check Out
Sub-Total
Mo/Day/Year
Horse Name
Color
Age
Height
Judges' Signatures
DIVISION
OPEN NOVICE C/P
☐ HWT. ☐ HWT. ☐
☐ LWT. ☐ LWT.
☐ JR. ☐ JR.
PENALTY POINTS (explain fully)
TOTAL
PLACE
Number
Breed
Registration Number
Sex
Weight
Name of Ride
Attn. Riders: REVIEW ADDITION AND REPORT ERRORS TO MANAGEMENT
Sweepstakes ☐

Figure 19 A North American Trail Ride Conference (NATRC) horse judging card.

1995 _____ EASTERN COMPETITIVE TRAIL RIDE ASSOCIATION

| HORSE ELIMINATED: | OVERALL ON RIDE | PLACING IN | DIVISION | RIDER'S # |
| Comments: | (Exclude Juniors) | DIVISION | | |

Judge's Initials _____

NAME OF RIDE _____ MILES _____ TOWN _____ STATE _____ DATE ___/___/____

RIDER _____ ADDRESS _____

OWNER _____ ADDRESS _____

HORSE _____ AGE ___ SEX ___ COLOR ___ BREED ___ REG # ___

INITIAL EXAM	FINAL EXAM	MAX PTS OFF
TACK AREA - Back, Girth, Chest and Head - Bumps, Rubs, Soreness etc.		10
RIGHT LEFT		
LEGS - Self-inflicted trauma: (Interference, swelling, windpuffs, scratches, filling etc.)		15
RIGHT LEFT		

LAMENESS	(Circle One)	(Circle One)	25
SOUND	0	0	
1 DIFFICULT TO OBSERVE	1 2 3 4	1 2 3 4	
2 CONSISTENT IN SOME CIRCUMSTANCES	5 6 7 8 9 10 11	5 6 7 8 9 10 11	
3 CONSISTENTLY OBSERVABLE	ELIMINATE	LOW 25 (above Low) ELIMINATE	
4 GRADE 4	ELIMINATE	ELIMINATE (Numbers 12 thru 24 _____	
5 GRADE 5	ELIMINATE	ELIMINATE may not be used)	

FATIGUE - Mechanical (Circle One in Each Category and/or COMMENT)		(Circle One in Each)	20
	EXT +AVG AVG -AVE	NC SL MOD SEV Deterioration	
LGTH OF STD	A B C D	0 1 2 3	
(Impulsion)			
HGTH OF STD	A B C D	0 1 2 3	
(Animation)			
OVERALL BODY CARRIAGE	A B C D	0 1 2 3	
WILLINGNESS	A B C D	0 1 2 3	
TOE DRAGGING	NONE, SL, MOD, EXT	0 1 2 3	
MUSCLE SORENESS (Other Than Back)	NONE, SL, MOD, EXT	0 1 2 3	
COORDINATION	COORD, SL UNC, MOD UNC, EXT UNC	0 1 2 3	
OPTIONAL			
MUSCLE TONE	A B C D	0 .5 1 2	

FATIGUE - Metabolic	(Circle One in Each Category)	(Circle One in Each)	10
	SECONDS > 0 1 2 3 4 5 6	0 1 2 3 4 5 6	
SKIN PINCH	0 .5 1 1.5 2 2.5 3	0 .5 1 1.5 2 2.5 3	
CAPILLARY REFILL TIME	0 .5 1 1.5 2 2.5 3	0 .5 1 1.5 2 2.5 3	
GUM COLOR	YELLOW PINK-PINK 0, PALE-RED 1, WHITE-GRAY 2	0 1 2	
GUM MOISTURE	WET 0, STICKY 1, DRY 2	0 1 2	
*GUT SOUND- NORMAL 0, SL DIM/HYPER .5, MOD DIM/HYPER 1, ABSENT 2		0 .5 1 2	
**ANAL TONE- TIGHT 0, SL LOOSE .5, MOD LOOSE 1, FLACCID 2		0 .5 1 2	

20 MINUTE HOLD PASS/FAIL	1st DAY 10 MIN, 20 MIN. TEMP	2nd DAY 10 MIN, 20 MIN, TEMP,	5
Pulse Parameter: 60-Min./64-Max	PULSE _____ _____ MANDATORY	PULSE _____ _____ MANDATORY	
Respirations: None, allowed to	RESP _____ _____ OVER 103	RESP _____ _____ OVER 103	
fall where they may.	1 Hold - 5 Points ELIMINATE	2 Holds - 2.5 Points ELIMINATE	

INITIAL	FINAL 1st DAY	FINAL 2nd DAY	FINAL 3rd.DAY	10
PULSE 44 TEMP _____ (Optional)	PULSE _____	PULSE _____	PULSE : _____	5
RESP 24	RESP _____	RESP _____	RESP _____	

BEHAVIOR Rearers, Biters, Strikers and Kickers ONLY (Judged through out the Ride.)	
PENALTY	CONDITION SCORE 100 - ___=___
May Eliminate in extreme cases	BEHAVIOR PENALTY(max 5) - ___

ON TRAIL COMMENTS: 1st DAY	2nd DAY	3rd DAY	THUMPS PNLTY(0 or 5)- ___
			TIME PENALTY - ___
			FINAL SCORE ___
FINAL:	FINAL:		Judge's Signature

* = Optional 1-Day ** = Optional 1-Day & 2-Day

Figure 20 An Eastern Competitive Trail Riders Association (ECTRA) horse judging card.

VETERINARY RECORD CARD

Competitor Number: _____

RIDE NAME.. On.................................19..........

RIDER.. CLASS...

HORSE... AGE.............. HEIGHT.............. COLOUR............ SEX.......

Inspection	Heart Rate 1	Heart Rate 2	Skin Dehydration Score (Secs)	Other Lesions/ Remarks	Pass/ Fail	Reason For Fail	Vet's initial
1st Inspection							
Average Speed							
2nd Inspection (Halfway Halt)							
3rd Inspection (if applicable)							
Final Inspection 30 mins after finishing							

IF RETIRED, STATE REASON.. FIT TO TRAVEL? YES/NO

DETAIN FOR ....HOURS.   Signature of Official Veterinary Surgeon...

Distribution: White copy - ERG Office   Yellow copy - Competitor

Figure 21 A British Endurance Riding Association (BERA) veterinary record card.

AMERICAN ENDURANCE RIDE CONFERENCE
ADMINISTRATIVE OFFICE:
701 HIGH STREET, SUITE 203 • AUBURN, CA 95603
(916) 823-2260

RIDER NO.

BEST CONDITION EVALUATION

RIDE NAME _____ REGION _____ DISTANCE _____ RIDE DATE _____

RIDER'S NAME _____ **RIDER'S WT _____ FINISH PLACE _____

RIDER'S FINISH TIME _____ (hrs) _____ (min) HORSE'S NAME _____

***The Rider's finishing weight is determined at the conclusion of
the ride with tack and the same clothes worn during the ride.*

A. VETERINARY SCORE SHEET	MAXIMUM SCORE 500 POINTS

STANDING EVALUATION
Recovery:
*Base upon ability to demonstrate recovery; e.g.: the Cardiac Recovery index; Recommend use the CRI
taken 10 or 15 minutes post-finish time. Base the respiratory aspects on quality of respiration as determined
visually and by auscultation*   SCORE 1-10 _____

Hydration Factors:
*Use all the metabolic parameters that indicate the state of hydration, i.e.: Skin Tenting, Mucous Membranes,
Capillary Refill Time, Jugular Refill Time and Gut Sounds*   SCORE 1-10 _____

Lesions Producing Pain and Discomfort:
*Major concerns are Back Pain and pain/swelling in Joints, Tendons, and Ligaments that may be indicative
of potentially serious pathology. Also consider Girth, Saddle, and other Tack-Induced Lesions and all
Wounds. Note: do all but cursory palpation after the movement phase*   SCORE 1-10 _____

MOVEMENT EVALUATION
Soundness:
*Note: Not eligible for consideration for B.C. if there is a pathologial gait aberration greater than grade II.
Consider: Regularity of gait and movement*   SCORE 1-10 _____

Quality of Movement:
*Consider: Attitude, Coordination and Impulsion (deterioration exhibited as a reluctance or refusal to
trot, stumbling, leg weariness, muscle fatigue and stiffness)*   SCORE 1-10 _____

SUBTOTAL _____

TOTAL VETERINARY SCORE = SUBTOTAL X 10

Parts B and C to be completed by Ride Management ONLY (To be done after veterinary completion of Part A)

B. TIME FACTOR	MAXIMUM 200 POINTS (Awarded to Fastest Rider)

Riding Time of THIS rider _____ *(Value one point per minute)*

Riding Time of Winner _____ MAXIMUM _____ 200

Difference: _____ LESS DIFFERENCE (-)

(calculate time in minutes - exclude hold times) TOTAL TIME SCORE

C. WEIGHT FACTOR	MAXIMUM 100 POINTS (Awarded to the Heaviest Rider)

Weight of Heaviest Rider _____ *(Value one/half point per pound)*

Weight of THIS Rider _____ MAXIMUM _____ 100

Difference ÷ 2 _____ LESS DIFFERENCE ÷ 2 (-)

TOTAL WEIGHT SCORE

TOTAL SCORE = A + B + C =

RIDE MANAGER _____ HEAD VETERINARIAN _____

*This score sheet must accompany AERC Ride Results for Winner to be eligible for Regional and National Awards.
Mail original copy to AERC with Ride Results, second copy to Ride Manager, Third copy to rider.*

AERC B.C. FORM: 11/96

Figure 22 A Best Condition judging form for endurance rides.

horse accordingly. (The time score contributes up to 200 points, while the weight score provides a maximum of 100 points. The fastest time of the top 10 finishers is the value against which the other 9 horses are measured. This is determined in minutes, and each rider's time is deducted from the fastest speed. This calculation is subtracted from a possible 200 points. A similar method is used with weights of the top 10 riders, with the heaviest rider receiving more points. However the difference in weight of the heaviest rider and each other rider is divided by 2, then subtracted from 100 possible points.) Upon adding together the veterinary score, the time score, and the weight score, the horse and rider with the most points wins the coveted Best Condition award.

10 Trailering the Distance Horse

Transport Stress

A long-distance horse that actively competes spends a great deal of time in a horse trailer. Most of us and many of our horses accept trailering as part of a standard routine. However, without sensible planning on your part, long distance transport can impose some adverse effects on your horse.

We are all familiar with the effects of daily stress on our own bodies — that exhausted feeling of malaise, an upset stomach, suppressed appetite, and a propensity to contract colds and flus. Horses experience similar physiologic changes when stressed. But, you can minimize the stresses created by trailering. Just knowing that your horse is traveling more comfortably should reduce the stress load on you as well. Our goal is to enable each horse to cope better with long hauling stretches while tightly confined in a small metal tube. Months and years of conditioning bring out the best of a horse's athletic potential, but the state in which a horse arrives at an event determines how well he will perform on a given day.

The Trailer Environment

Numerous studies have shown that confinement within a horse trailer for more than several hours has a pronounced impact on a horse's respiratory health. A trailer trip imposes at least a mild form of stress on even a well-adjusted horse. Let's look closely at the unique environment that develops inside the trailer.

As you cruise down the road on a summer day, your gelding is munching on the hay you've placed in the manger or hay net. Everything is going along pretty well until several hours have passed. The sun is rising higher in the sky, and the inside of the trailer is growing hotter and more humid. Your horse has been getting a bit tired from the constant acceleration and deceleration of the truck as it negotiates a twisting road. He's not much interested in eating anymore because he's thirsty and hot.

If your horse could talk to you, he might have the following things to say:

- He wants a drink of water.
- He wants the trailer to stop moving so he can rest his muscles.
- He wants to stretch his neck and back to loosen kinked muscles.
- He wants to roll to scratch away the itches that developed from sweating in the trailer.
- He needs to cough, and the only way he can do that is to stretch his neck down.
- He'd like his world to stop swaying, so he can comfortably stretch and balance to urinate.
- And, he'd like to get in some good punches to these irritating flies that have hitched a ride in the trailer along with him.

We all know that horses don't complain much about their lot in life. This may seem like an unreasonable number of requests. Yet, if you have ever spent any time riding in the back of a horse trailer, you will find it is not the same as what you experience while sitting in the truck cab rocking to tunes on the radio, with a soda and sandwich snuggled beside you on the seat while the air conditioner softly whirs away.

So, now that we've peeked a little at the larger picture of your horse's discomfort, let's look a little at the effects the trailer environment creates on your horse's internal system.

Stress and the Immune System

Everything about a trailer journey creates some form of stress on your horse. His muscles are weary. He may be sweating and loosing fluids and electrolytes, without a chance to replenish water. His bladder may be full. In general, as the miles go by, your horse may become more and more uncomfortable. Add to this a novice traveler, or one that is traveling solo and has just left his pasture companions at home. What about the horse that has just completed a 50 or 100 mile competition, whose muscles are fatigued, and who is dehydrated and energy depleted? For any of these individuals, discomfort can easily turn to distress. Simply said, stress suppresses a horse's normal immune response. The airways and lungs have specific defenses against invading viruses and bacteria. One type of defense works as follows: a type of white blood cell, called an *alveolar macrophage*, is instrumental in ingesting and neutralizing foreign organisms. But, anxiety created by traveling stress stimulates increased production of *corticosteroids* by a horse's adrenal glands, which depress the function of immune cells such as alveolar macrophages.

Respiratory Health

In addition, a horse trailer becomes a hothouse for the growth of microorganisms. The longer a horse remains within a trailer, the higher the temperature and humidity become, and the more bacterial organisms accumulate from dropped feces. Hay contains plentiful fungal spores. Dust and mold spores are blown into a horse's airways as he stands with his nose perched over a filled hay manger. Ammonia fumes from urine collect inside the trailer, while gas vapors such as carbon monoxide, nitrous oxide, and hydrocarbons filter back from the exhaust of the towing vehicle.

The combined effect of all these inhaled irritants is to destroy at least partially the cells lining the respiratory tract. The lining cells are responsible for moving particles and debris in a mucous layer out of the inner spaces of the respiratory tissue. Loss of the integrity of the respiratory lining ruins its protective function. This situation, coupled with a poorly functioning immune system, creates an environment that is conducive to the growth of viral and bacterial invaders. Increased humidity and temperature also compromise a horse's ability to clear the respiratory tract.

Your horse is more likely to develop a full-blown respiratory disease if he already has some form of pre-existing respiratory problem. Even the slightest little cough or sniffle can turn into a life-threatening pneumonia when transport stress is superimposed on a mild respiratory condition. Progressive dehydration, exposure of the lungs to accumulating microorganisms, and increasing temperature, humidity, and numbers of microorganisms progressively tilt the balance away from a healthy horse to a sick horse.

The long-distance horse does not have to get sick for his performance to suffer. An excellent functioning lung capacity is essential to the success of an endurance athlete. Any compromise to a horse's ability to take in plenty of air and oxygen can radically alter the outcome of his performance.

Many of these high risk features can be minimized with appropriate hauling management, coupled with tactics to improve the hygiene of the trailer environment.

Management Strategies for Respiratory Health

Summertime is the popular time of year to travel with our horses, but the warmth of the days poses some added challenges to improving the trailer environment. Not only does a hot day warm the inside of the trailer, but a horse's body heat, breathing, and urinations also add to the heat and humidity within.

CLEAN AIR

The first issue to address is clean air. For starters, make sure there is adequate ventilation through the trailer to minimize temperature, humidity, and bacterial count. This is especially important during the summertime in a hot and humid climate. A horse that travels in an enclosed trailer during hot, humid weather is also at risk of overheating and developing heat stroke. Leave windows and vents open where possible. Air movement through the trailer helps maintain a relatively constant temperature and humidity. In one study, horses were loaded into a trailer on a cool, but mild, winter day with a temperature of 44°F (8°C). Within three hours of travel, the temperature inside the horse trailer had elevated to 55°F (12°C). Humidity started at 71% and rose to 94%. During that same time period, the bacterial count increased from negligible to numbers similar to what you would find in a stall.

VENTILATION IN HOT WEATHER

If a trailer is stationary for a period of time, heat and humidity rise significantly, as do the numbers of bacterial and fungal organisms. When crossing state or international boundaries, have all the required paper work ready for inspection to minimize delays. The faster you are processed through these stations, the less time your horse must remain cooped up in a stationary trailer.

Anytime you must stop the trailer for an extended time, try to unload the horses to give them a chance to stretch their muscles and breathe fresh air. Use the rest stop as an opportunity to scoop wet bedding and feces out of the trailer. This will cut down on the bacterial count and the ammonia fumes.

Removal of feces from the trailer and continued movement of air within the trailer will diminish the number of flies that annoy your horse. When traveling through highly infested insect areas, you may need to use a fly sheet (the ventilated kind with many holes), or a nontoxic (to horses) type of fly spray. (Skin-So-Soft® by Avon mixed with vinegar and water works well.)

FEEDING ARRANGEMENTS

Mangers should always be cleaned after each trailer trip. Feed left in a manger will spoil, leading to proliferation of mold spores within the trailer. A trailer that has no manger is probably better for a horse's respiratory health in many respects. Without a manger, a horse's head is not confined in a nest of hay dust and mold spores while traveling. In addition, the absence of a manger allows a horse room to stretch his neck to snort or cough and blow debris from the upper airways. Greater freedom of movement also enables your horse to periodically adjust his body position to loosen tight muscles.

This is not to suggest that you run right out and trade in your horse trailer with a manger for one without a manger, but if you have the option of using a roomier, more open trailer that allows you to hang a hay net or hay bag, then do it. Remember that hay nets should not be hung so low that a horse's leg can get entangled in the net. Hay nets allow chaff and dust to fall down away from a horse's airways, and that in itself is an improvement over a manger type of arrangement. If you have a manger setup, be sure to use excellent quality hay, and maybe even dampen it slightly before you hit the road.

MUFFLER SYSTEMS

It is difficult to tell if exhaust fumes are collecting in the trailer. Probably the best way to determine this as well as to find out about your trailer in general is to take a ride in the trailer yourself. (Note: It is illegal in some parts of the country for a person to ride in a trailer being towed. Check your area's vehicular laws.)

Inspect under your truck and examine the position of the tail pipes, making sure the muffler exhaust is vented away from the trailer. All parts of the muffler system should be intact with no leaks.

VACCINATION SCHEDULES

Probably one of the most critical management tools to ensure sound respiratory health of your horse is the use of routine vaccinations against common respiratory viruses. A horse that is on an aggressive vaccination schedule stands a better chance of withstanding minor insults to his respiratory tract. It is best to vaccinate about two weeks prior to long distance transport to give your horse's immune system the greatest opportunity to respond with protective antibodies. A frequent traveler or a steady campaigner should receive equine influenza and rhinopneumonitis boosters every three to four months to provide the best protection possible. Check on specific vaccines that may be needed for the region to which you will be traveling. You can call the veterinary offices for the specific state, or contact a veterinarian in your intended destination to gather this information.

Transport stress and the trailer environment are not the only reasons to vaccinate your horse. New geographical environments harbor viral organisms to which your horse may have never before been exposed. Contact with horses from different geographical regions also exposes your horse to a variety of infectious organisms that other horses may carry in their respiratory secretions. A horse does not have to be clinically ill to be able to transmit an infectious disease to another horse.

Competition horses often share water sources. Also, many people handle many horses throughout the course of an event, increasing the likelihood of transmitting infectious material from horse to horse. One way to protect your horse is to immunize regularly against viral respiratory diseases.

VENTILATION IN COLD WEATHER

If you find that you must travel with your horse during cold winter weather, it is best to leave vents open to allow fresh air to continuously replace stale air. In many cases, it would be better to blanket your horse to minimize the chilling effect of small drafts than to close the trailer up too tightly, locking in stale air.

Strategies for Minimizing Fatigue

Cushioning the Ride

A trailer with a good suspension provides a smoother ride, which will minimize a horse's muscle fatigue. Floor mats also cushion the ride, especially if they are of solid, heavy rubber. Use a mat that is heavy enough to not shift or roll at the edges, so the horse has a stable surface for his feet.

Bedding on top of the mats adds to the cushion. It also absorbs urine moisture, and its presence encourages your horse to urinate while the trailer is in motion. Shavings or paper bedding are preferable to straw, since wet straw is slippery. Straw also contains mold spores that add to the microorganism contamination in the trailer.

After each road trip, clean out the bedding, remove mats, and let the floor boards dry. This allows you to check for floor rot, while cleaning away sources of bacterial and fungal contamination that are detrimental to respiratory health.

Balancing

Muscle enzymes have been shown to increase in horses transported distances of as little as 30-150 miles. A horse's muscles must do a great deal of work in the act of balancing and adjusting for acceleration and decelerations. To achieve stable footing and balance, a horse must be able to spread his legs.

Unfortunately, a full partition (one that extends to the floor) in a trailer does not allow a horse to do that. A partition rail between two horses allows each horse to spread his legs, but keep in mind that there is a possibility that one horse might step on another if he has to make a hasty adjustment. Shipping boots can protect against leg injuries.

In various studies, it has been demonstrated that horses that travel facing backward ride more comfortably and experience less muscle fatigue. If you don't want to invest in a new trailer designed for this, you can haul your horse backward by using a stock-type trailer. If you are a proponent of tying your horse's head to the side of a trailer, then tie the horse to one of the middle posts. Then he can swing his body forward and backward to adjust for vehicle movement. In this type of rig, a horse generally rides backward as the vehicle goes forward. As the truck turns corners, a horse also turns with the vehicle in an attempt to position his center of gravity to his advantage. A horse's ability to align his body in the direction of easiest balance minimizes muscle work during rapid decelerations. As a compromise, slant-load trailers offer a more comfortable balance position as compared to front-load trailers.

A horse that has a small window to see out of may have an easier time balancing. As the horse focuses on the outside scenery it achieves better equilibrium.

Tying the Head

There are various reasons why you should tie your horse's head, and just as many reasons why you should not. Everyone has their own preference, and you must decide what works best for each individual horse. The type of trailer you use also helps you decide this matter. Just remember that a horse that tries to turn around in too small a space can wedge his shoulders, head, and neck in a potentially life-threatening position. A horse that is tied too tightly is cramped and muscle weary by the time you arrive at your destination.

Rest Stops

One method to minimize your horse's muscle fatigue is to stop periodically (about 15-30 minutes for every four to six hours of travel). In hot weather, it is not enough just to stop the trailer for a break. As discussed on page 214, lack of air movement inside the trailer causes the temperature, humidity, and microorganisms to escalate. If a particular rest stop area seems to be an inappropriate place to unload, then at least open all the doors and windows to improve air flow.

Whenever possible, try to unload your horse every four to six hours to let him move around, roll, drink, eat, and urinate. Movement helps clear the lungs of mucus and debris. You can massage stiff muscles, or do some stretching exercises with your horse's legs to loosen him up. As a courtesy to other people, don't forget to pick up any droppings or leftover hay before you leave a rest stop.

Driving Technique

Your driving technique greatly affects how well your horse weathers a trip. Try not to speed through any turns. Erratic driving practices use up your horse's valuable energy and muscle reserves. Go reasonably slowly, and negotiate turns and stops smoothly.

Strategies to Minimize Dehydration

Summertime Transport

Many times the distances traveled to a base camp encompass at least a day or more in the horse trailer. In the summer, this has far-reaching repercussions on the state of your horse at the start line on race day. Just the heat inside an enclosed horse trailer stimulates enough sweat losses to bring your horse below optimum performance by the time you pull into the ride site. Muscle fatigue created by balancing over many miles in the trailer is comparable to working part of a tough trail.

An obvious strategy for summertime hauling would be to drive at night when it is coolest, or to stop during the heat of the day. No matter what, it is smart to stop frequently to water your horse, to sponge him down, and as previously mentioned, unload him from the trailer whenever possible. Park in the shade and open all the trailer doors and windows to allow a breeze to flush out the hot air. It's not just the ambient heat that causes temperatures to climb inside the trailer; your horse is putting out a great deal of body heat during the drive from the muscular work of balancing and from the sheer amount of *metabolic heat* generated by being alive.

Recently it was suggested that aluminum trailers might tend to retain heat a lot more than the older style steel trailers with wooden floors. Even with rubber mats on the aluminum floors, it has been reported that the floors transfer heat to a horse's feet during a long highway drive in exceptionally hot weather. Heat from the road may be absorbed by the aluminum floors, far more than what you'd see with a wooden floor. With that in mind, consider bedding the trailer floor with lots of shavings. Dampening the shavings could also keep your horse's feet and legs cooler.

Ice blocks in the mangers might help a little to cool the local air around the head. In hot weather, they don't last long, but every little bit helps.

The Significance of Dehydration

It is not uncommon to see a horse arrive at its destination in a mild state of dehydration after a long trailer trip. Over a twelve hour period, a horse may be at least 3% dehydrated even if the best of care has been taken. A horse with nervous diarrhea or one that sweats due to anxiety during the trip will lose even more fluid and *electrolytes*.

Any degree of fluid and electrolyte loss in the long-distance athlete puts his performance at a serious disadvantage. A horse that is dehydrated and/or stressed may not eat well, either. Weight loss and a poor appetite decrease the fuel reserves needed for a competition.

Methods of Offering Water

Before you leave on a long distance journey with your horse, offer hay and water for at least six hours in advance, giving your horse plenty of time to drink and eat his fill. Once in the trailer, hang a water bucket with bungee cords. A small amount of water may remain in the bucket and not slosh over the side. Even six inches of water in the bucket allows your horse to sip a little, or at least wash his mouth out. Some horses like to dunk their hay, and this gives those individuals an opportunity to cleanse their mouths. When you stop, refill the bucket to a level where the water doesn't just slosh out over the side. A couple of gallons intake is much better than none at all. For very long distance hauls, it is possible to locate automatic waterers that are filled from a pressurized water tank. Either setup allows your horse to drink at leisure, and will minimize the development of dehydration.

Trailer Conditioning

Trailer conditioning is important for the novice or nervous horse. You might consider feeding and watering an inexperienced horse in the parked trailer so he learns to associate the trailer as a place to eat and drink. Without continuously replenishing its fuel and water, a long-distance competitor cannot easily excel. Train the horse to travel comfortably for short distances before subjecting him to the stress of a long haul. Accustoming your horse to the feel of movement and the annoyance of highway noise ultimately pays off in the form of less overall stress. During the trailer conditioning process, a horse learns to load and unload quietly, and learns to look forward to feeding and watering

Photo 99 Many trail riders travel with these pipe fence sections which are easily erected alongside a trailer to create a pen where a horse can move around at will.

rituals. It may be an advantage to bring along a mellow companion horse to calm a horse that is learning the ways of the road for the first time.

Once at Base Camp.....

When you set up your camp site, think of the coolest options for your horse. Orient the pens behind the trailer so there is as much shade for as long as possible during the day (Photo 99). Or, put up shade awnings to give some respite from the sun.

If you have more than one horse with you, it is best to place them in separate pens. In that way you can monitor exactly how much each horse drinks, eats, and manures. You can examine the manure for quantity and consistency each day. This eliminates any guesswork as to whether or not each horse is processing normally.

What is normal water intake?

An idle horse needs about five to seven gallons of water a day just to maintain normal physiologic function. When you put that horse to protracted endurance exercise, he needs to drink at least 20 gallons of water each day to keep up with the losses. Over 100 miles of trail, he can easily lose 10 gallons of "water" in his sweat. Performance suffers with just 3% dehydration which is equivalent to a loss of four gallons of body "water." For most horses, the demands of a typical endurance race result in 4-6% dehydration by the end of the race.

Early Arrival at the Competition

When possible, particularly before a 100 mile endurance competition, try to arrive a couple of days early. This allows your horse some rest and an opportunity to replenish fluids, *electrolytes*, and energy. A relaxed and happy campaigner is able to give a more brilliant performance. The horse that starts a competition in its most vital state stands a better chance of maintaining well through the miles. This gives both you and your horse a chance to do your very best.

11 How to Avoid Common Mistakes Made at Competitions

Over many years, I've had the opportunity to watch and listen to all levels of inexperienced and experienced riders take on the challenge of a competition. Despite the advances made in the endurance world, some common mistakes and misconceptions persist. Many solutions to these problems are based on a generous dose of common sense, but as so often happens with fallible human beings, it is hard to recognize how to apply things to our own lives. It's easy to give advice, and recommend that folks should "Do as I say, not as I do." But, as you read through this, think about how some of these situations apply to you and your horse, not just to Joe or Josephine Rider on the next farm. If you recognize one or more things as something you have done in the past, look at these comments as a rung in the learning ladder, and use this as an endurance primer.

Prior to Arrival at a Competition

Ride Frequency

Probably the hardest decision for any rider is how much to ride and how often. This dilemma applies both to training and competition schedules. Even before a rider has left for a competition, it is possible that excessive wear and tear have been placed on a horse. Occasionally, you might see a horse arriving at an event looking slightly dull, fatigued, and in thin body condition. Legs and joints may be puffy. The horse lacks luster. More commonly, the horse looks all right, albeit a little gaunt and slightly drooped in posture. He starts a race with abundant energy, but tires quickly. Performance failure occurs for three reasons, each of which ends in the same result.

The first reason is due to a lack of commitment to a conditioning program appropriate to the level of competition. Remember that it takes about three years to build a foundation for a 100 mile horse. Before your horse tackles his first 100 miler, he should be at least seven years old. A young or novice horse new to long-distance sports should be conditioned diligently over four to six months before even taking on a slow 50 mile training ride. Conditioning for a 50 mile event requires that your horse is occasionally ridden 20-30 miles. I have seen horses put to the task of a 50 mile mountain ride, never having done more than 7-10 miles in a training ride. Don't shortcut the conditioning process; your horse will pay the price.

A second reason for general fatigue is created by the opposite problem: overtraining and literally riding a horse into the ground. Once you have a solid conditioning foundation on your horse, it isn't necessary to ride him hard four or five days a week. Exercising him at some stress level **twice** a week is usually sufficient to maintain a level of condition. You can ride him another day that week at a light hack or work on dressage or cavalletti exercises. As a rule of thumb, keep your training mileage to less than 90 or 100 miles within a two week period. And give your horse several days off from training rides before you go to an event.

A third reason for "tired horse syndrome" results from excessive frequency of competition. It is unreasonable to ask your horse to compete in 100 mile events every two weeks. That is also too frequent an expectation for 50 mile events. A horse should **not** be competed at 50 milers more than once every two to four weeks. This rule of thumb applies even if you ride him slowly through a competition. For 100 mile competitions, give your horse six to eight weeks between events. His body needs ample down time to heal and recover. If you push him too much, he may slowly wear down, looking tired and strained by the end of the season, even if his musculoskeletal system survived.

Remember that there are always those unusual horses who are so efficient in their work that they are able to campaign on a more frequent schedule and they prove the exception to the rule. Ambition is an applaudable trait, unless it compromises your horse. Ultimately, every horse will deteriorate from persistent stress of travel and competition unless given sufficient rest time. Just don't get overzealous in your planning or your expectations. Sometimes it's best to sit one out. If you want to go to an event, be a volunteer, and leave your horse at home.

Keep Things Consistent

Another phenomenon that overtakes an endurance rider is the need to always improve on the details. This is great in theory and in practice, but remember not to change your routine within two weeks prior to a ride. This includes shoeing, tack and equipment, even your own riding clothing.

If you are considering some acupuncture work, chiropractic, or massage therapy for your horse, don't do it just prior to a competition. Most performance horses have some kind of musculoskeletal ailment as is common to all athletes. Your horse has learned to compensate for both the little and the big problems. If you have one of these therapists alter your horse's way of going, you have to allow time to accommodate this new pattern. You will have affected his compensatory mechanisms, and he needs time to repattern himself. The time to apply alternative therapies is definitely not the day before a race, or even within the week ahead. Try to get the larger adjustments worked out during the noncompetitive season.

The same applies to shoeing modifications. Your horse needs time to adjust to a trim, the new angles on his feet, the weight of the shoes. Think about how you might feel if you are used to running in your sneakers and suddenly switch to a pair of hiking boots; your muscles and joints will feel the difference. It is best to build up to a shoeing change gradually, and not ask your horse to accommodate the new shoeing over the course of 50 or 100 miles.

Travel to and Arrival at the Ride Site

Lead Time

Because many of us have to work to support our riding passion, it is often hard to get away many days before a competition. We find ourselves loading the camper and bundling our horses into the trailer either Thursday night or early Friday morning to make it to check-in for a Saturday event. Not only does this add stress to our lives, but it may affect some people's driving as they feel rushed. Your driving techniques radically affect how well your horse comes through the traveling experience. Similarly, the match and suitability of your truck and trailer create either a rough or a pleasant ride. And, each horse responds differently to the trailer experience (see Chapter 10 for more on trailering).

Many horses bounce back right away when they get off the trailer, having eaten well and drunk regularly throughout the trip. A comfortable trailer allows many horses to doze on the road, and they arrive rested and well hydrated. But more commonly, there has been some stress related to transport. Ideally, you'd like to arrive two to three days before a 100 mile event. Since this is rarely possible, just keep in mind that you may need to adjust your demands on your horse's performance on ride day, and give him more time to rest and eat at vet checks and along the trail.

Feed Changes

Often when you must travel long distances to rides and are gone for more than five or six days, you may need to purchase hay from local sources. Whenever you change the diet, your horse's intestinal tract needs time to make adjustments. Different hay sources and different hay types will affect your horse's assimilation of the altered nutrition. Typically you won't notice any difference, but certain situations are predisposed to problems.

When you remove a horse from pasture and feed dry hay instead, the effects of dehydration suffered at a ride are amplified. It is best to accustom your pastured horse to eating hay at home for several weeks prior to a ride, and continue this practice throughout the season.

Also, don't think that all of a sudden you need to increase your horse's supplements in the few days preceding a ride. Adding too many *nutraceuticals* and vitamins to the diet increases urination and puts an added burden on the intestinal tract. Supplementing with additional grain creates more gas in the bowel. Besides, your horse often experiences a rebound hypoglycemia within four hours of eating a large grain meal: subsequent to ingesting carbohydrates like grain, insulin is released into the bloodstream. This drives sugars into the cells, making it less available in the bloodstream for muscular work.

Your operating rule of thumb: Keep the diet constant! The competitive season is not the time to start experimenting with new and different feeds like rich alfalfa or added grain or pellets. If you must use hay bought from local sources, blend it half and half with your regular hay to ease the transition.

Water Intake

Many horses don't drink well when traveling or even after arriving at a ride site. The type of water container you offer your horse may dramatically affect his water intake because the taste of the water is affected by the bucket you put it in. Some horses prefer rubber buckets, some prefer plastic buckets, while others drink best from a galvanized bucket. Experiment and give your horse choices.

Pre-ride Check-in

Sign-In at the Office

When you arrive at the campsite, get your horse comfortable and then go check in with ride management. Pick up your ride packet and make sure all the information about you and your horse is correct. Also ask if you will be weighing in before or after the ride, and find out where the scales are. Make sure you have checked in at the ride office, have paid, and have your rider packet with your rider card and number in hand **before** entering the vetting area.

Presentation

With paper work in hand, head toward the veterinary check-in area. Don't wait until the last possible moment to check in. A big word of advice: have your horse warmed up prior to presentation to the veterinary staff. Don't just pull your horse off the trailer and run right over for your exam. At least hand-walk or longe your horse for 10 or 15 minutes to get his circulation going, to loosen muscles and joints, and to give him the opportunity to show at his soundest. In many premier rides, you won't get a second chance to come back into the vetting area.

How do you perform the trot-out? (See Chapter 9, page 195 for more detail.) Remember, practice trotting your horse in hand at home, and train your horse to be obedient. Stay to the side of your horse on the straight line, and concentrate on making your circles **round** and large enough to maintain your horse at a trot. Don't rush, but on the other hand, don't take forever to trot your figures. Don't go so far away from the veterinarian that he or she needs binoculars to see you. Performing this well gives you a chance to show off your horse, and your efforts are most appreciated by the veterinarians. Other competitors also appreciate a steady flow through the vetting area, as delays keep people from attending to their other chores and social time.

Before Leaving the Vetting Area

At an endurance ride, don't run off before having a number crayoned onto your horse's hindquarters once you have received the go-ahead from the veterinary staff. This number identifies your horse as part of the event. In some situations, you will be given a rider pinney to wear, and a bridle tag for your horse.

The Ride Meeting

The main thing to be said about ride meetings is you had better go! Many times there are changes in the trail, in the hold times at vet checks, all kinds of things of which you should be aware. Management will tell you what you can expect on the trail, obstacles or hazards you may need to negotiate, gates to open and close. You will be directed on how you and your horse will be returned to camp should you be pulled. You need to hear this information so there are no misunderstandings.

On the same note, remember that if you are pulled or voluntarily decide not to continue on course, you must notify ride management immediately so dedicated volunteers aren't out in the wee hours of the night searching for you, thinking you lost in the wilderness. Don't just pull out and leave. Management must know where you are as long as you are part of the event.

The ride meeting is a good opportunity to set your watch to official time.

Ride Day

Settling Your Nerves

Only the coolest of the cool don't suffer from nervous butterflies just before an event. Even riders planning to stay at the back of the pack often experience rattled nerves. It's a lot of trail out there, and you just never know what will unfold. But, if you adhere to a consistent routine from the minute you rise to the start of the race, each time the process will get easier, and you'll have confidence that you didn't forget anything.

Feed, dress, saddle in a consistent protocol. Have all your clothing and gear laid out the night before. Use that same old familiar equipment that both you and your horse are used to. Have your water bottles filled and your packs loaded with energy bars, *electrolytes* for your horse, and don't forget that oral syringe!

Check that your flashlight and head lamp batteries are functioning if you will be spending time on the trail in the dark. Have your reflective gear, like stirrup bars and brow bands, already installed. Have your glow sticks packed if you like to dangle those from the breast collar.

Despite a weather forecast of hot and dry, don't believe it. You know the saying: "If you don't like the weather, just wait five minutes." Be ready for the worst, making sure you've got rain gear, or at least a large plastic garbage bag tucked into your cantle pack. It's no fun being wet and cold with many miles to go, even in summer. Of course, make sure your horse is okay with you wearing a plastic garbage bag, or you might find yourself with a long, lonely hike to the next vet check.

It doesn't hurt to carry along a basic first aid kit on your person in case you do get thrown off and separated from your horse. Include basic anti-inflammatory medications for yourself, a couple of flares, a whistle, and a space blanket if you've got room. You just never know....

Saddled Up and Ready to Ride

Can you believe this? All these comments and the trail hasn't even opened for competition! Well, before it does, think through your riding strategy. Start with a plan, and be prepared to adjust it as the ride unfolds.

Start by warming your horse up for 10 or 15 minutes to get circulation moving in his muscles, and to warm up his tendons and joints. Don't hover around the start line since the confusion there often adds to your tension and affects your horse as well. Your watch should already be set to official ride time, and you only need to show up at the start line a couple of minutes before the send-off.

You're Off and Running!

With luck, you won't be bolting with the front of the pack, and you will set off at a nice quiet pace. Remember, it doesn't hurt anything to hang back for 15 or 20 minutes so your horse will go out relatively quietly.

Sometimes riding with the pack fuels your horse with adrenalin, and he puts out more than he is capable of at the beginning. Adrenalin often masks signs that he is getting tired until he is **too** tired. As a rider, it is easy to get caught up in the excitement of the group, causing you to go faster than you intended.

Another situation often occurs in the more elite endurance rides when riders who have finished in the Top Ten at local rides and have therefore qualified for the more prestigious rides end up thinking they will be in the Top Ten all the time. But when the littler fishes meet the bigger fishes, sometimes those valiant horses are allowed to move along too fast in the beginning, and they eventually fade.

The First Vet Check

One of the biggest mistakes is thinking that you've got to be in the first group into the first vet check. Statistics taken from four years of data from the Race of Champions (ROC) give us some invaluable insights. These are the results taken from the first 20 horses into the first check:

- 1992 Race of Champions (Colorado): 8 of the first 20 (40%) into the Vet Check 1 did **not** complete.
- 1993 Race of Champions (South Dakota): 6 of the first 20 (30%) into Vet Check 1 did **not** complete.
- 1994 Race of Champions (South Dakota): 9 of the first 20 (45%) into Vet Check 1 did **not** complete.

- 1995 Race of Champions (Utah): 7 of the first 20 (35%) into
  Vet Check 1 did **not** complete.

In summary, it looks like few people are paying close attention to these figures: if you are in the top 20 arriving at the first vet check, you have close to a 40% likelihood that your horse will be pulled during the ride. The lesson in this: if you burn up the trail early on, you may well burn up your horse.

Getting Lost

People who get lost tend to think they've got to make up time. If you lose your cool, you'll have a tendency to override to try to catch up. Try to think steady and only ask your horse to travel at a reasonable speed consistent with your original plan.

Listen To Your Horse

Pay attention to all those subtle signs your horse is giving you. Don't ignore problems, and don't cook up excuses for your horse's waning performance. Take these indications to heart. If your horse is tiring, then slow down and allow him food, water, and rest breaks along the trail. You don't need to move forward continuously. Similarly, at the vet checks, there is no reason you need to leave when the out-timer calls your number. Just advise the out-timer that you'll be remaining a little longer to give your horse more time to eat and drink. Be sure to tell the out-timer when you leave so management knows you are back on the trail.

In many competitions, you will have a cutoff time for reaching each vet check. For example, consider a ride starting at 5am. Vet Check 1 may be positioned at 18 miles, and it will be open from 6:15am to 8:40am. Vet Check 2 at 27 miles would be open from 7:30am to 11:30am. For an endurance ride, these cutoff times are usually calculated on an average pace of 4.7 mph. This is the **average** speed you need to maintain to finish a 100 mile ride in 24 hours assuming there are 3 hours of hold time along the trail. Everyone's horse should be up to traveling at that pace or they are perhaps not well prepared for a 100 miles of trail. In some parts of the trail you will go faster; in other parts you may need to go slower, depending on the terrain. Part of your strategy is knowing when you can afford to give your horse extra rest time, knowing that once he has gained a second wind you will move along more efficiently and with less danger to your horse. Listen carefully at the ride meeting for information on specific sections of trail that will be really rocky, or free-going. This will be part of developing your strategy. Don't ask your horse to work long periods at speeds for which you haven't trained. On many an occasion, competitors canter a good portion of a race, never having done so in training. Or, they canter a horse downhill for the first time ever. Tendons, ligaments, and joints really take a beating from this lack of preparation, and muscles tire quickly.

Using a Heart Rate Monitor

A heart rate monitor is an invaluable tool that helps maintain your horse within an *aerobic* working heart rate. Be sure you have trained with one at home so you know how to interpret the readings. Also rely on your instincts to tell you if your horse is not doing well despite a working heart rate that remains below 130-145 *bpm*, and reasonable *heart rate recoveries*. A heart rate monitor does not always tell you if your horse is getting into trouble, either *metabolically* or *musculoskeletally* (see Chapter 6 for more detail on using a heart rate monitor). An additional word of caution: don't try to ride off of someone else's heart rate monitor. Your horse is an individual and no two horses respond to the stress of working in exactly the same way.

Using a heart rate monitor like a tachometer invites injury. If there are rocks along the trail, or the footing becomes deep or treacherous, don't try to go fast enough to keep the working heart rate up around 130 or 140 bpm; slow down and walk if need be!

Taking Care of Yourself

To keep your sensibilities throughout the ride, you must remember to drink well and to eat high energy foods. If you get fatigued, you are more likely to make judgment errors, and you won't be as sensitive to your horse. Take care of yourself! This seems pretty logical, but along about 60 miles or so, you won't be thinking this clearly. It helps to have a feeding/drinking plan for yourself before you start the ride, and then just follow this program all the way through to the finish line.

Entering Vet Checks

The Approach

Your objective as you approach the vet check is to have your horse's heart rate down as quickly as possible so you can pass the pulse criteria immediately. Slow down as you near the check. Pour any remaining water from your bottles over your horse's neck. Dismount, loosen the girth, and lead him in. Often this signals your horse that he is approaching a rest stop and it is time to relax. Without your weight on top, he doesn't have to expend as much energy carrying you.

Once at the check, immediately loosen the breast collar so he can comfortably get his head down to drink. Then start pulling off your tack to improve heat dissipation. In hot weather, head for any available shade.

Ideally, you'd like to enter the vet check at a heart rate of 72 bpm or less. Allow your horse to drink if he wants, but don't allow him to eat prior to P&Rs or going through the veterinary exam. Eating slows his heart rate recovery. You should train your horse at home to patiently accept this waiting process so he's not anxious about having food withheld, and so he doesn't pull on you to get to food. You shouldn't let him scratch and itch; he should stand quietly while you go through the cooling down process and while the P&R volunteer counts his heart rate.

Cooling

To summarize, you'll need to soak the front part of your horse until his chest feels cool to the touch. Be sure to check the temperature of the water you use to sponge with, as warm water in a hot, humid climate actually delays heart rate recovery. On the other hand, if you over-cool, your horse will get chilled and the heart rate will stay elevated.

If the air temperature is cool or there is a breeze, your horse may do better having his haunches covered with a light rug so muscles don't cool down too quickly and cramp. Muscle cramps lead to pain, and pain leads to a persistently elevated heart rate. If it is warm and the air is still, don't throw a cooler on your horse. Read the weather, and think.

It is best to walk your horse intermittently and sponge. A horse that is allowed to stand too long will have heat continue to build in the muscles. *Lactic acid* also won't be flushed out of the muscles by the circulation in the standing horse, so when suddenly you move your horse to the P&R or the veterinary area, his heart rate will spike, possibly over criteria.

If your horse is taking more than five or ten minutes to reach criteria — usually 60 or 64 bpm — you are probably riding too fast for this horse's level of fitness, or something is wrong metabolically or he is experiencing pain somewhere in his body. Start looking for problems. If there are none, plan to seriously slow your pace on the next leg of trail.

P&R and the Veterinary Exam

As you enter the vet check stations, remember to keep your horse away from others. Bunching horses together with hindquarters close to one another is not only poor horsemanship, it risks injury to people and horses. Keep your space, and be considerate of other people's space.

Have your rider card ready to present to the P&R person, and to the veterinary recorder. Once the P&R person records the start of your hold time, check your card to make sure you agree with the time written down. Also check your watch and remember that your horse must "pass" through the veterinary criteria within 30 minutes of the start of your hold time. Normally, you will flow directly from the P&R to the veterinarians, and this gives you the full hold time to attend to your horse and yourself. But if you are asked to return to the veterinary exam area for a second *cardiac recovery index* or re-examination of a particular concern, keep track of the time. I have seen too many people wander back in about 40 minutes after the start of their hold and be disqualified because they missed the time cutoff. Not fun!

When you present to the veterinarian, remember to use the same trot-out procedures you did at the pre-ride check-in; that is, stay to the side of your horse so the veterinarian can evaluate your horse's gait and not yours. Then you won't have to repeat the trot-out and you'll proceed through the check quickly.

Watch the traffic flow through veterinary presentation areas. Keep an eye out as you start your trot-out so you don't interfere with another rider's presentation to another veterinarian. Your crew should be clear of the presentation area so people moving about don't cross in front of the veterinarian's line of sight.

COMMUNICATION

Back in the older days of endurance sports, riders used to try to get problems past the veterinarians. Fortunately, this antagonistic relationship is mostly a thing of the past. Most riders are quite up front about their concerns. They realize it is to their advantage to point out issues to the veterinarians, and to approach the veterinary exam as a team effort in determining what is best for the horse. More often than not, there is a true comraderie between the veterinarians and the riders. The point after all, is to have fun while competing.

By the same token, don't misinterpret veterinary criticism. Keep an open mind, and don't be defensive. Rarely are comments directed personally. Most veterinarians are very concerned, caring individuals, looking out for your horse's welfare. If you don't understand or agree with a veterinary judgment, then ask why the determination was made.

When you read through your rider card, don't get too carried away with a literal interpretation of the grading scores on your horse. The A's, B's, and C's are meant to communicate a relative physiological state to the next veterinarian down the line, or to remind that veterinarian of what was seen at a prior vet check. Each veterinarian will use the grading scale a little differently, but the scores will be consistent within that person's way of judging. Remember that an A is what is expected of the normal, unstressed horse at rest. Most horses will experience some deviation from this "normal" after traveling many miles down the trail. B scores are expected, and certainly do not detract from the capability of a horse as *fit to continue*.

The biggest mistake I see is a rider storming off in a huff after being pulled, reeling off a scathing repertoire of foul language about how unfair the world is and how so-and-so veterinarian should go get "stuffed," or worse. This may well be the essence of poor horsemanship. It makes that rider look bad, and makes it appear that the event is more important than the well-being of the horse. Not all veterinary decisions are entirely correct all of the time, but if you are there to play the game, then you must play by the rules of the game. Every horse is examined with the same scrutiny, and most veterinarians are as fair and objective as they can be. If your tendency is to complain first and never ask questions, then control yourself, or have a friend help you out by being your spokesman. Similarly, if you see a friend of yours having problems accepting veterinary information, step in and try to bring a sense of calm to the situation.

Understand that many times a veterinarian will pick up on an impending problem long before you do. As rider and owner of a horse, it is all too easy to lose your objectivity, especially as you become more fatigued and low on blood sugar during the course of a ride. Keep your expectations realistic. Practice the art of communication, which means that you should open your mind and listen, and engage in a sensible discussion. Look at each veterinary exam as a new learning experience. Look at the well-being of your horse as **the** most important issue.

Refueling at the Vet Checks

FOOD AND WATER

Once your horse has passed through pulse criteria and the veterinary exam, get him some food and more water. Try to feed wetted hay and watery mashes to improve water intake. Greedy horses sometimes grab too large a mouthful of hay, so sometimes it's best to fluff up the hay or feed directly from a bale to prevent choke. The chances of choking are greater as a horse becomes more dehydrated through the course of a ride and has less saliva present in his mouth.

Please refer to the chapter on Intelligent Nutrition for concerns about the type and amount of hay and grain to feed and what to avoid.

ELECTROLYTES

Ideally, you have been administering small but frequent doses of *electrolytes* along the trail every time your horse takes a good drink. This reduces the lag time for absorption of these salts from the bowel so your horse is being replenished as he goes long. Once in the check area, let your horse eat and drink for a while before you administer more electrolytes. You don't want to do anything that might interfere with his eating or drinking at the vet check.

Some riders prefer to give the electrolytes just before leaving the check. Practice at home and know your horse's preferences. Have the electrolytes prepared in film canisters or a small container in advance. Mix with applesauce to make them into a more pasteable mixture.

It is possible to give too much electrolytes. A horse might get a loose stool as a result, or become more dehydrated if not drinking enough water. (For more information, refer to Chapter 8.)

Back on the Trail

Preparing to Leave

Be tacked up and ready to go at least five minutes before your out time. Both you and your horse should stretch. If you plan to take off at a fast pace, then warm up your horse for five minutes before you hit the trail hard. This is especially true if you had ice boots applied to the legs, as collagen stiffens and the tendons lose their elasticity when cooled down (see Chapter 8).

As you set off toward the next vet check, remember to keep that constant rhythm and pace that allows your horse to work efficiently. Random speeding up and slowing down uses up valuable energy reserves.

Riding Along the Trail

Practice good horsemanship throughout the ride. Be courteous to other riders by letting them know if you are coming alongside to pass. Only pass if there is sufficient room to get by without endangering your horse or another's horse by pushing them off the trail. If you are in front of a group of riders, use hand signals to communicate if you need to slow down suddenly due to rocks or trail hazards. Nothing is more important than safety and courtesy to others. This may be a horse race, but a win should not be at the expense of horses or riders.

The Last Leg

As you leave the last vet check toward the finish, don't be tempted to override the last miles, especially if you are not competing for "Top Ten." I have seen many a horse burned up in the last few miles, only to be sadly pulled at the finish. The criteria of "sound at the trot" at the finish was established to prevent people from blowing their horses out in the last miles with a crazy race to the finish. I remember one horse who was pretty tired, and the rider was cautioned to go easy in the last stretch. Unfortunately, she got swept up in the grand finale, raced for the line, and her horse broke his leg.

I'm sure we all have heard similar horror stories. These tragedies don't happen very often, but they stick in everyone's mind for many, many years. Interestingly, it is harder to remember who won what race, or when. So, measure whether a placing is worth the risk. Most of the time, the horses pushed hard at the last make it across the finish line just fine, and they receive a completion with no problem, but you can be guaranteed they are tired. Keep this in mind when addressing your post-ride care, and allow adequate rest time following a competition.

Post-ride Care

Monitoring Metabolics

Your job is far from over once you cross the finish line. There is still a lot to do to take care of your super athlete. Throughout the next several days, you want to carefully monitor your horse's heart rate, *capillary refill time*, attitude, appetite, water intake, and bowel movements. The *heart rate recovery* gives you a check on hydration, level of exhaustion, or pain. In judging Best Condition horses the day after a tough ride, it has been interesting to note that the more tired horses breathe faster, with an accelerated respiratory rate. This is another parameter every rider should track during the post-ride period.

Offer your horse soupy gruels of bran or pelleted feed with electrolytes. Give him as much free choice grass hay as he wants to eat. Often as I peruse the trailers at the end of a ride, I see horses that are out of hay, and more importantly, out of water! Make sure multiple buckets of water are available at all times. Leave a couple of full buckets near where your horse is parked so roving veterinarians can top off the water in the wee hours of the night if you happen to be sleeping. But don't rely on other people to keep your horse well watered. That is your responsibility.

Minimizing Soreness

Your goal in managing your horse immediately after you dismount is to minimize inflammation and keep your horse as comfortable as possible. Parking him next to the trailer causes tired muscles to tighten. You can minimize his stiffness and muscle soreness by periodically hand-walking him around the campsite. This keeps you loose and supple, as well. Massage his big muscle groups to soften the muscles and to encourage circulation. Carefully do leg stretches to maintain range-of-motion through the joints and ligaments.

Clean dirt and sweat from your horse's coat, including his legs. Check girth, saddle, and bit areas for chafing. Apply Desitin® or an antibacterial salve to keep abraded skin from drying and hurting.

Icing the legs after a tough workout helps reduce the inflammatory response, and keeps the puffs and swellings to a minimum. Just don't forget that a tired horse is likely to chill easily, so don't just slap on those ice boots and leave them. Either put them on and off at about 10 minute intervals, or massage the legs with ice cubes. After icing the legs, apply standing bandages to continue support of the tissues and further prevent lower leg swelling.

Medications

Many people think they can give medications to their horse once a race is done and they have received their completion, unless they are showing for Best Condition. This is **not** the case. Although nonsteroidal anti-inflammatory drugs like phenylbutazone or Banamine® are effective in combating inflammation, swelling, and muscle soreness, **don't give any of these drugs until at least 8 hours post-ride**. These drugs are toxic to the kidneys in a dehydrated horse. You need to allow your horse enough time to rehydrate and return to normal kidney function before you administer these anti-inflammatory products.

If you ride your horse intelligently and pay careful attention to post-ride management of icing legs, massaging muscles, and intermittently walking your horse, you shouldn't need to rely on anti-inflammatory medications.

However, because the joints take a tremendous punishment over the course of 50 or 100 competitive miles, it would benefit your horse to receive an intramuscular dose of Adequan® to minimize the inflammatory products in the joints. Adequan® is a medication that improves nutrition and lubrication within the joints by stimulating the production of naturally occurring substances produced by joints. It also has some anti-inflammatory properties. Allow your horse to relax and refuel for some hours before you give the Adequan®.

Returning Home

Just as your trailer trip to the ride site may slightly compromise your horse in his hydration and create muscle fatigue, consider that you need to allow him sufficient rest time and rehydration before you travel home. This is especially true if you anticipate many hours or days of driving. Your horse just put forth a Herculean effort, and he is probably exhausted. Don't be too hasty in packing up camp and leaving.

At Home

Well, we've come full circle. Give your horse sufficient healing time after a ride. A general rule of thumb: **Allow 1 day of rest for every 10 miles of trail**. If you don't have adequate pasture turnout, you may need to lightly ride or pony your horse for 20-30 minutes each day to loosen him up so he's not just stiffening up as he stands in a small paddock.

In Conclusion

Did you recognize any of your own follies in this sketch of a ride? Not a single person is exempt from making any of these mistakes. The trick is not to repeat them. I hope that as you read through this you gleaned some valuable tidbits of what to do and what not to do to bring your horse through an event safe and sound. It's the details that allow your horse to excel!

Glossary

Adenosine diphosphate (ADP) Breakdown product of *adenosine triphosphate* created during the release of energy from muscular contraction; used to synthesize adenosine triphosphate.

Adenosine triphosphate (ATP) Energy fuel used for muscular contraction; formed from the synthesis of *adenosine diphosphate* combined with phosphate molecules.

Aerobic capacity Intensity of exercise a horse can perform before crossing the anaerobic threshold.

Aerobic metabolism In the presence of oxygen, fats or carbohydrates are metabolized to generate energy in the form of *adenosine triphosphate*. This form of *metabolism* is used in low or moderate intensity exercise for prolonged periods.

Alveolar macrophages Immune cells that scavenge and inactivate bacteria, viruses, or debris within the lungs.

Ambient temperature Surrounding environmental temperature; temperature of the air.

Anaerobic metabolism Carbohydrates are metabolized to generated *adenosine triphosphate* (energy) in the absence of oxygen with *lactic acid* as a by-product.

Anaerobic threshold Intensity of exercise at which *anaerobic metabolism* significantly contributes to the production of energy; *lactic acid* in the blood-stream exceeds four mmol/liter.

Anhidrosis Inability to sweat even in conditions that normally stimulate sweating.

Autonomic nervous system (ANS) A branch of the central nervous system that involuntarily controls function of all body tissues.

Bpm Beats per minute.

Breakover The period of time measured from the time the heel leaves the ground until the toe leaves the ground.

Breakover Point A point on the end of the toe, evident by greater wear. Ideally, this point is in the center of the hoof wall of the toe.

Broken back hoof-pastern axis The angle of the pastern is steeper than the angle of the front of the hoof, causing excessive stress on the rearward portions of the foot and limb.

Capillary refill time The rate at which blood perfuses back into the tissues of the mucous membranes (gums) after being pressed with a fingertip.

Cardiac recovery index (CRI) A standard-ized method of evaluating the *heart rate recovery*: A resting heart rate is taken and then the horse is trotted out 250 feet. Exactly one minute from the start of the trot, the heart rate is again taken and compared to the resting rate. The expected value is for the horse to return to resting rate or below, although 4 *bpm* faster may be acceptable.

Cardiovascular (C-V) Relating to the heart, arteries, veins, and capillary beds that deliver oxygen and nutrients throughout the body.

Central sulcus Central groove in the frog.

Conduction Direct transfer of heat from a hot surface to a cool surface.

Convection As cool air passes across a horse's skin, heat is transferred from the skin to the air.

Coronary corium The active tissue of the coronary band that is responsible for hoof growth.

Corns Pressure points at the angles of the bars of the hoof that result in necrosis of the underlying tissues of the sole, often accompanied by pain and lameness.

Corticosteroids (steroids) Naturally occurring hormones from the adrenal gland; synthetic forms are injected into the vein, the muscle, or the joint as anti-inflammatory treatment. A side effect is depression of the immune system.

Desmitis Inflammation of a ligament.

Effective temperature See *heat index*.

Egg bar shoe Oval shaped horseshoe that provides rear support to the foot.

Electrolytes Body salts that are normal components of blood and tissue that contribute to muscle contractions, nerve impulses, oxygen and carbon dioxide transport, etc. When lost in the sweat they must be replaced to maintain normal fluid and electrolyte balances.

Endocrine glands Glands in the body that secrete hormones into the bloodstream.

Endotoxin The outer cell wall of a bacteria that is released during intestinal inactivity due to dehydration or colic; circulation of this substance in the body contributes to laminitis, shock, and even death.

Evaporative cooling Transfer of heat from the skin to the air as water vapor that is excreted from the sweat glands.

Exhaustion syndrome A set of symptoms related to the combined effects of dehydration, electrolyte imbalances, energy depletion, and acid-base (pH) imbalances.

Fartlek (speed play) High speed sprints alternated with moderate intensity exercise to touch the *anaerobic threshold*; speed play brings the working heart rate to between 160-175 *bpm* for several minutes.

Fasciculations Quivering or twitching of the muscles.

Fast twitch high oxidative muscle fibers Muscle fibers that are capable of using both *aerobic* or *anaerobic* metabolism for energy production.

Fit to continue At veterinary checks, assessment of metabolic and soundness factors should fall within an expected standard to allow a horse to continue in competition.

Glycogen A form of carbohydrate stored in liver and muscle tissue.

Heat index (HI) Combination of environmental temperature (degrees Fahrenheit) plus percent humidity to give a number that is used to determine the amount of exercise that permits safe cooling of the horse.

Heart rate recovery Rate at which the heart rate falls to an expected value or to the resting rate after exercise ceases.

Heat bumps Small welts created by excess temperature in the skin.

Hematocrit See *packed cell volume.*

Hemoglobin Protein of red blood cells that transports oxygen within the blood to the tissues.

Ileus Absence of intestinal activity, normal peristaltic contractions, or gut sounds.

Impulsion Characteristic of a horse's gait indicating strength and energy while in motion.

Inertia A property of matter by which it remains at rest or in uniform motion in the same straight line unless acted upon by some external force.

Interval training (IT) A form of conditioning that breaks exercise into brief work periods of high intensity, followed by rest periods of lower intensity to allow partial recovery of heart and respiratory rates and removal of toxins (*lactic acid*) from the muscles. Trains muscles to function under *anaerobic* conditions without incurring damage to *musculoskeletal* tissues.

Jugular refill time Period of time (in seconds) that it takes the jugular vein to refill after blood flow has been blocked at the bottom or middle of the neck.

Lactic acid Toxic by-product of *anaerobic metabolism*; contributes to fatigue.

Laminitis Inflammation of the tissues within the hoof caused by circulatory disturbance to the feet from concussion, trauma, or *endotoxin.*

Lever arm A rigid piece that transmits and modifies force or motion when forces are applied at two points and it turns around a third point.

Long slow distance training (LSD) First phase of cardiovascular conditioning program that stimulates improvement in heart, circulatory, and respiratory tissues while promoting adaptive responses in the musculoskeletal tissues (joints, feet, tendons, ligaments, and muscles).

LTLH Low toe, low heel

Metabolic alkalosis Subsequent to loss of electrolytes in the sweat, especially of potassium and chloride ions, a horse's kidneys compensate by retaining bicarbonate ions that alter the blood pH to a more basic or alkaline status.

Metabolic heat Heat generated from normal resting metabolic processes such as eating, digestion, and breathing.

Metabolic problems Metabolic problems refer to a departure from normal physiological function of the *cardiovascular* system, the neurologic system, the digestive system, and/or the muscular system. In the exercising horse these are usually a result of dehydration, *electrolyte* imbalances, energy depletion, or acid-base (pH) imbalance.

Metabolism Chemical changes in living cells by which energy is provided for vital processes and activities. Metabolism accomplishes the following:
- Obtains chemical energy from fuel molecules
- Converts nutrients into building blocks of cellular components.   *(cont.)*

Metabolism *continued*
- Assembles building blocks into cells and tissues.
- Forms and degrades molecules required in the specialized function of cells.

Mitochondria Cellular "factories" that use enzymes in the presence of oxygen to produce energy from nutrients.

Musculoskeletal Relating to the muscles and the skeleton, including the interaction of these structures to create locomotion.

Myoglobin Protein in muscle tissue that stores oxygen; if released with muscle damage (*myositis*), it filters through the urinary system to give a reddish color to the urine; since it is a large molecule, it can plug kidney tubules and induce kidney failure.

Myositis Inflammation of muscle tissue, often accompanied by cramping.

Neuroendocrine A neuroendocrine response refers to the function of the nervous system in response to hormonal substances secreted by *endocrine* glands. Hormones are chemical substances secreted by endocrine cells into the body fluids; these chemicals then regulate the function and metabolism of other organs and tissues in the body.

Neuromuscular Relating to the nerves and the muscles, including their interaction to provide agility, coordination, and strength of movement and locomotion.

Nutraceuticals Food additive supplements that allegedly alter the function or structure of a horse's body.

P & R Pulse and respiration.

Packed cell volume (PCV) Represents the percentage or concentration of red blood cells in blood; also called hematocrit.

Pedal osteitis Inflammation of the coffin bone.

Periople Protective waxy covering at the top of the hoof that grows down from the coronary corium.

Radiation Heat transfer from a warm body to cool air.

Radiograph The image created on special x-ray film by passing x-radiation through a body part.

Rebound hypoglycemia After eating a large grain meal, glucose released from digestion stimulates insulin secretion to drive the glucose into the cells, temporarily making less glucose available in the bloodstream.

Recovery parameters A collection of data obtained from physical exam that indicate that a horse has recovered sufficiently from the recent stress of exercise to continue to work.

Respiratory cooling A means of dissipating heat through the respiratory tract by rapid breathing. Moves heat from the body through the blood vessels of the lungs to the lung tissue to be expired into the cooler air; contributes as much as 33% to heat loss.

Roughage Food in the form of plant fiber, as in hay or pasture.

Scratches Dermatitis usually occurring on the back of the pasterns or in white haired areas of the lower legs.

Seedy toe Separation of the white line due to an inflammatory or infectious process of the hoof.

Sheared heels One heel bulb is driven higher than the other by excessive impact over time.

Shearing forces Stress resulting from applied forces that causes two contiguous parts to slide relative to each other.

Skin pinch test The rate at which the skin snaps back into position after it has been squeezed between the fingers; rapid return to normal indicates adequate "water" in the tissues; a delayed response may indicate significant dehydration.

Slow twitch muscle fibers Muscle fibers that rely on *aerobic metabolism* to transform carbohydrates and fats into energy.

Stance phase The period of a gait when the foot is in contact with the ground.

Standard exercise test (SET) A standardized test that evaluates a horse's level of fitness.

Submaximal work *Aerobic* exercise.

Synchronous diaphragmatic flutter (SDF) Rhythmic contraction of the diaphragm at the same rate as the heart beat; the nerve supplying the diaphragm crosses the atrium of the heart, and when sensitized by *electrolyte* imbalances of calcium, potassium, and magnesium will contract at the same rhythm as the heart; seen as a flutter or thumping in the flank.

Tendinitis Inflammation of a tendon.

Thumps See *synchronous diaphragmatic flutter*

Tying-up syndrome See *myositis*

Total digestible nutrients (TDN) A term used to describe the energy content of food matter. TDN accounts for the total percent of digestible fat, protein, and carbohydrate in feed. One pound of TDN approximates 2000 kcal of digestible energy.

V 160 Velocity your horse is traveling when working at a heart rate of 160 *bpm*.

Volatile fatty acids An *aerobic* energy source produced from fermentation of *roughage* in the large intestine.

White line disease Infectious process, usually caused by yeast or fungus, that embeds within the white line of the hoof.

Appendix I

Conversion Tables

MILES VS KILOMETERS

Miles	Kilometers
1	1.6
2	3.2
3	4.8
4	6.4
5	8.1
10	16.1
11	17.7
12	19.3
13	21
14	22.5
15	24.1
16	25.7
17	27.4
18	29
19	30.6
20	32.2
25	40.2
30	48.3
35	56.3
40	64.4
45	72.4
50	80.5
55	88.5
60	96.5
65	104.6
70	112.6
75	120.7
80	128.7
85	136.8
90	144.8
95	152.9
100	160.1

Miles per hour (mph)	Kilometers per hour (Kmphr)
0.62	1
1	1.6
2	3.2
3	4.8
4	6.4
5	8.1
6	9.7
7	11.3
8	12.9
9	14.5
10	16.1
11	17.7
12	19.3
13	21
14	22.5
15	24.1
16	25.7
17	27.3
18	29
19	30.6
20	32.2

Appendix II

Distance Riding Associations

United States

American Endurance Ride Conference
701 High Street #203
Auburn, California 95603-4727

Eastern Competitive Trail Ride Association
PO Box 738
Kent, Connecticut 06757

Equestrian Trails Inc.
13741 Foothill Boulevard #220
Sylamar, California 91342

Gold Country Endurance Riders
PO Box 3412
Auburn, California 95604

Great Lakes Distance Riding Association
23378 Nine Mile Road
Reed City, Michigan 49677

Middle of the Trail Distance Riders Association
699 East 57.5
Lawrence, Kansas 66047

Mountain Region Endurance Riders
1000 Salida Street
Aurora, Colorado 80011

National Association of Competitive Mounted Orienteering
503-171st Avenue, SE
Tenino, Washington 98589

Nevada All State Trail Riders
PO Box 100
Virginia City, NV 89440

North American Trail Ride Conference
PO Box 2136
Ranchos de Taos, New Mexico 87557-2136

Old Dominion Association
149 Spring Street
Herndon, Virginia 20170

Orange County Distance Riders
24811 Buckskin Drive
Laguna Hills, California 92677

Pacific Coast Long Riders
955 Olympic Way
Nipomo, California 93444

Pacific Northwest Endurance Riders
PO Box 1774
Clackamas, Oregon 97015

The Ride and Tie Association
11734 Wolf Road
Grass Valley, California 95949

South Eastern Distance Riders Association
PO Box 302
Mims, Florida 32754

Southern Utah Endurance Riders
Association
HC76, Box 350
Beryl, Utah 84714

Upper Midwest Endurance & Competitive
Rides Association
455 Moore Heights
Dubuque, Iowa 52003

Vermont Equine Riding & Driving
Association
RR 1, Box 124
South Woodstock, Vermont 05071

Western States Trail Foundation
701 High Street, #228C
Auburn, California 95603

Canada

Canadian Long Distance Riders
Box 160
Javie, Alberta
T0GM 1H0

United Kingdom

British Endurance Riding Association
British Equestrian Centre
Stoneleigh Park
Kenilworth
Warwickshire
CV8 2LR

The Endurance Horse & Pony Society of
Great Britain
Mill House
Mill Lane
Stoke Bruerne
Towcester
Northamptonshire
NN12 7SH

Irish Long Distance Riding Association
188 Ballynahinch Road
Ballykeel
Dromore
County Down
BT25 1EU

Scottish Endurance Riding Club
9 Elliot Road
Jedburgh
Roxburghshire
TD8 6HN

France

CNREE
Logis de Seneuil
79410 - Cherveux

Endurance Long Distance Rides
Conference
Rue Clandeyer
Port Blanc
22 710 Penvenan

Germany

Verein Deutscher Distanzreiter (VDD)
und Fahrer E.V.
Habichtstr. 77
45527 Hattingen

New Zealand

New Zealand Endurance Riding
Cl - Kevin James
Cliffs Road
RD 14
Timaru

Australia

Australian Endurance Riders Association
PO Box 144
Nanango QLD 4615

Spain

Spanish Equestrian Federation
Plz. Marques de Salamanca No. 2
28006 Madrid

Recommended Reading List

American Endurance Ride Conference. *Endurance News*. Auburn, California: American Endurance Ride Conference, ongoing monthly publication.

Clayton, Hilary, DVM. *Conditioning Sport Horses*. Saskatoon, Saskatchewan, Canada: Sport Horse Publications, 1991.

Denoix, Jean-Marie and Jean-Pierre Pailloux. *Physical Therapy and Massage for the Horse*. North Pomfret, Vermont: Trafalgar Square Publishing, 1996.

Dorrance, Tom. *True Unity*. Tuscarora, Nevada: Give-It-A-Go Enterprises, 1987.

Dynamics of Equine Athletic Performance: Fifth Annual Scientific Meeting for Equine Sports Medicine. Veterinary Learning Systems Co., Inc., 1985.

Edwards, G.B. *Anatomy and Conformation of the Horse*. Croton-on-Hudson, New York: Dreenan Press, Ltd., 1980.

Ethics in Endurance. European Long Distance Riders (ELDRIC) and Federation Equestrian International (FEI), 1993.

Focus on Endurance. Guelph, Ontario, Canada: Equine Research Centre, University of Guelph, 1995.

*Gillespie, J.R. and N.E. Robinson, Ed. *Equine Exercise Physiology 2: Proceedings of the Second International Conference on Equine Exercise Physiology*. Davis, California: ICEEP Publications, 1987.

*Hodgson, David and Reuben Rose, Editors. *The Athletic Horse*. Philadelphia: W.B. Saunders Company, 1994.

*Jones, William E., Ed. *Equine Sports Medicine*. Philadelphia: Lea and Febiger, 1989.

Loving, Nancy S., DVM. *Veterinary Manual for the Performance Horse*. Grand Prairie, Texas: Equine Research, Inc., 1993.

Midkiff, Mary D. *Fitness, Performance, and the Female Equestrian*. New York: Howell Book House, 1996.

Müseler, W. *Riding Logic*. New York: Simon & Schuster, 1985.

*Robinson, N.E., Ed. *Equine Exercise Physiology 4: Proceedings of the Fourth International Conference on Exercise Physiology*. Newmarket, Suffolk, UK: Equine Veterinary Journal, 1995.

Rooney, James R. *The Lame Horse: Causes, Symptoms, and Treatments*. New York: A.S. Barnes and Company, 1974.

Savoie, Jane. *Cross-Train Your Horse for Performance and Pleasure: Volume I. Simple, Basic Dressage for all Disciplines, Volume II. Build a Better Athlete with Dressage Techniques.* North Pomfret, Vermont: Trafalgar Square Publishing, 1998.

Savoie, Jane. *That Winning Feeling!: Program Your Mind for Peak Performance.* North Pomfret, Vermont: Trafalgar Square Publishing, 1992.

Swift, Sally. *Centered Riding.* North Pomfret, Vermont: Trafalgar Square Publishing, 1985.

Tellington-Jones, Linda with Sybil Taylor. *Getting in TTouch: Understand and Influence Your Horse's Personality.* North Pomfret, Vermont: Trafalgar Square Publishing, 1995.

Trail Blazer Magazine. Bend, Oregon: Trail Blazer Publications, ongoing bi-monthly publication.

*Veterinary Clinics of North America, Equine Practice. *Exercise Intolerance.* December 1996, Vol. 12, No. 3, Philadelphia: W.B. Saunders Company, 1996.

*Veterinary Clinics of North America, Equine Practice. *Exercise Physiology.* December 1985, Vol. 1, No. 3, Philadelphia: W.B. Saunders Company, 1985.

Wanless, Mary. *For the Good of the Horse.* North Pomfret, Vermont: Trafalgar Square Publishing, 1997.

Wanless, Mary. *The Natural Rider.* North Pomfret, Vermont: Trafalgar Square Publishing, 1996.

*Reading of a more technical nature.

Index

About the Author

Dr. Nancy Loving's intense interest in horses began at a an early age and continues to figure prominently in both her professional and personal life. She discovered the challenges and pleasures of distance riding in 1983. Prior to that she competed in both eventing and dressage. Dr. Loving graduated from Colorado State University Veterinary School in 1985. Since graduation she has practiced equine medicine and surgery exclusively, currently at her own Loving Equine Clinic in Boulder, Colorado where she is sole practitioner.

In addition to regularly judging endurance rides in Colorado, Nevada, and California, Dr. Loving has officiated at such notable rides as The Old Dominion, The Vermont 100, and The Race of Champions since 1992. Internationally, she has served as a support veterinarian to the United States Endurance Team at the World Equestrian Games in Holland in 1994, as a member of the Veterinary Commission for the North American Championships in 1995 and 1997, and was Treatment Veterinarian at the 1996 World Championships Endurance Race in Kansas. She also judges competitive trail ride competitions for the North American Trail Ride Conference (NATRC), and she is a certified Eastern Competitive Trail Ride Association (ECTRA) judge.

Horse Illustrated and the *International Arabian Horse Magazine* are among the publications Dr. Loving writes for regularly. She is Medical Editor for both *Trail Blazer* and *Horse & Rider.* Her previous book, *Veterinary Manual for the Performance Horse,* was published in 1993.

Dr. Loving lives in Boulder, Colorado where she keeps two Arabian horses. One is her endurance ride partner of many years and the other is a young horse who is starting his competitive endurance career.